An
Anthology
from
X

An Anthology from X

A Quarterly Review of Literature
and the Arts, 1959–1962,
edited by Patrick Swift
and David Wright

Selected with an introduction by
DAVID WRIGHT

OXFORD UNIVERSITY PRESS
1988

Oxford University Press, Walton Street, Oxford OX2 6DP
Oxford New York Toronto
Delhi Bombay Calcutta Madras Karachi
Petaling Jaya Singapore Hong Kong Tokyo
Nairobi Dar es Salaam Cape Town
Melbourne Auckland
and associated companies in
Berlin Ibadan

Oxford is a trade mark of Oxford University Press

Introduction and selection © David Wright 1988

All rights reserved. No part of this publication may be reproduced, stored in a retrieval system, or transmitted, in any form or by any means, electronic, mechanical, photocopying, recording, or otherwise, without the prior permission of Oxford University Press

British Library Cataloguing in Publication Data
An Anthology from X.
1. English literature—20th century
I. Wright, David G. II. X : a quarterly review
820.8'00914 PR1148
ISBN 0-19-212266-5

Set by Colset Private Ltd.
Printed in Great Britain
at the University Printing House, Oxford
by David Stanford
Printer to the University

CONTENTS

An Introduction *by David Wright*   xi

List of illustrations   x

I

1. GEORGE BARKER
   Circular from America   1
2. ANTHONY CRONIN
   The Notion of Commitment   6
3. HUGH MACDIARMID
   Reflections in a Slum   15
4. PATRICK SWIFT
   Official Art and the Modern Painter   16
5. FRANK AUERBACH
   Fragments from a Conversation   22
6. SAMUEL BECKETT
   L'Image   26
7. PATRICK KAVANAGH
   Living in the Country   28
   Lecture Hall   30
8. STEVIE SMITH
   The Last Turn of the Screw   31
   Thoughts about the Person from Porlock   33
9. ALBERTO GIACOMETTI
   The Dream, the Sphinx and the Death of T.   35
10. DAVID GASCOYNE
    Remembering the Dead   44

II

1. GEORGE BARKER
   How to Refuse a Heavenly House   45
2. ANTHONY CRONIN
   Goodbye to All That   52
3. MICHAEL ANDREWS
   Notes and Preoccupations   58
4. POETS ON POETRY
   Hugh Macdiarmid   63

Vernon Watkins	64
Patrick Kavanagh	66
Stevie Smith	68

III

1 BRIAN HIGGINS

Cartons	71
My Mother was a Burler	72
The Social Realists	73
I Have No Comrades	74
The Only Need	74
Letter to a Literary Professor	75

2 ROBERT GRAVES

November 5th Address	75

3 PATRICK KAVANAGH

The Flying Moment	81

4 DAVID BOMBERG

The Bomberg Papers	86

5 ANDRÉ MASSON

Dissonances	94

6 DAVID WRIGHT

Adam at Evening	101

IV

1 EZRA POUND

Conversations in Courtship	103

2 C. H. SISSON

Money	107
Moriturus	107
Sparrows Seen from an Office	108
Ightham Woods	108
Family Fortunes	109
Epictetus	110

3 CRAIGIE AITCHISON

Fragments from a Conversation	111

4 ANTHONY CRONIN

A Question of Modernity	114

5 PATRICK SWIFT

The Painter in the Press	124

CONTENTS

V

1	C. H. SISSON The Profession of Letters	135
2	GEORGE BARKER III Roman Odes	140
3	C. H. SISSON Natural History	144
4	GEOFFREY HILL Annunciations	152
5	JOHN MCGAHERN The End or the Beginning of Love	153
6	DANNIE ABSE The Magician	164
7	ANTHONY CRONIN Getting Wurred In	165
8	STEVIE SMITH Thoughts about the Muse	173
9	VERNON WATKINS Poem for Conrad	173
10	ON THE MARGIN	175

VI

1	MALCOLM LOWRY Be Patient for the Wolf Delirium in Vera Cruz Reading Don Quixote	177 178 179
2	ART AND MORALITY Prefatory Note George Barker: The Hippogryph and the Water-Pistol Patrick Swift: Mob Morals and the Art of Loving Art Anthony Cronin: It Means What It Says C. H. Sisson: Leisure and the Arts Patrick Kavanagh: On a Liberal Education	179 180 187 192 199 204
3	JOHN HEATH-STUBBS Use of Personal Pronouns	211
4	BRIAN HIGGINS On Going into the City Unfinished Autumnal	214 214 215

CONTENTS

5 JAMES LOVELL
 Alive, Alive O!   216
6 ANTHONY CRONIN
 'Fairway's' Betting Office, Dublin, 1949   222
 Responsibilities   222
7 CLIFF ASHBY
 The Reduced Nanny, Smell of Talcum Powder   224
 In the Twilight of her Time   225
8 ON THE MARGIN   225

VII

1 MARTIN SEYMOUR-SMITH
 The Administrators   227
 Request on the Field   228
 Found on a Building Site   229
 Living by the River   229
 The Execution   230
 History Lesson   231
2 GEORGE BARKER
 On a Distant Prospect of English Poetry & Downing College   232
3 WILLIAM CLARKE
 The Widow   235
 Old People's Home   236
 Mission Hall   236
 Military Cemetery   236
4 MARTIN SEYMOUR-SMITH
 C. H. Sisson   237
5 C. H. SISSON
 The Nature of Man   246
 Things Seen   246
 Adam and Eve   246
 By the Lift Gate   247
 Great Down   247
 Grandmother   248
 A Young Woman   249
 The Nature Lover   249
6 BRIAN HIGGINS
 A Triumvirate   250
 The Corrupt Man in the French Pub   250
 The Accidental Purity   251
 Baedeker for Metaphysicians   251

7 MARTIN GREEN Coming Up for Air	252
8 CLIFF ASHBY Please Don't Laugh Fountains Abbey	253 254
9 PATRICK KAVANAGH The Cattle Fair	255
10 THOMAS BLACKBURN A Small, Keen Wind Teaching Wordsworth	257 258
11 PATRICK KAVANAGH Mermaid Tavern	260
12 HUGH MACDIARMID In Memoriam James Joyce	261
13 ON THE MARGIN	261
ACKNOWLEDGEMENTS	265
INDEX	267

LIST OF ILLUSTRATIONS

Plates

Patrick Swift: *Portrait of George Barker*
Portrait of C. H. Sisson
Portrait of David Wright
Portrait of Patrick Kavanagh
David Bomberg: *Self-portrait*
Michael Andrews: *The Gardener*
Frank Auerbach: *Head of E. O. W.*
Craigie Aitchison: *Tree and Wall Landscape*
Chrysanthemums

Drawings

Alberto Giacometti: *Head* — 38
plans for 'The Dream, the Sphinx and the Death of T.' — 40–3
André Masson: illustrations for *'Dissonances'* — 98–9

AN INTRODUCTION

X, a quarterly review of literature and the arts, flourished, or at any rate existed, between the years 1959 and 1962. It took its name from the algebraic symbol for the unknown quantity—'incalculable or mysterious factor or influence' as the *Concise Oxford Dictionary* defines it. Neither manifesto nor editorial introduced the first number: its contents were the manifesto. The unstated object of the magazine was to make war on mediocrity, and to provide a platform for individual vision rather than second-hand avant-gardism or accepted attitudes. How far it succeeded is to be judged by the present anthology, for which I have selected, so far as space and other considerations allow, what seems to me to be the best of the work published in the seven numbers of *X* that appeared.

Patrick Swift and I did, however, make our aims explicit in a foreword to the bound volume containing the first four numbers of *X*, published by Barrie and Rockliffe in 1961:

Many people deplore the lack of public interest in the arts. Yet the most dangerous thing for the arts is in fact the interest taken by the public. For there is never any lack of talented mediocrity ready and willing to satisfy the demand for what the public is prepared to regard as a work of art, and it is the productions of those who serve the mass that deflect attention from the real thing, the productions of the individual vision.

Nobody expects that society under whatever persuasion is going to turn around and single out with accuracy the genuine artists, praise them and support them for their works. Nobody is likely to pretend even that it would be a great social blessing if something of the kind were to happen. For there is a paradoxical aspect to the situation of the artist: by definition it does not accommodate this sort of thing. And yet, again paradoxically, it is for these very reasons that there must exist an outlet for those productions of the individual vision which, because of the social bias and necessary social conservatism of any State, are most likely to suffer neglect or be suppressed altogether.

If two things are granted, and they are not often denied, (i) that the products of the true artist are vital to a healthy society, (ii) that even in the best societies there is the constant risk that these very things will wither and die for want of the minimum support, then the collection of writing, poetry, and art brought together here needs no further apology.

There was a time when the manifesto was a useful and amusing weapon. Nevertheless, looking back on the great days of manifesto-making, what chiefly strikes one is the general failure to live up to claims.

There is at the heart of any interesting idea of art or poetry an anarchic volatile centre—a sort of living principle—which will not tolerate categoric definition so that even the wildest of surrealist or anti-art proclamations militate against the sort of freedom the artist values.

This does not mean that we exist to initiate a drift from principle and clear proposition. It means that only propositions sufficiently accurate to include the necessary complexity of any interesting artistic viewpoint are good enough for us. And that any attitude based upon the notion that there exists a total and rational explanation for the artistic impulse and activity is for us the enemy of real poetry.

And so it is that throughout all the critical articles published in this journal will be found a questioning and sceptical curiosity about the prevailing and fashionable conceptions which now dominate the scene.

It may well be that there was a time in history when evil inhabited a single house and went by a simple name. But the real enemy now is probably confusion-general; complete intellectual confusion with a prevalent readiness to pounce on anything that looks like a moral issue provided it be simple, accessible, and public enough—in short, safe.

In these circumstances it becomes as much the duty of a watchdog to look to the credentials of the official opposition as to question the claims of the Establishment.

If we allow ourselves a convenient division of purpose the first aim, to bring to the light of day the work of the best with the qualification that preference be given to the unknown and the neglected or the known but unhonoured, is a clear and basic function which demands absolute precedence, while the second, to question and expose the nature of prevailing and fashionable theory and practice, is a more complex function difficult to perform.

The hardest thing that anybody can do is to think for himself, to like something because he likes it and not because he knows or is told that ten or ten thousand or ten million other people do. The artist is a man who experiences for himself and believes in the validity of that experience. One of the editors of this magazine was once told by a well-known contemporary poet-pundit: 'I read novels in order to find out the kind of world I am living in.' He should have said: 'I write novels in order to find out the kind of world I am living in.' It is those who are capable of making the second remark or its equivalent that we have published in *X*. They are individuals, not a group; not even a group of individuals. And if they have anything in common it is the seriousness with which they take their art—not that lugubrious dedication one associates with people who confuse art with social amelioration, but the apparent frivolity with which they ignore the terrible worries of our time in favour of the apparently selfish delight of creating some image of personal vision, some faint echo of the eternally liberating 'I am'.

The true begetter and leading light of *X* was Patrick Swift. A painter of genius, he was to die in Portugal in 1983 of a brain tumour at the early age of 55. On his death he left behind him a magnificent *œuvre*, hundreds of canvases, paintings of trees, landscapes, and portraits. He would seldom exhibit, for he distrusted celebrity, regarding it as a distraction and a nuisance; but much of his work is to be reproduced in a memorial volume currently in preparation. He also founded an internationally famous pottery, the Olaria Porches in Algarve, for which he designed many remarkable *azulejos*, and which has recently been made a National

INTRODUCTION xiii

Heritage by the Portuguese government.

I met Swift in (to quote his words) 'the Bohemian jungle of Soho, where practitioners of arts and letters were thick on the ground, though not professors of these activities'. And in a sense X was born in that Bohemian jungle, a society which, as I now realize, was as extraordinary as it was short-lived. Nothing is left of it today bar a few ageing survivors; but in the spring of 1953, when Swift and I met, it was still going strong, though the best days were over.

The pubs in Dean and Old Compton Street, and those in Rathbone Place, were then a rendezvous for the arts, and even the sciences, where you could, by day or night, encounter poets, painters, and musicians—Francis Bacon, Lucian Freud, and Malcolm Williamson among others—and such survivors of Montparnasse (of which Soho was the lineal descendant) as Nina Hamnett; not to mention odd-bods such as the Librarian of the House of Lords and the rightful king of Poland. It was in those days the kind of 'convivial university' that Ivan Illich was later to advocate; a successor to the informal gatherings of poets and artists that had been going on since the 1890s in places like the Café Royal, the Eiffel Tower in Percy Street, Fitzrovia, and the pubs near the British Museum. At any rate it was in Soho that I received the best part of my education, from people as diverse as W.S. Graham, Roy Campbell, John Heath-Stubbs, Hugh MacDiarmid, and not least from Swift himself.

Soon after we met Swift disappeared, having won a travelling grant from the Irish Committee of Cultural Affairs on the strength of the success of the first and penultimate exhibition of his paintings that he gave in the course of his short life. Meanwhile I had got involved, first as adviser, then as associate, and finally as co-editor, with a 'little review' called *Nimbus*, founded and edited by a young businessman, Tristram Hull, whom I encountered in the same Soho pub where I had run into Swift. I looked on my connection with *Nimbus* as an opportunity to get into print work that I knew was good but not the fashion of the day (these were the years of 'consolidation' and 'commitment'). Thus, when I took up the reins as co-editor, *Nimbus* published a batch of fourteen poems by Stevie Smith whom, *mirabile dictu*, the literary periodicals of the day ignored, apparently because her work did not jibe with the notion of poetry as currently received. The next number printed another batch of nineteen poems by Patrick Kavanagh, now generally regarded as the most considerable Irish poet since Yeats, but whose work was then disregarded for much the same reason.[1] Their publication in *Nimbus* led to

---

[1] These poems had been posted to me by Swift, whose brother James had invaded the poet's flat in Dublin, gathered up the trampled manuscripts scattered about the floor, and had them sorted, typed, and bound. One of the carbon copies was sent to me.

the appearance of Stevie Smith's *Not Waving But Drowning*, and of Kavanagh's *Come Dance with Kitty Stobling*, and to their eventual and belated recognition by what Swift and I used to call the Reviewage.

But after a year as co-editor of *Nimbus* my connection with it came to an end. Early in 1957 I resigned and Christopher Logue took over; thereafter *Nimbus* concentrated on the products of politically committed afflatus, in which I took no interest. However, eighteen months later, when I was living on fish and chips in one of the dressing-rooms of the Theatre Royal at Castleford, where my wife, Phillipa Reid, was leading lady in James Lovell's Commonwealth Players company, a letter arrived from Swift inviting me to come in with him to edit a new magazine on the lines that he and I had wanted *Nimbus* to follow.

Through the poet David Gascoyne, Swift had become acquainted with an extraordinary old lady, one of the last survivors of Bloomsbury. This was Mary Hutchinson, a cousin of Lytton Strachey, and—as the multifarious chronicles of the Bloomsbury group have since informed me—the sometime mistress of Clive Bell, and friend of practically every twentieth-century artist or writer of note, from George Moore to Alberto Giacometti and Samuel Beckett. It had long been her ambition to start a magazine devoted to literature and the arts, and as editors Swift and I seemed to her to be the answer. This was before the days when literary magazines could get financial backing from the Arts Council—not that Swift, who held the view that cultural institutions tend to promote mediocrity ('it may even be that this is their true function', as he once wrote) would have wanted to have much to do with that body. However, Mrs Hutchinson and he were confident that she would be able to find a backer for the venture.

I was sceptical—but also determined, after my experiences with *Nimbus*, which had had to pay its printers vast sums and could therefore offer only derisory fees to its contributors, that it should not merely be a printing firm that benefited from the new magazine; enough money must be found, or guaranteed, to pay contributors properly. My doubts began to wane when I found that Mrs Hutchinson seemed to be intimate with almost everybody of importance in what was then called 'The Establishment'—indeed, one of her daughters was married to a Rothschild.

From Castleford I returned to London to meet Swift and Mrs Hutchinson for dinner at her Bayswater flat, high over Hyde Park Square. We were sumptuously entertained in a room hung with Matisse odalisques, for which, I was given to understand, Mrs Hutchinson had been the model. The old lady—she was nearing her eightieth birthday—impressed me immensely. She was very much a *grande dame*, a slight, erect figure, Victorian in bearing, holding herself straight as an arrow—I never once saw her lean back in a chair. She had a determination that more than once made me think of Yeats's lines on Lady Gregory:

> They came like swallows and like swallows went,
> And yet a woman's powerful character
> Could hold a swallow to its first intent.

And, sure enough, Mrs Hutchinson eventually succeeded after no more than a few months in finding a backer for the magazine.

He turned out to be a most unlikely patron for the kind of venture that Swift and I projected. Our benefactor was Michael Berry, now Lord Hartwell, the owner of the *Daily Telegraph*. He undertook to guarantee the first four numbers of *X*, and proved to be an ideal backer—he never interfered. Indeed, I never even met him. We were able to draw a small salary for our work as editors, and apart from Swift and myself there was no other staff, for we had determined to cut out all unnecessary expenses. Thus there was no grand launching party, and for an office we rented, at about £5 a week, an attic room in New Row off Covent Garden— ironically enough, the same room that had once been the office of *Nimbus*. This office really served as an accommodation address, for we were rarely in it except to collect mail and answer correspondence. The latter activity mostly consisted of inserting rejection slips into stamped addressed envelopes containing unsolicited manuscripts, of which huge quantities arrived daily. Our real offices were the saloon bars of the nearby Salisbury public house or the White Swan just opposite: here we met, and conferred with, contributors whose work we were interested in.

The first number of *X* was carefully planned, and well received. Philip Toynbee hailed it in the *Observer* as 'an event, if only because a literary magazine of this kind has not existed for a long time. The admirable impression of a review devoted to attacking both the corruptions of an established avant-garde and the dreary "retrenchments" of the age is reinforced by every article and poem which appears here'. In a leading article the *Times Literary Supplement* was also laudatory: 'A concern for "rethinking" about the nature of literary and artistic experience is apparent throughout the pages of *X*, and gives the whole of the first issue a unity uncommon among periodicals now.' About 3,000 copies of the first number were sold, and the circulation of *X* remained at this figure, more or less, until its demise. Much of its impact was due to the layout that Patrick Swift designed, and to its unusual format, which was in fact determined by the dimensions of a menu card in a caff off Victoria Station where we happened to be having a cup of coffee.

To begin with we were resolved to avoid insularity. Poems, essays, and graphics by European writers and artists like Robert Pinget, Yves Bonnefoy, René Daumal, Ghika, Oskar Kokoschka, André Masson,

O. V. de L. Milosz, Philippe Jaccottet, Jules Superveille, H. A. Gomperts, and others appeared in our pages—though in the present anthology considerations of space and copyright difficulties have precluded me from representing them as I should have wished.

Swift was, of course, responsible for the art side of the magazine. These were the boom years of abstract art. Swift, twenty years ahead of his time, launched a series of penetrating attacks on the cult, which he diagnosed as the official art of the day, as well as promoting the work of then unknown or unfashionable figurative painters, among them the young Frank Auerbach, Michael Andrews, and Craigie Aitchison, and such as-yet uncanonized painters as Lucian Freud, Francis Bacon, and the forgotten David Bomberg. Examples of their work were reproduced; more importantly, it was Swift's idea that the artists should speak for themselves, which was achieved either by transcribing their tape-recorded conversation (not 'interviews', wherein questions loaded with some obtuse interrogator's impercipience tend to darken counsel), or by publishing their notes. Swift's unearthing and editing of David Bomberg's outspoken and apocalyptic *pensées*, scattered about in his miscellaneous papers, was an outstanding contribution.

All exercises in criticism or exegesis published in *X* were written, be it noted, by practising painters, writers, or poets; a deliberate policy, for already a cloud no bigger than the dead hand of academe was hovering over the arts. Hence the series 'Poets on Poetry' where, again, we abjured 'interviews', and invited the poets—Hugh MacDiarmid, Stevie Smith, Vernon Watkins, Patrick Kavanagh, Jules Superveille, Yves Bonnefoy, Henri Thomas, and Philippe Jaccottet to speak for themselves.

Our first two numbers were filled with work by writers and artists we knew, or knew of. But by the time the third number of *X* appeared we were starting to attract unpublished writers of the kind we were looking for, but had begun to despair of finding. Thus, *X* was first to recruit three new, and widely different, poets who, given the climate of the day, certainly would not have been afforded a hearing elsewhere—this I know for a positive fact, for during the three years that *X* operated none of those I am about to name was able to get work accepted by any other literary periodical. The odd thing is that during the same period all three found publishers for their first books of verse. At that date, by some reversal of natural law, publishers took risks that editors of professedly advanced literary magazines didn't, or wouldn't; nor, come to that, would the Arts Council itself. For one of these poets had his first book chosen by the selectors of the Poetry Book Society (admittedly, I was one of the selectors for that year), only to have it disallowed by the Arts Council for fear of being involved in a possible action for libel—a fear which the publisher of the book, who would have been the first target of such action, either didn't share, or managed to overcome.

Its author was the late Brian Higgins, who died in 1965 of a rare heart condition at the age of 35, after what may justifiably be called a meteoric progress. In the five years from 1960—when he first appeared, the day after we had accepted his poems, in the office of *X*, having emigrated from Hull with all his worldly goods in a knapsack, along with an Anglo-Saxon typewriter of indeterminate ownership, thereafter to be put up, and up with, by one or other of us for the rest of his life—Higgins published three books of poems. The last of these, posthumously and ironically, was permitted to be made a Poetry Book Society Choice. Higgins was perhaps the only true *poète maudit* of our day—by which I do not mean that he took drugs—a bloody nuisance, a pitiless scrounger, yet one whose verse was alive with fire and bad taste. Higgins called himself 'a realist who wished to be romantic'; was Yorkshire-Irish working-class ('only I don't work'); a mathematician, and a one-time Rugby League full-back. He was, as Martin Seymour-Smith remarks in his *Guide to Modern World Literature*, 'a hit-or-miss poet . . . who had too little time to exercise control over his considerable intelligence'. But one or two of his later poems sustain a comparison with Blake, that otherwise might seem fatuous, made by a reviewer of his last, and posthumous, book in the *New Statesman* (which, of course, never printed a line by Higgins when he was alive, despite, or because of, the abusive letters he used to hurl at its editor). Higgins's first book, *The Only Need*, was published by Abelard-Schuman; the second, *Notes While Travelling*, by Longman; the third and last, *The Northern Fiddler* (ah, that title!), by Methuen. No publisher would bring out more than one book by Higgins—their nerves couldn't stand it. More than once Swift and I had to sit on his head to stop him writing furious letters full of impossible pecuniary demands to whichever was the unfortunate publisher of the moment. Higgins would say, with impenetrable logic: 'Look, it's going to cost them £500 to publish these rubbishy poems. Why don't they give me £500 and not publish?' Useless to speculate what Higgins might have done, or been, had he lived; but with his going there closed a window which would have let fresh air into the literary hothouse—and some of us might have felt the draught.

The second of these poets appeared in the fourth number of *X*. He should have been the job-evasive Higgins's natural enemy, for at that time C. H. Sisson was an Under-Secretary in the Ministry of Labour. In fact the two got on very well, even exchanging verse-letters, for they complemented one another while sharing an intellectual savagery that didn't, and still doesn't, sit easily with the soft thinking of the day. Sisson was 47 when we first came across his work in the form of a privately printed pamphlet entitled *Twenty-One Poems* which lay in the office for weeks unglanced-at (because printed, and therefore, we assumed, published). Patrick Swift and myself were confabulating in the New Row garret, and lamenting the impossibility of finding a new poet worth publishing, when Anthony Cronin happened to pick up the pamphlet from among the staggering piles of identikit verse under which the editorial table was groaning. We hardly needed to read further than the opening poem to realize that here we had found what we were looking for. That poem was 'Ightham Woods'. An ashamed editor wrote that very day to the mysterious Mr Sisson at the address printed on the verso of the title-page of his pamphlet. It was soon clear that we had stumbled upon a gold-mine, so far as *X* was concerned, for Sisson proved to be that rare phenomenon, a first-rate literary critic (and good critics are rarer than good poets). It also turned out that he had written a novel, *Christopher Homm*, a chapter of which we printed in *X* no. 4, together with six of his poems. As with Higgins, Sisson was unable to get anything published by any other periodical. However, Abelard–Schuman brought out his first collection, *The London Zoo*, in 1961, although his rebarbative novel, reminiscent of Jonathan Swift in its combination of obsidian prose and ferocious irony (a well-known literary agent, to whom I gave the manuscript, was so horrified that he refused to handle it), had to wait another five years before Methuen published it simultaneously with *Numbers*, Sisson's second book of poems, and his collection of critical essays, *Art and Action*. Since then, of course, Sisson has become an established literary figure.

But it was not till the penultimate number of *X* that the poems of Cliff Ashby, who described himself as a Yorkshire cowman, came our way. Like Higgins, he became one of C.H. Sisson's sparring-partners—for despite differences of temperament and background all three had their feet firmly on the ground, used language as she is spoken, and shared an uncompromising and discomposing honesty. Ashby, ignored like the other two by current literary periodicals, nevertheless published his first collection, *In the Vulgar Tongue*, in 1967, and his collected poems, *Plain Song*, in 1985. This includes a remarkable autobiographical essay in Skeltonics, 'The Tied Cottager'. To wind up the list of *X* 'firsts', another writer that it discovered before its demise was the novelist John McGahern. A chapter from his first novel, printed in *X* no. 5, led to its publication by Faber soon afterwards.

X survived for nearly three years, and ended with its seventh number. After our first year, when his original guarantee expired, Michael Berry generously agreed to back a further two numbers while we looked around for another Maecenas. Though optimistic about our prospects—after all, as someone remarked, we had won our first backer with nothing but a nimbus and a swift tongue—wherever we tried we drew a blank; and to tell the truth, we did not try very hard. If our efforts were lukewarm, it was not because we felt the job we had set out to do with *X* was anything like accomplished; it was because neither of us felt we could stand much more of the stress and pressure to which we were subjected. Besides, we had our own work to get on with. Mary Hutchinson, without whom the magazine would never have come into being, proved to be its old lady of the sea. Almost daily letters, almost twice-daily telephone calls, conveying an endless succession of notions, suggestions, and sometimes demands that the work of so-and-so be included, and some key essay or article thrown out to make room for it, emanated from that quarter. Some of the suggestions were invaluable, but 90 per cent stemmed from her reading of current Sunday papers, and were nonsenses out of which she had to be politely argued, an exercise that often occupied us for a large part of the day. I am not sure if Mrs Hutchinson ever really grasped our aims, and the standards we had determined to set. She tended to be hypnotized by reputations, and despite her sharp mind was susceptible to intellectual and cultural waffle, especially if respectably dressed in *la langue française*. My deafness saved me from the telephone, and it was Swift, who had the golden tongue, who bore the brunt. Many a time I would call at his studio to find him chained like a dog to the telephone for half the day, cajoling and persuading. There was not a page of the magazine that we did not have to pay for with hours of argumentation, till in the end Swift had to give up answering his telephone altogether; when it rang, some other member of his household, or a visitor, had to pick up the receiver. This well-meant harassment finally inhibited us from any serious effort to continue the magazine, although, financed by the sale of old letters and manuscripts that had accumulated from past numbers, we did manage to bring out a seventh, and valedictory, issue. This accomplished, Swift and I were free to pursue our different avocations.

DAVID WRIGHT

August 1985

In memory of
PATRICK SWIFT
1927–1983

I

GEORGE BARKER

Circular from America

Against the eagled
Hemisphere
I lean my eager
Editorial ear
And what the devil
You think I hear?
I hear the Beat
No not of the heart
But the dull pulpitation
Of the New Art
As, on the dead tread
Mill of no mind,
It follows its leaders
Unbeaten behind.
O Kerouac Kerouac
What on earth shall we do
If a single Idea
Ever gets through?
The English have seventy
Gods and no sauce
(The French have Voltaire
And Two Maggots of course)
But ½ an idea
To a hundred pages
Now Jack, dear Jack,
That ain't fair wages
For labouring through
Prose that takes ages
Just to announce
That Gods and Men
Ought all to study
The Book of Zen.
If you really think

So low of the soul
Why don't you write
On a toilet roll?
And as for Rexroth
That angry king
He'd court anyone
Or any thing.
If you pick your judgements
Up in the street
Why be so bloody
Indiscreet
As to display 'em
Like a dirty sheet?
O pen is alive
I beg you tell 'em
What wouldn't we give
For some cerebellum?
Whole chapters and verses
Of bric-à-brac
Will bring Carlos Williams
And not a dove back.
'I first met Dean
Not long after my wife
And I split up.'[1]
Gawd, what a life.
I'm a Dharma Bum.
Gawd, I'm a toad.
I'm wide. I'm out.
I'm off the Road.

But on Third Avenue
(Like Rome only more so
A street as gregarious
As any Corso)[2]
The shady bars
Open at morning
Like nenuphars
And the Beats yawn in
From their motor cars.
O its early to bed
You story tellers

---

[1] The opening of *On the Road*.   [2] Gregory Corso, author of *Gasoline*.

If you're not on Fulbrights
Or Rockefellers.
And only the blondes
In their skin tight jeans
Are living on private
Or pubic means.
Whaddya want?
A spade?[1] A fink?[2]
Don't goof, cripple.
Man, I stink.
And the silver towers
Of vanity sink
Into the golden
Seas of drink,
And round and round
At the fiery brink
Fly those who do every
Thing but think.
And all the while
From Maine to Utah
The virgins arrive
On foot and scooter
With bags that will never
Again be neuter.
Yes, far away
On the other side
Of the Middle Worst
And the Great Divide
There, there on the gilded
Coasts of the West
The Great I Am's
Are the happiest—
For somewhere in Yonkers
They're shocking amoeba
With a cyclotron
Or the Queen of Sheba.
O beautiful
America
I have a feeling
I've come too far—
Did the plane put down

[1] Negro.   [2] Homosexual.

On the right star?
O tell me where the Statue
Of Libertines is—
In the middle of Erewhon
Or Atlantis?
And the dead whores glitter
In Central Park
Just before every
Thing goes dark.

Down in the Village
The parvenu
Dreams of Madison
Avenue
And on Madison
The copywriters
Dream of the calm
Nights of St Vitus
As in the arms
Of their advertisers
They gollop down
Their tranquillisers;
And the workmen burrowing
Into the sidewalk
('Dig we must—
For growing New York')[1]
Chaw ten-inch cigars
As they work,
And dogs and children
On long lists
Attend their psycho
Analysts.
The automobiles
As large as whales
Sweep up and down
Like hearses. Tales
Of Offmen softly
Echo over
Streets choked up with
Four leafed clover,
Yet oh us lucky

[1] Stencilled on all roadmenders' trestles.

Eleven million
Would give it all
To be one simple
Nice Sicilian.

And, every week,
Like a public crime
We sit in our toilets
Glued to the slime
Of the last issue
Of a loose Time.
And high on their pinnacles
The Committees sit
Denouncing all sanity
In the name of God
And unanimity.
And the ghost of a great
Democratic conception
Shrieks out: 'I confess
To a little deception
But I meant well—
Make me an exception.'
O Gawd once again
I hear the beat
Of the rock and rolling
Paraclete:
Man, you know
Our attitude
Ain't a defeat,
It's a beatitude.
We all mean well,
Yeah, we all mean well
Like the Esso pipeline
That goes to hell.
For brother, brother,
The Am Express
Has illegalised
Human distress
And in the end
All our ills
Succumb to a bottle
Of vitamin pills
And the logic of

The formal mind
Acknowledge it's super
Annuated
By IBM
Incorporated.
Till the voice of the Turtle
Or the New Yorker
Intones the verses
Of Garcia Lorca:
'The jungle of To-morrow.
Ah, that's it, man—
All caught up in
The beard of Whitman.'
And 'Enough!' enunciates
The Spectre of James
'Don't spare the horses.
Throw out the dames.
Just drive like mad
Straight through the flames
And we'll all take tea
At the Court of St James.
The pyrotechnics
Of shall I say Hell
Have reached Minneapolis
And St Paul as well:
So lower the curtain
At all the borders
And close my books
Until further orders.'

ANTHONY CRONIN

The Notion of Commitment: An Aesthetic Inquiry

Nearly all the facts about a man, including his beliefs, will, if he can surmount the technical problems involved, go into poetry without doing it much damage. The most difficult to include are those that are to his credit. This is particularly true to-day, the age of the advertiser: i.e. the man who proclaims his own merit.

W.H. Auden has said that there are two theories of poetry: 'Poetry as a magical means of inducing desirable emotions in oneself and others, or Poetry as a game of knowledge, a bringing to consciousness, by naming them, of emotions and their hidden relationships. The first view was held by the Greeks, and is now held by M.G.M., Agit-Prop and the collective public of the world. They are wrong.'

Two techniques, two words, both perfectly serviceable and more or less agreed upon; (a) Poetry, (b) Prophecy. Poetry: a statement of fact and an examination of the relationship between facts. Prophecy: a statement of the desirability of changing the facts, an interpretation of the will of God, or History, or what have you.

If you can argue with a poem it ceases to be one.

No-one can command the imagination. We do not choose our obsessions; they choose us. The demand for a certain kind—any kind—of poetry is therefore almost certainly a demand for an inferior kind.

There is not and never could be in art any such thing as a hierarchy of subjects in order of importance. That there is so is an auctioneer's belief, and it retains its essential mendacity whether presented in the interests of religion or politics or anything else. Whatever the unwearying, enthusiastic mind of the journalist may conceive, no other fact or set of facts can render the facts in a true poem unimportant. Conversely neither theology, the bomb, analytical psychology, the future of the human race nor anything else can make a poem important if it is not so of its nature.

Prophecy: the poetry of possibility, though 'poetry' here is used really in the sense in which people use it when they speak of the poetry of industry, the prairies, etc., i.e. 'glamour', 'romance'.

What am I to do? Consult a priest, a wise man, a prophet; buy a handbook.

What should I feel? Consult a psychiatrist.

What do I feel? Read a poem.

Anything which calls for a resolution in action of a situation is not a poem but, in varying degrees, prophecy, rhetoric or plain fraud.

> For those that love the world serve it in action,
> Grow rich, popular and full of influence,
> And should they paint or write, still it is action:
> The struggle of the fly in marmalade.
> The rhetorician would deceive his neighbours,
> The sentimentalist himself; while art
> Is but a vision of reality.

In a recently published memoir of his brother, Professor Stanislaus Joyce says that since we know nothing whatever about Jesus's handling of all the difficult relations in life the validity of his teaching is seriously weakened. What it certainly does is to place his words on a plane other than poetry.

When we ask for an illumination of the reality and are offered only an indication of the putative possibility or a reiteration of the ideal (as by Lawrence, Whitman, etc.) we find we are in the wrong shop. They share with the greatest of all poets of the possible (that is, properly speaking, orators or prophets), Christ, the fact that they are no aid to the sufferer who cannot believe that his circumstances will change. He asks for bread and is given a magic stone.

Poetry, by naming it, celebrates what is.

'I have sinned.' The priest says: 'Repent or burn.' The politician: 'We will re-make ourselves and the world so that there shall be no more cruelty or injustice.' The poet: 'Alive, alive O.'

There is one grave moral charge which, as a result of his function, the poet must bear. Every time a lamentable situation is described in a poem and a reader involved in it feels, as he will feel, only elation and calm as a result, the poet must suffer the accusation of encouraging for every such reader a continuance of being rather than a process of becoming. However, though he is unlikely to act differently, the reader feels differently for knowing how he feels, so that in a sense he has become something else as a result of the poem, though the situation the poem describes has not changed. Otherwise the charge is just. The only way to remove the danger would be to abolish the art, a course suggested by Plato, Stalin and the believers in commitment.

Has poetry, then, no social function at all? Several, some of them most important, though since they are *necessary* functions which it *uniquely performs*, the question of their importance is, so to speak, of no philosophical importance.

Two poets, Sweeny and Murphy. Sweeny and Murphy grow up together in an atmosphere begrimed by servitude, superstition and poverty. Both are exposed to hardship, worry, the contagion of sexual shame and a simultaneously irrational dread of the supernatural and the neighbours. Both, having the temperament of poets, survive. Murphy devotes his genius to the composition of verses urging people to be free, to strike for freedom, to destroy within themselves and in the world the effects of poverty, lies and superstition. Arise, ye starvelings, he thunders, more or less eloquently.

Sweeny meanwhile probes his wound. With scrupulous honesty he analyses the nature of his sufferings, his fear of life, his adolescent traumas, his adult failures, his crippled love.

It will be seen at once that Murphy serves an important social purpose. He belongs to an admirable profession, if a somewhat overcrowded one. According to the level of his talent he is either a publicist using verse as his medium (and with accordingly less persuasive power than many lesser men) or a prophet exercising that incalculable but probably somewhat dubious influence on events that we may attribute to such mediocre poets but good(?) prophets as Shelley, Whitman, or Swinburne in his republican vein.

Meanwhile poor 'subjectivist' Sweeny, though patently no dandified aesthete, is very likely to be accused—probably by Murphy, in the columns of the *New Statesman*—of fiddling while the fuse burns. 'No, not art for art's sake', he might well reply, 'but art for my sake', meaning that his kind of poetry remained necessary to him whatever his position vis-à-vis the militant masses of Asia. However, that his, even his, poems have a function also is a proposition it may be possible to prove as follows.

The impulse towards self-expression: the need to express the effect the operations of external reality have had and are having on the self. The poet: someone who combines this need with a natal love of words and a desire to be associated with them. Poetic statement: one made as a result of this need and this love.

The reader benefits by this statement (1) because it is almost as good for the soul as confession and confers on him freedom from the terrible fear of being unique, a fear which is at the root of most insanity and (2) because many things can not be seen until they are first pointed out or known until they are named, so the reader will probably be indebted to the poem for a knowledge of what his feelings are. This is before there is any question of insight. But of course, granted the love of words and the need to state truly, that is to understand, there will almost certainly be special insights. Words, the instruments of thought and feeling, have, in the hands of an honest user, a probing quality of their own. They are difficult to satisfy. Nor could any true poet be content to rest on blind knowledge without insight, which is the saving grace of knowledge, for mere confession of the facts is generally a falsification, like evidence in a police court.

This kind of information about what he really feels or has felt which the poem gives the reader is what Wordsworth spoke of when he referred to the poet as 'binding together with passion and knowledge the vast empire of mankind', and of, 'passions which do more nearly resemble the passions produced by real events than anything which, from the motion of their own minds merely, other men are accustomed to feel in themselves'; and Johnson, when he called poetry a statement of 'that which, though not obvious, is upon its first production acknowledged to be just, that which he that never found it wonders how he missed'.

Its effect is to create a species of honour among thieves. Love is a luxury which we can seldom afford; charity a moral duty which we can seldom perform. Compassion on the other hand is simply a faculty, attendant on and inseparable from full knowledge of ourselves and others, our common weakness, dishonesty and hope. The poem, literally, reveals the extent of our common humanity. It literally makes our excuses and even occasionally states the grounds of our pride for and to each other. Just how bad luck, bad weather and bad faith brought this about the poem will say, for one and for all, how much choice there was and how little. The poem in fact consoles.

This is what Rilke had in mind when he made that dangerous and intriguing remark about all good poems arising out of self-pity. The suffering of an egotist is rather more likely to make good poetry than the humane pity of an honest man (of course the boasting of an egotist is another matter). Through introspection and fidelity to personal experience the poem will tell us, what oddly enough we probably did not know, where in fact the shoe pinches and provide that basis of compassionate understanding which only it can provide.

The poem of personal failure is therefore a more valuable production politically (i.e. tending to the general good) than the poem of assumed nobility and exhortation.

To say all this is of course to leave out poetry's obvious function of giving pleasure (though this deepening of our consciousness, this stabbing self-knowledge is perhaps the acutest pleasure it gives). As Dryden said 'pleasure follows of necessity, as the effect does the cause, and therefore is not to be put in the definition'.

Apart however from this provision of illumination and consolation poetry has three other social functions the importance of which it would be difficult to exaggerate.

(1) Without the repeated recognition of the real nature of objects, surfaces, relationships and proportions which both poetry and painting give in their different ways, certain faculties would atrophy.

(2) Poetry maintains the language as a living instrument of communication. (It is arguable that the poetry which remains closest to the speech and speech rhythms of its own day does this best, all else tending towards rhetoric, otiosity and decoration.)

(3) The proof which poetry continually provides that the mangy old facts about ourselves can be wedded indissolubly, truly and with honour to the supremest beauties and felicities, can become beautiful themselves, is its chief glory and the only justification it needs.

I have referred to all these characteristics of poetry as social functions, for such in fact they are. However I do not wish to suggest anything in the nature of accountability. Good poetry does most of these things, though God forbid that the poet should set out to. This is a specialised argument. Charges of 'triviality' have been made against 'subjective' verse. What I have called functions are simply characteristics.

Nearly all good poetry has these characteristics in varying measure whatever the object of the poet. There are perhaps only two kinds which cannot of their very nature possess them: very abstract lyrical poetry and verse which sets the poet up as above the battle, in possession of a morality superior to that of the rest of men.

We have heard a great deal about Commitment recently as if it were a new thing, though the notion has appeared several times in other decades under other names. Oddly enough we never hear of Mr Eliot as committed, or Ezra Pound or Yeats, though the verse of all three is passionately, profoundly and fundamentally committed to the truth of certain views about the moral basis of civilisation and the importance of the kind of society we live in. These beliefs are not, however, made the occasion for boasting or hectoring, nor are they presented as if the mere holding of them were a feat deserving of great acclaim. They take their place in fact among the tensions, the human contradictions and the heart-searchings of the verse in a way that does not, so far as one can judge, meet the requirements of those who propagate the word commitment. It, in fact, is reserved by its adherents for a certain kind of propagandist, socialist, querulous and superior verse of which there seems to be only one practitioner, the advertiser of the movement himself. The blurb of Mr Christopher Logue's *Songs*[1] reads as follows:

'At a time when poetry has drifted into schools, one specialising in resolute titivation, the other in the frank pursuit of triviality—like two bald men fighting over a comb—Christopher Logue's work has shown that life outside the ego and the library is not only a possible subject for poetry but a meaningful one. Many have come to feel, after reading the work he has published in the last three years, the only meaningful one. Nowadays, when a poet's work is described as 'engaged' or 'committed', fears are immediately aroused that he is reading us an 'ought' and 'should' lesson. But in Christopher Logue's case the lay content is served by his vivid lyrical gift which critics of his earlier works have praised.'

This is a very odd document, with its supposititious reference to cohorts of other committed poets from whom Mr Logue may be distinguished by the vividness of his lyrical gift, and the lame falling back on the 'gift' itself when a positive, poetic—as opposed to some other kind of—virtue is sought for. What makes it most odd however is the phrase about 'life outside the ego' for in fact the most noticeable characteristic of Mr Logue's verse is precisely and simply his insistent and insatiable egotism:

> you say
> Logue grinds his axe again. He's red.
> Or cashing in. And you are right.
> I have an axe to grind. Compared to you
> I'm red and short of cash. So what?

[1] London. Hutchinson, 1959 (12s. 6d.).

> I think, am weak, need help, have lived,
> And will with your permission live.
> Why should I seek to puzzle you with words
> When your beds are near sopping with blood?
>
> And yet I puzzle you with words.

The assumption of importance here is startling; and the claim to be poorer than anybody else is significant as well as dubious. Statements on the level of 'I think, am weak, need help, have lived' are, as they stand, of no interest whatever, 'lay' or poetic, except as evidence of the kind of exhibitionism which generally accompanies the role of saviour—a suggestion of martyrdom is presumably intended both by them and by the elephantine irony of the request to be accorded permission to go on living.

This resolute self-regard is the principal impression left by Mr Logue's propagandist poems. They are glumly insistent that Mr Logue is the only one who cares:

> Men of the future think of me
> Living at a time when one by one
> Our kings gave way to businessmen,
> Our poets wrote to make men bother less,
> Our wisemen, fat with caution, spoke of death,
> And most died twice from individuality,
> In this time on earth given by men to me.

Apart from egotism, the passage displays only the threadbare nature of Mr Logue's social thinking—the romantic cliché, worthy of Noel Coward, about kings giving way to businessmen, and the communist jargon about people dying twice from individuality—truer to say they are dead from mass-production—but the utter unoriginality and clumsiness of the language are also of interest: the filling out of the line previous to the kings by the redundant 'one by one' and the unpoetic use of the word 'fat' as a term of abuse—a loutish puerility.

A long poem, supposed to be a prayer, which was read by the author in a religious programme for teenagers on TV (and from which incidentally the usual bullying note is not absent)

> Note particularly
> Those who declare themselves to be
> Uncommitted
> And remember their names, for
> When our troubles begin—it is soon—
> Such neighbours will betray their neighbours

ends on a mystical note, the author promising himself a future as legend:

> I wrote this song
> For those of you who will be born
> In the time we call New Year
> For I am among you there
> Even as you are here.

Many of the sentiments expressed in Mr Logue's poems are undoubtedly admirable, if unoriginal; what is wearisome is the constant claiming of so much credit for possessing them. The language is a mixture of turgidity and old Georgian frivolity about kings and princesses with a few words like 'turd' and 'shit' thrown in, apparently in the hope of achieving an uncompromising modernity. The real modern world never appears; for all the indication the (mostly literary) imagery of the poems gives we might as well be living in the Middle Ages. We learn nothing from the poems about Mr Logue's attitude to any of the difficult relations in life, so that, one may say so without blasphemy, the validity of his teaching is seriously weakened. The vivid lyrical gift which is supposed to provide the jam on the pill, the separable poetry, when not a fearsome misuse of Yeats (and some other very odd influences, including Dame Edith Sitwell), turns out to be a compound of all the sweepings of the Georgian anthologies. Here is Mr Logue in lyrical vein and the manner of Rupert Brooke:

> For God's sweet sake give me back part of that
> I gave. Part of a part? One loving jot?
> Child I am no Elizabethan hack
> Spicing his dalliance in a sonnet's pot . . .

Or like Rupert Brooke with an incongruous echo of Yeats:

> Who will, if I do not, remember her?
> Cast me again—as King; and then again—
> A beggarman; and then again and when
> I have been crying through a dozen selves . . .

Sometimes the verse is like the weak side of De La Mare, but weaker:

> Fine faggots, fair ladies
> And a bright-eyed
> Clayboned beggarman mad, O
> Mad in the street, my ladies.

And at others the model seems to have been the late Mr John Drinkwater:

> My heart is a bell
> Rung by a loon
> Called darlin' Tom
> Off bedlam straw . . .

This remote moonshine, far removed from the sane speech of men ever or anywhere, presumably represents Mr Logue's attempts to come to grips with what the apostles of commitment call, in a noticeable tone of self-congratulation, 'reality'. Complacent, trivial and boring, it reflects nothing but an ultimate unconcern with life. Poetry as an expression of adult matters which involve other people is not Mr Logue's medium.

An aspiration towards poetry certainly predicates certain other attitudes. That freedom is a good and he who is not free an exile is a belief almost certainly inherent in the minds of all who seek release in words; but that true freedom depends on self-knowledge and a recognition of necessity as much as on the destruction of external barriers will equally be found to be a belief inherent in most of the great poetry written since Baudelaire.

Though it is obviously not necessary to share a poet's beliefs in order to be affected by his poetry and clearly not necessary to be a party to any particular set of beliefs yet, so far as we know, formulated in order to write great poetry, it is difficult to imagine a receptive reader of contemporary poetry, or a possible great contemporary poet, who enjoyed living in a spiritually desolate civilisation such as our own.

Most poets, like most decent people, possess some vision of the just city. Yet a poet can not propagate it without extreme danger of ceasing to be a poet and turning into a prophet or a charlatan. The three most influential poets of the century, Yeats, Pound and Eliot are, as was said, all deeply committed to beliefs of varying kinds. But their poetry is primarily a profound statement of the human condition. Their beliefs enter into it because their beliefs are part of them and of humanity. In most truly great poetry the non-existence of the just city is simply a fact like other facts about the poet and his circumstances. The poetry of Yeats springs out of the whole man 'in all his loneliness and pain'. Anger and a passionate hatred of injustice everyone may feel who has 'climbed that stairs to eat that bitter bread', or felt 'the oppressor's wrong, the proud man's contumely, the insolence of office'. But only those poems where such abstractions appear in the garb of experience, which are about man with his visions as he is; where, as in Yeats, the petty and the ridiculous, the humiliations, niaiseries and failures of the poet are set down as well, will answer us, when we question them, as poems. It may be simpler to say that all true poetry aspires towards an ultimately untroubled acceptance of the poet's own nature.

Provided then that they enter his poems like any other facet of his being, and provided also that he can surmount the technical difficulties of tone and the human difficulties of asserting what is to his credit, a poet's protests, his beliefs, and his visions of possibility, have a part, like anything else, in his poetry. Much of the poetry of Mr David Gascoyne, for example, derives its power from a contrast of the vision with failure. But it is a failure from which the poet himself is not exempted and the statement of it ultimately perhaps says more for man than the conception of the vision itself. Ezra Pound has said that 'the arts are noble only as they meet the inner need of the poor'.

HUGH MACDIARMID

Reflections in a Slum

A lot of the old folk here—all that's left
Of them after a lifetime's infernal thrall
Remind me of a Bolshie the 'whites' buried alive
Up to his nose, just able to breathe, that's all.
Watch them. You'll see what I mean. When
Found his eyes had lost their former gay twinkle.
Ants had eaten *that* away; but there was still
Some life in him . . . his forehead *would* wrinkle!
And I remember Gide telling
Of Valéry and himself:
'It was a long time ago. We were young.
We had mingled with idlers
Who formed a circle
Round a troupe of wretched mountebanks.
It was on a raised strip of pavement
In the boulevard Saint-Germain,
In front of the Statue of Broca.
They were admiring a poor woman,
Thin and gaunt, in pink tights, despite the cold.
Her team-mate had tied her, trussed her up,
Skilfully from head to foot,
With a rope that went round her
I don't know how many times,
And from which, by a sort of wriggling,
She was to manage to free herself.

Sorry image of the fate of the masses!
But no one thought of the symbol.
The audience merely contemplated
In stupid bliss the patient's efforts
She twisted, she writhed, slowly freed one arm,

Then the other, and when at last
The final cord fell from her
Valéry took me by the arm:
'Let's go now! She has ceased suffering!'

Oh, if only by ceasing to suffer
They were able to become men.
Alas! how many owe their dignity,
Their claim on our sympathy,
Merely to their misfortune.
Likewise, so long as a plant has not blossomed
One can hope that its flowering will be beautiful.
What a mirage surrounds what has not yet blossomed!
What a disappointment when one can no longer
Blame the abjection on the deficiency!
It is good that the voice of the indigent
Too long stifled, should manage
To make itself heard.
But I cannot consent to listen
To nothing but that voice.
Man does not cease to interest me
When he ceases to be miserable.
Quite the contrary!
That it is important to aid him
In the beginning goes without saying,
Like a plant it is essential
To water at first,
But this is in order to let it to flower
And I *am concerned with the blossom.*

PATRICK SWIFT

Official Art and the Modern Painter

Il faut être absolument moderne—Arthur Rimbaud

The famous case of the Impressionists has made the notion of the man in advance of his time, misunderstood, neglected, but finally triumphant, a commonplace easily acceptable and known to everyone. There is also the popularisation of the idea in fictional romance and biography. People quite readily understand that the painter must suffer and that his work must be obscure.

It is beyond doubt that there is a real historic basis for this view.

The suffering, ignominy, and death of Rembrandt though due to special causes and differing in its chronology to that of more famous and recent cases has about it an archetypal quality. It is the case of a man triumphant over terrible circumstances through the exercise of his art. When the great painter, old, bankrupt, his wife's servant, suffering those nervous diseases of a person in grave stress (asthma, fibrositis, hayfever, etc.), stood at his easel and looked, like Swift in his old age, into the mirror and made out of his situation a masterpiece of painting, he was demonstrating in a monumental way the heroism that we are all so familiar with in the lives of the modern masters.

Thus it was when he had failed to conform to the requirements of Parisian success that Paul Cézanne retired to those places of his boyhood to demonstrate in another way the same heroic capacity.

Art, profound and original, created in solitude and in anguish, by men outside and ahead of their times is something we can now conceive of and be prepared to look for. It is an acceptable axiom that the man who dares to be modern in a personal and obscure way must risk the immediate historical consequences, i.e. his own neglect and derogation.

The list is a long and formidable one of those who, destined to create an art truly original in its character, were also called upon to endure the consequences of this fidelity to their temperaments. The prototypical great painter, it may be, bears a closer resemblance to John Constable than to Sir Joshua Reynolds. In this age his name is Paul Cézanne and he did not live to profit from his efforts. In his life we see the destiny of the truly modern painter work itself out with exceptional purity.

There would seem to be a law involved. For even when the pattern has not the purity of Cézanne's life, or of Van Gogh's, the historical situation is not wholly evaded. The relationship between a man's life and his work is very mysterious, and the falling away in quality of the work of so many great men in their old age, after they had received the rewards of their youthful heroism, is of interest in this respect. Nor is the picture always clearcut. Baudelaire remarks that at a time when Delacroix had difficulty in finding a buyer for a canvas at 1000 francs, the little figures of Meissonier fetched ten or twenty times as much. Vermeer had a moderately successful life, but died grossly in debt and had to wait two hundred years before it was realised that he was one of the greatest painters who lived.

The truth no doubt lies in the deeper nature of the relation of art to society. It is not necessary to subscribe to the tiresome conception of the artist as rampaging Bohemian to understand that the activity of painting is socially useless, or at best occupies a dubious position. (I take it as unnecessary to remark on the futility of the notion of art as a social function of man.) In the remote purity of his solitariness, where the work of art is made, the artist is supremely the anti-social creature. This solitariness is not necessarily achieved in the country or by the seaside, one can be very much alone on the top of a bus, etc. The artist, as artist, occupies a position that is fundamentally neither social nor amenable to social arrangement.

Society has always honoured this fact in one way or another. Despite the effect of the great men of the late 19th century, who it might be thought would have rendered the world safe for those who came after them, it was still possible even for Picasso to spend some time in the wilderness. The situation in the early years of this century was still characteristically difficult.

The social relevance, or one social relevance, of this difficulty is reflected in the salesrooms of the great cities to-day. A picture bought for £4 fetches £36,000 a mere thirty-five years later. This is an absolute reality socially because it is a financial reality.

It may be coincidental, but it is of interest that the art dealing business as it exists to-day dates from that period when the difficulty of the modern (or let us say Progressive, since it is truer to the current jargon) painter was most evident and first exploited. This fact cannot be viewed as simply pejorative. No one can deny the honour due to Vollard, or later to Kahnweiler or Uhde.

Nevertheless the consequences are there. It is not necessary to labour the point. The extraordinary and alarming increase in the number of art galleries is exactly equalled by the extraordinary and depressing increase in the number of Progressive artists who fill them monthly, yearly, recurrently, with progressive pictures.

It may be remarked that this system which after all is there as much to serve the good as the bad (unhappy terms, my objections are not really puritan) has very likely a demoralising effect on the young painter. Quite apart from the temptation to adapt his temperamental inclinations to the situation for financial reasons there is the more insidious temptation to overproduce. I hesitate to trot out the name of that much belaboured young man (who besides was a painter of talent at the age of eighteen) but Bernard Buffet supplies a classic example of the unhappy consequences of this latter evil.

It would be phony, however, to pretend too great a concern for the effects of the system of selling pictures on the character of contemporary painters. It is very likely unhealthy and occasionally disastrous even to some people of real talent. Yet the nature of art is so strange, so unpredictable, and the circumstance of its production so remote from the world of commerce that it would appear the truth is less alarming than the facts might lead one to suppose. It is possible that the occasions of corruption being so frequent the flowering of genuine vision is all the more intense, the more purified, and consequently more valuable than ever. Still one is entitled to one's concern, and it may not be altogether useless to attempt to keep a proper perspective on the situation. It would be hopeless as well as pointless to attempt the role of posterity, but quite interesting and useful to observe the pattern, bearing in mind the history of that odd animal nowadays called the Progressive Painter.

To-day it is not uncommon to hear art experts predict the next step in the history of painting. Not only journalists (who may be said to preserve a greater sanity, by and large) but dealers and museum directors are addicted to this game.

A common recent claim of this kind, for instance, has been that America has 'taken the lead' from Paris, or Europe simply, and that certain American painters are making the sort of pictures which shall determine the next direction the art of painting will take (though it must be noticed that it is a plain fact such pictures are also being made in Japan, Bulgaria, Chile, etc.). These claims nearly always deal in large numbers of painters at once under the cover of 'movements'. Any one with a small knowledge of history must realize how far the number of great painters involved in these movements exceeds that of the richest period ever recorded.

A situation has occurred wherein a premium is put on any work qualifying for the term 'progressive'.

Recent large-scale international exhibitions and competitions demonstrate this beyond doubt. The whole machinery of organised culture—museums, institutes, councils, societies for the spread of culture, etc., all compete to produce and to patronise 'modern and progressive' art.

In fact we have now a new official art to the furtherance and protection of which the whole Establishment is committed. It is the new academicism and it is open to doubt whether in the end it is more amusing or desirable than the old.

It has traditionally been the position of the modern artist that he has found himself outside the world of official encouragement. His art was unconventional, disturbing, etc., and he was driven to work out his salvation alone and apart.

This at any rate is a fair approximation to the truth. It will not be difficult to find partial or perhaps occasional real exceptions.

Still, it was in fact because of his rejection from the official world that Paul Cézanne retired 'to work in silence until the day when I should feel myself able to defend in theory the results of my attempts'. There is no doubt he tried hard to be accepted first. Then after years of silent and courageous effort during which the public saw nothing, when to destroy had as much relevance to the progress of the work as to preserve or show, etc., it inevitably happened that the world was drawn to the strange and powerful vision so heroically engineered in isolation. The purity of the circumstance in which the work was created contributed to the intensity of the quality in the final structure. Leonardo da Vinci remarked: 'Truth is never where men shout and scarcely ever where they speak.' And if the isolation of Cézanne has a relation to the quality of his work it may be of interest to ask whether that isolation would be required to-day. For it may be that every artist is conditioned, can be diminished or increased, by the action of circumstance. It may be that a law of dialectics operates in art too.

I am not about to advocate starvation and neglect as a recipe for powerful art. One cannot choose one's fate. If a man is not isolated from the universal involuntarily, then the tragedy is bogus, as Kierkegaard points out.

Certain facts require explanation. Rembrandt's great work occurs in his old age, not in any sense a happy old age. This is not true of Braque, it is not true of Picasso. The heroic effects of Van Gogh, Gauguin, or the remarkable Seraphine, were not called forth by the action of any council for culture. The question is, what kind of painter is likely to be called upon to suffer the circumstances which will require heroism. It is not merely a social question, but is symptomatically thus observable.

Those painters who to-day work under the banner or label of the Modern, the Progressive, can hardly accuse the public of not taking notice. They are the spoiled children (Baudelaire's phrase in 1859 for the established) of a vast culture-loving audience. What they inherit is the enthusiasm which these people would have showered on the neglected masters had they but known, etc. Above all they inherit the developed taste for certain qualities in the art of painting. Particularly the appreciation of what everybody knows to be the sensual qualities of paint. This phrase, alas, has not any obscene connotations, and the whole idea is thoroughly healthy, eminently acceptable in the suburbs.

The suburbs are also thoroughly familiar with the postulates of the New Art.

It would be a waste of time for me to undertake the task of describing what is already so well known. A typical quotation will do to indicate what I have in mind when I use the phrase New Art. This, from an old newspaper review of the vast Documenta exhibition at Kassel: 'Almost all the painting and sculpture is non-representational, it is either non-figurative or if figuration is admitted, the artist is more concerned with imagery than with representation. . . . The abandonment of representation has not meant the abandonment of the visible world. If he wishes the artist can still refer to things that are real . . . colour, light, space, shape, texture, movement. He can even make reference to actual objects without needing to represent them. . . . There is a comparable situation in music and it must be admitted that the new art like the new music makes considerable demands on those trying to familiarise themselves with it.' There is also this serious sentence: 'there is no room for off-beat artists and for developments the significance of which is not yet apparent on an international level.'

The first thing which occurs to me, when faced with this sort of journalism, is how very nice it would be if the claims made were true. If only it really was a new art and had not in fact reached its real point of extremus in 1915 with those very great men Kandinsky and Mondrian, not to speak of the earlier orphism, rayonism, nonobjectivism, suprematism, etc., all about 1915. Secondly, if only it were difficult to familiarise oneself with it, if it were not so very familiar already. And then if only we could be spared the exclusive puritanism throughout.

For I am not interested in taking a stand on the grounds of aesthetics (one respects Mondrian) except to say these techniques which lay claim to freedom and to releasing powers of an imaginative order depend in fact on a strict aesthetic both narrow and constricting. And here we have the prime characteristic of an Official Art. It is noticeable that rejection and selection no longer operate in terms of merely quality but depend on kind. This is exactly the situation confronting the Impressionists who attempted to show their works in the salon of 1865.

It may be that never before has the Official Art of the day been so conformist and so uniform in character. Perhaps after a period of great discovery this is inevitable. It seems to me a reasonable proposition that the extraordinary depth of Cézanne's achievement has not been assimilated yet, nor has the full meaning of the great Cubist pictures been understood.

Behind all the muddle that fills the philosophical justifications for the new art there lurks another old bogey it would be well to drag into the air for a minute.

It is the idea of progress in the arts; the notion that we move forward from one good thing to another in a simple progression and in a single direction.

Baudelaire dealt so profoundly with this particular idiocy that it requires a certain arrogance to set up an attack on it from any other angle. Also Wyndham Lewis in a more muddled way, but still forcefully and with vigour, exposed its pernicious effects. But this can be said: if there were such a thing as a direct and simple progression from the work of one generation to the next the historical difficulty of the Progressive Artist could not exist.

In the light of the New Art one must ask: has history relented on the painter and ceased to require that servitude to suffering which has previously been the fate of the artist who dared to obey the categoric imperative to be contemporary?

I cannot believe that the activity of any number of institutes, councils, societies, etc., can change the relation, the deep and perverse character of the relation, of the artist to society.

Put it grandiosely; I cannot believe History is to be so easily cheated of her prize victims or that art will condescend to reveal her mysteries without demanding her ancient tribute.

The point is this; it may well be time some one informed the art-loving public that the popular notion of the Progressive Artist and the New Art may not after all be the last word on a complex subject. That there may be, even to-day, and in spite of the vast activity surrounding the painter, such a thing as the *absolutely modern*. That as before it may be something unexpected, and not completely accounted for in the arrangements for encouraging the arts.

For to be contemporary is not necessarily to be part of any movement, to be included in the official representations of national and international art. History shows that it may well be the opposite. It may be that it is the odd, the personal, the curious, the simply honest, that at this moment, when everyone looks to the extreme and flamboyant, constitutes the most interesting manifestation of the spirit of art.

Certainly the quality of unique and heroic effort which is so much a part of the real activity of painting is more likely to be found outside the vast international movements of anonymous styles that form the common character of the so called modern from Eastern Poland to Western California. *It may be necessary to be absolutely modern.*

FRANK AUERBACH

Fragments from a Conversation

Painting is a practical day-to-day thing I think. One might say something clever, one might say something big, but one does something limited. It is a serious thing—like religion—like love—one does the persistent thing, and then the really remarkable happens when something's there that wasn't there before. The consciousness—the strictness—and then the image. The image, the good painting, is the result of conscientious experimentation—conscientious roots—one has to be true to that, I mean the object, then one's more likely to get a unique result.

If one paints somebody one knows—I've painted the same person thirty times (one's got to use small words)—one's even more got to know—one can tell ... with someone one knows one's got to destroy the momentary things. At the end comes a certain improvisation. I get the courage to do the improvisation only at the end—a gaiety ... a serious word ... Miro is a gay painter.

But painting is a practical thing, and words are so windy. The subject—places one knows, things one loves—it's almost a guilty secret which one keeps in painting ... or it might destroy the spontaneity. I'm always much more interested in people painting their toenails—but there's a borderline where the conscience takes over. One must be perpetually willing to destroy. It's a surprise to me ... one starts with an ordinary idea ... one might do the feeble thing again and again ... but you've got to be left with something that wasn't there before ... it's got to be a revelation ... (they're always lies, one's bad pictures). In the case of Rembrandt (every body loves Rembrandt, but one must use these big words) ...

There is an urgency apart from people. Intimate circumstances ... some things can be obviously untrue ... there is a false courage, a false meticulousness. In painting one destroys everything, in life one can't do it—the day-to-day crudities destroy all the things one's used to ... known already. It's a sort of rage ... I always finish pictures in anger ... it's exacerbated conscience. One never has power over anything, can never do anything clearly or purely.

This moment of somebody's being able to destroy all the relevance—it works, maybe, but it doesn't quite work, because it doesn't relate to one's experience ... it isn't moral. That's why one paints the things one loves because one is aware of all the relevances; maybe, it's the only way to get power over the things one loves ... that's why in the Jewish religion it's forbidden to make images ... because one worships *them* not the things they are images of. One gets suspicious of love, of religion, of everything. In the end it's impossible. In painting one can destroy it.

Everybody has a certain amount of energy. It *is* a question of energy. Sometimes I think it weakness, madness, a disease, but it's the only creative thing anyone does except the thing women do ... it's a question of getting up in the morning ... before one can say anything one's got to learn the language ... I could tell you the date at which I reached it, finding the image—strange and new to me. In the morning I'd been working, very, very conscientiously, painting a building site ... suddenly I was conscious of something underneath it ... this building site, I'd done it again and again, I knew it intimately ... and then there suddenly was the image underneath it . I'd destroyed all the reminders (that is, of painting) to get a unique thing ... it began to operate by its own laws ... but it's senseless and irrelevant unless it's tied, anchored, to truth. It's a question of freeing the possibilities of improvisation which contain the mysteries.

What happened on the building site?

Every other activity is useless, awkward—one hopes to destroy merely in painting. Worrying about a specific painting one uses cunning, common sense, lying, deceit, acceptance of things . . . it may be a useless activity, painting. The thing that gives me a thrill about other people's paintings—paintings that I'd cross the road to see—is a vision pushed to its extreme. One doesn't care at all about idiom—manner. Personality consists in this thing of conscience. Van Gogh . . . Degas (blind)—formal problems express a question of conscience—being true to oneself, which means finding unique forms—their feelings about clouds above cornfields, aloneness, blindness . . . it's all contained within their paint-marks. One can feel how it's been done if one is at all alive to anything—the moral quality's always there.

Cimabue . . . negro sculpture seem new, art is always new. It is impossible to do something good that is repetitious. Rembrandt is not better than Cimabue, nor is Cimabue better than Rembrandt. One's got to make a new problem, to make it one's own—the identity is new, that is one of the points about it. All important discoveries are made in the course of autobiographies . . . sometimes an extreme situation drives one—once or twice in one's life if one's lucky.

One tries to do what one can't do—painting is a very specific thing, even the painting I've done in the past is impossible to do. In the act of trying—the new look—it sometimes happens by opposites . . . bright colours suddenly look brittle, so one tries to push it further—strongly divided in black and white . . . suddenly turned the brown to yellow . . . destroy it, and so on. But it happens in specific ways—by a hair's breadth (these are windy running words), but I think one should never *try* to do anything new. Big words—all they can do is stir one's conscience.

An artificial activity (like marriage, etc.)—made by discipline . . . one can push painting a long way oneself by discipline . . . then one gets one's reward. Without discipline, rigours, rules, the discovery wouldn't mean anything at all.

Rembrandt and others seem alive because they are reaching out for something. Bad painting sets itself too low an aim—not difficult enough (I won't say complex, because one's trying to do a simple thing and can't). There are two absolutely distinct things in painting; 'this is *not* like this it's like *that*' . . . not academic or boring, but introducing interesting things, opening the door to new ideas (or not ideas, perhaps *facts*) . . . seeing that a nose is longer introduces a new fact. But if that were enough the painting would be repetitious—there is the image one's striving for. These two things, the fact and the image, one tries to tie up (lock the stable door . . . clinch the image . . . have the truth in it . . .) the conflict between the image and the object—in the most scrupulous way. Truth will always be different from what one's already achieved.

Then of course one always has physical needs—food—love—peace. Painting is a form of action, moral action—the bad is intolerable. I often feel it's a disease, a form of weakness that makes me turn to painting . . . to do something unnatural in order to . . . but it's also entertaining. One has energy that needs to act.

What I like to know about painters is where they live, what time they get up in the morning, and all those things. I always take a long time over everything, three or four years over a painting—sometimes it's lack of energy, sometimes it's seeing everything again. I prefer my idiom versatile so that I can do a painting quickly or slowly. I can admire the pernickety (like, say, Michael Andrews) but for myself I like the greatest possible freedom . . . surprise may condition the painting, it looks different every day, even from an hour before . . . it may be white in the morning . . . unrecognisable . . . colours change—but that's a personal idiom. I can see other ways one could work—that could be equally workable. I like painting quickly again and again and again (I'm slow-witted)—one tries to get everything in (Delacroix's drawings). And it's partly the financial thing, if one has money, canvases . . . one's always limited by one's canvases, one's models, etc., etc.

It's conceivable I could have painted differently, but the quality of the personality remains. Friends . . . influences . . . Bomberg taught me a lot. Courageous people teach one. Good painters have courage, that makes them good painters, and of course the fact that they prefer painting to anything else. Painters if not committed to painting might spend their energy on other things. Painting is my form of action. Many people taught me. And I suppose Bomberg taught me as much as anyone. Then Rembrandt in the National Gallery—I went every day for a long time. I drew from paintings then drew them as if I'd drawn them myself . . . I looked at them again and drew over them. Turner, Tintoretto, Poussin—Tintoretto has tremendous brilliance, tremendous energy . . . Rembrandt and Tintoretto seem to be the polarity of what can be called good painting—the gaiety of Tintoretto, the conscientiousness of Rembrandt, his doggedness, though of course the excitement was bound to be there, they were poles apart, but there is no difference. If one's got to make distinctions—Tintoretto gets by one way, he exacerbates us, Rembrandt gets by by doggedness—pushing and pushing until he gets there.

Other people taught me. Someone sent me outside to draw. I'm grateful for that . . . other people too . . . the thing is to get other people's rules and destroy them and get one's own. But I'm grateful to all the people who taught me.

After ten years working in isolation, I was surprised when other people began to see it. I had to adjust myself to the fact that people wanted to see my paintings . . . one destroyed their teaching in order to be able to work. The only possible progress is to destroy . . . then one's left with nothing one began with but a new fact.

SAMUEL BECKETT
L'Image

La langue se charge de boue en seul remède alors la rentrer et la tourner dans la bouche la boue l'avaler ou la rejeter question de savoir si elle est nourrissante et perspectives, sans y être obligé par le fait de boire souvent j'en prends une bouchée c'est une de mes ressources la garde un bon moment question de savoir si avalée elle me nourrirait et perspectives qui s'ouvrent, ce ne sont pas de mauvais moments me dépenser tout est là la langue resort rose dans la boue que font les mains pendant ce temps il faut toujours voir ce que font les mains, eh bien la gauche nous l'avons vu tient toujours le sac et la droite eh bien la droite au bout d'un moment je la vois là-bas au bout de son bras allongé au maximum dans l'axe de la clavicule si ça peut se dire ou plutôt se faire qui s'ouvre et se referme dans la boue s'ouvre et se referme c'est une autre de mes ressources, ce petit geste m'aide je ne sais pourquoi j'ai comme ça des petits trucs qui sont d'un bon secours même rasant les murs sous le ciel changeant je devais être malin déjà, elle ne doit pas être bien loin un mètre à peine mais je la sens loin un jour elle s'en ira toute seule sur ses quatre doigts en comptant le pouce car il en manque un pas le pouce et me quittera je la vois qui jette ses quatre doigts en avant comme des grappins les bouts s'enfoncent tirent et ainsi elle s'éloigne par petits rétablissements horizontaux c'est ce que j'aime m'en aller comme ça par petits bouts et les jambes que font les jambes oh les jambes et les yeux que font les yeux fermés assurément eh bien non puisque soudain là sous la boue je me vois je dis me comme je dis je comme je dirais il parce que ça m'amuse, je me donne dans les seize ans et il fait par comble de bonheur un temps délicieux ciel bleu d'oeuf et chevauchée de petits nuages je me tourne le dos et la fille aussi que je tiens par la main le cul que j'ai, à en juger par les fleurs qui émaillent l'herbe émeraude nous sommes au mois d'avril ou de mai j'ignore et avec quelle joie d'où je tiens ces histoires de fleurs et de saisons je les tiens un point c'est tout, à en juger par certains accessoires dont une barrière blanche et une tribune d'un rouge exquis nous sommes sur un champ de courses la tête rejetée en arrière nous regardons j'imagine droit devant nous immobilité de statue à part les bras aux mains entrelacées qui se balan-

cent, dans ma main libre ou gauche un objet indéfinissable et par
conséquent dans sa droite à elle l'extrémité d'une courte laisse conduisant
à un chien terrier couleur de cendre de bonne taille assis de guingois tête
basse immobilité de ces mains-ci et des bras correspondants, question de
savoir pourquoi une laisse dans cette immensité de verdure et naissance
peu à peu de taches grises et blanches auxquelles je ne tarde pas à donner
le nom d'agneaux au milieu de leurs mères j'ignore d'où je tiens ces histoires d'animaux je les tiens un point c'est tout dans un bon jour je sais
nommer quatre ou cinq chiens de race totalement différente je les vois
n'essayons pas de comprendre surtout, au fond du paysage à une distance
de quatre ou cinq milles à vue de nez la masse bleutée d'une longue mon-
tagne de faible élévation nos têtes en dépassent le faîte, comme mûs d'un
seul et même ressort ou si l'on veut de deux synchronisés nous nous
lâchons la main et faisons demi-tour moi dextrorsum elle senestro, elle
transfère la laisse à sa main gauche et moi au même instant à ma droite
l'objet maintenant un petit paquet blanchâtre en forme de brique des
sandwichs peut-être bien histoire sans doute de pouvoir mêler nos mains
de nouveau ce que nous faisons les bras se balancent le chien n'a pas
bougé j'ai l'absurde impression que nous me regardons je rentre la langue
ferme la bouche et souris, vue de face la fille est moins vilaine ce n'est pas
elle qui m'intéresse moi pâles cheveux en brosse grosse face rouge avec
boutons ventre débordant braguette béante jambes cagneuses en fuseau
écartées pour plus d'assise fléchissant aux genoux pieds ouverts cent
trente-cinq degrés minimum demi-sourire béat à l'horizon postérieur
figure de la vie qui se lève tweed vert bottines jaunes coucou ou similaire à
la boutonnière, nouveau demi-tour vers l'intérieur soit de nature à nous
amener fugitivement pas fesses mais face à face au bout de quatre-vingts
degrés transferts rattachement des mains balancement des bras immobilité du chien ce fessier que j'ai, trois deux un gauche droite nous voilà
partis nez au vent bras se balançant le chien suit tête basse queue sur les
couilles rien à voir avec nous il a eu la même idée au même instant du
Malebranche en moins rose les lettres qu'avais alors s'il pisse il le fera
sans s'arrêter j'ai envie de crier Plaque-la là et cours t'ouvrir les veines,
trois heures de pas cadencé et nous voilà au sommet le chien s'assied de
guingois dans la bruyère baisse le nez sur sa bitte noire et rose pas la force
de la lécher nous au contraire demi-tour vers l'intérieur transferts rattachement des mains balancement des bras dégustation en silence de la mer et
des îles têtes qui pivotent comme une seule vers les fumées de la cité
repérage en silence des monuments têtes qui reviennent on dirait reliées
par un essieu bref brouillard et nous revoilà qui mangeons les sandwichs à
bouchées alternées chacun le sien en échangeant des mots doux Ma chérie
je mords elle avale Mon chéri elle mord j'avale nous ne roucoulons pas
encore la bouche pleine Mon amour je mords elle avale Mon trésor elle

mord j'avale bref brouillard et nous revoilà qui nous éloignons de nouveau à travers champs la main dans la main les bras se balançant la tête haute vers les sommets de plus en plus petits je ne vois plus le chien je ne nous vois plus la scène est débarrassée quelques bêtes les moutons qu'on dirait du granit qui affleure un cheval que je n'avais pas vu debout immobile échine courbée tête basse les bêtes savent bleu et blanc du ciel matin d'avril sous la boue, c'est fini c'est fait ça s'éteint la scène reste vide quelques bêtes puis s'éteint plus de bleu je reste là, là-bas à droite dans la boue la main s'ouvre et se referme ça aide qu'elle s'en aille, je me rends compte que je souris encore ce n'est plus la peine depuis longtemps ce n'est plus la peine, la langue resort va dans la boue je reste comme ça plus soif la langue rentre la bouche se referme elle doit faire une ligne droite à présent c'est fait j'ai fait l'image.

PATRICK KAVANAGH

Living in the Country

Opening

It was the Warm Summer, that landmark
In a child's mind, an infinite day
Sunlight and burnt grass
Green grasshoppers on the railway slopes
The humming of wild bees
The whole summer during the school holidays
Till the blackberries appeared.
Yes, a tremendous time that summer stands
Beyond the grey finities of normal weather.

[The Main Body]

It's not nearly as bad as you'd imagine
Living among small farmers in the north of Ireland
They are for the most part the ordinary frightened
Blind brightened, referred to sometimes socially
As the underprivileged.
They cannot perceive Irony or even Satire
They start up with insane faces if
You break the newspaper moral code.
'Language' they screech 'you effing so and so'
And you withdraw into a precarious silence

Organising in your mind quickly, for the situation is tense,
The theological tenets of the press.

There's little you can do about some
Who roar horribly as you enter a bar
Incantations of ugliness, words of half a syllable
Locked in malicious muteness full of glare.
And your dignity thinks of giving up the beer.
But I trained in the slum pubs of Dublin
Among the most offensive class of all—
The artisans—am equal to this problem;
I let it ride and there is nothing over.
I understand through all these years
That my difference in their company is an intrusion
That tears at the sentimental clichés
They can see my heart squirm when their star rendites
The topmost twenty in the lowered lights.
No sir, I did not come unprepared.

Oddly enough I begin to think of Saint Francis
Moving in this milieu (of his own time of course)
How did he work the oracle?
Was he an old fraud, a non-poet
Who is loved for his non-ness
Like any performer.

I protest here and now and forever
On behalf of all my peoples who believe in Verse
That my intention is not satire but humaneness
An eagerness to understand more about sad man
Frightened man, the workers of the world
Without being savaged in the process.
Broadness is my aim, a broad road where the many
Can see life easier—generally.

Here I come to a sticky patch
A personal matter that perhaps
Might be left as an unrevealed hinterland
For our own misfortunes are mostly unimportant.
But that wouldn't do.
So with as little embarrassment as possible I tell
How I was done out of a girl,
Not as before by a professional priest but by
The frightened artisan's morality.

It was this way.
She, a shopgirl of nineteen or less
Became infatuated by the old soldier,
The wide travelled the sin-wise.
Desdemona—Othello idea.
O holy spirit of infatuation
God's gift to his poetic nation!
One day her boss caught her glance.
'You're looking in his eyes' he said.
From then on all the powers of the lower orders—
Perhaps all orders—were used to deprive me of my prize
Agamemnon's Briseis.
It soured me a bit as I had
Everything planned, no need to mention what,
Except that it was August evening under whitethorn
And early blackberries.

In many ways it is a good thing to be cast into exile.
Among strangers
Who have no inkling
Of The Other Man concealed
Monstrously musing in a field.
For me they say a Rosary
With many a glossary.

Lecture Hall

To speak in summer in a lecture hall
About literature and its use
I pick my brains and tease out all
To see if I can choose
Something untarnished, some new news

From experience that has been immediate,
Recent, something that makes
The listener or reader
Impregnant, something that reinstates
The poet. A few words like birth-dates

That brings him back in the public mind,
I mean the mind of the dozen or so
Who constantly listen out for the two-lined

Message that announces the gusto
Of the dead arisen into the sun-glow.

Someone in America will note
The apparent miracle. In a bar
In Greenwich Village some youthful poet
Will mention it, and a similar
In London or wherever they are

Those pickers-up of messages that produce
The idea that underneath the sun
Things can be new as July dews—
Out of the frowsy, the second-hand won . . .
Keep at it, keep at it while the heat is on

I say to myself as I consider
Virginal crevices in my brain
Where the never-exposed will soon be a mother.
I search for that which has no stain,
Something discovered vividly and sudden.

STEVIE SMITH

The Last Turn of the Screw

I am Miles, I did not die,
I only turned, as on shut eye
To feel again the silken dress
Of my lovely governess.

Yes, it was warm, poetical and cosy
I never saw the other fellow when
I lolled on Lady's lap (I called her Lady)
But there were two of us all right. And both were men.

Yes, that's the oddest part. She made me feel
A hundred years more old than I was, than she was;
She'd had a sheltered life, of course, a vicarage,
Some bustling younger children, a father pious, I'm sure he was.

But two of us? Of me? I'll be explicit,
A soft boy, knowing rather more than boys should, lolling,
No harm in that, on Lady's lap; the other,
Source of my knowledge, half my self by now, but calling . . .

Some children are born innocent, some achieve it,
You scowl, that doesn't fit with your philosophy?
Can you by choosing alter Nature, you inquire?
Yes, my dear sir, you can; I found it fairly easy.

But calling (to go back a step) but calling?—
That proved he was not yet quite One of Us,
The vulgar little beast, the fellow Quint.
It was at first my lordly feelings held him off,
That dapper knowingness of his, for instance,
The clothes right, being my Uncle's, but worn wrong,
The accent careful, well he must be careful,
I daresay he had thumbed a book about it . . .
To spend ten minutes with a Thing like this
Would be too long.
So snobbery made the breach; religion followed . . .
Ten minutes? No, Eternity, with *Quint*,
This Quint, whose seedy sickness in my blood
I could detect (in time?) running to flood,
The sickliness of sin,
Oh yes, I saw quite plain by now
What was going in.
How did I fob him off? (now we know why)
When half my heart
Was panting for him and what he could teach,
Reaching for shame, and retching too,
(It was, as I have said, this squeamishness I had
First judged him bad.)
Oh there was still some rotting to go on
In my own heart
Before I was quite ready to cry 'Out!'
And see him off, though half my blood went with him.
I grow a shade dramatic here, none went at all,
My sinews have remained the same, my blood, my heart
Have not, as I'm aware, taken a taint,
I was not and I am not now a saint,
But I loved Virtue, and I love her still,

Especially as I see her in the dress
Of my sweetly fatheaded governess. . . .

Well, let's be plain, I fobbed Quint off
By simply failing to be clever enough,
By taking nothing in, not looking and not noticing,
I made myself as dull to the persuading
Of all that shabby innuendo as
The plainest ten-year schoolboy ever was;
And so I have remained, and by intent,
Quite dull. And shall remain
Sooner than chance such entering again.

I did not die, but bought my innocence
At the high price of an indifference
Where first I knew the most engaging love
That first through squeamishness made virtue move,
The love, now lost, of my sweet governess
Who cannot bear I should be so much less
The Miles she knew, or rather did not know.
Yes, I have lost my interestingness for Lady who
I fear as other innocent ladies do,
Hankered for something shady,
Well, say dramatic, not what I am now
An empty antic Clumsy, a mere boy.
She'll never know
The strength I have employed and do employ
To make it sure
I shall be this
And nothing more.

I am Miles, I did not die,
I only turn, as on shut eye
To feel again the silken dress
Of my lost and lovely governess,
And sigh and think it strange
That being dull I should feel so much pain.

Thoughts about the Person from Porlock

Coleridge received the Person from Porlock
And ever after called him a curse

Then why did he hurry to let him in?
He could have hid in the house.

It was not right of Coleridge in fact it was wrong
(But often we all do wrong)
As the truth is I think, he was already stuck
With Kubla Khan.

He was weeping and crying, I am finished, finished
I shall never write another word of it.
When along comes the Person from Porlock
And takes the blame for it.

It was not right it was wrong,
But often we all do wrong.

May we inquire the name of the Person from Porlock?
Why Porson, didn't you know?
He lived at the bottom of Porlock Hill
So had a long way to go.

He wasn't much in the social sense
Though his grandmother was a Warlock
One of the Rutlandshire ones I fancy
And nothing to do with Porlock.

But he lived at the bottom of the hill as I said
And had a cat named Flo.
And had a cat named Flo.

I long for the Person from Porlock
To bring my thoughts to an end
I am becoming impatient to see him
I think of him as a friend

Often I look out of the window
Often I run to the gate
I think, He will come this evening
I think it is rather late.

I am hungry to be interrupted
For ever and ever amen

O Person from Porlock come quickly
And bring my thoughts to an end.

I felicitate the people who have a Person from Porlock
To break up everything and throw it away
Because then there will be nothing to keep them
And they need not stay.

Oh this Person from Porlock is a great interrupter
He interrupts us for ever
People say he is a dreadful fellow
But really he is desirable.
Why should they grumble so much?
He comes like a benison
They should be glad he has not forgotten them
They might have had to go on.

These thoughts are depressing, I know. They are depressing.
I wish I was more cheerful it is more pleasant
Also it is a duty, we should smile as well as submitting
To the purpose of One Above who is experimenting
With various mixtures of human character which goes best
All is interesting for him it is exciting, but not for us.
There I go again. Smile smile and get some work to do
Then you will be practically unconscious without positively
having to go.

ALBERTO GIACOMETTI

The Dream, the Sphinx
and the Death of T.

Scared, I saw at the foot of my bed a huge brown hairy spider clinging to a thread which depended from the hangings directly above my bolster. 'No! No!' I exclaimed to myself, 'I couldn't bear such a menace over my head all night—kill it, kill it.' In my dream I spoke with as much repugnance as I should while awake.

At that moment I woke up; but I awoke in the dream, which went on. I lay in the same place at the foot of the bed: and at the very moment when I thought, 'It was a dream' I perceived—my eyes involuntarily looking for it—I perceived, as if displayed on a heap of earth or of shards or little flat stones, a yellow spider, ivory yellow, even more of a monster than the first, but sleek and as though covered with sleek yellow scales; with long thin claws, sleek and hard as bone. Terrified, I saw my companion's hand stretch out to touch the scales of the spider; she didn't seem to feel either fear or surprise. I cried out and took her hand away—as in the dream, I begged that the beast be killed. Someone I hadn't noticed until then smashed it with a long stick or spade—she hit at it violently and, turning my eyes away, I heard the scales crack and the queer squelching sound of the soft parts. It was only afterwards, while looking at the spider's remains collected on a plate, that I read a name very clearly written in ink on one of the scales. It was the name of one of a species of Arachnoid—I cannot give the name, I have forgotten it; I can only see the isolated letters, the black colour of the ink on the yellow ivory. It was the kind of lettering one sees on stones and shells in a museum. Obviously I was responsible for the killing of a rare specimen from the collection belonging to the friends with whom I was then staying. A moment later this was confirmed by the lamentations of an old house-keeper, who came in to look for the lost spider. My first impulse was to tell her what had happened, but I foresaw the unpleasant consequences and the bad odour I should be in with my hosts. I ought to have seen the name, and stopped it from being killed. So I decided to say nothing; to pretend ignorance and hide the remains. Carrying the plate I went out into the park and crossed it, taking care not to be seen (the plate in my hands would have looked odd), until I reached a piece of ploughed land hidden by briars at the foot of a slope. There, sure of not being observed, I threw what was left of the spider into a hole and trod it down, telling myself: 'The scales will have rotted before they can be discovered.' Just then, a little above me, I saw my host and his daughter riding by on horseback; they did not stop, but said something which surprised me; and I woke up.

For the whole of the next day I had this spider before my eyes: I was obsessed by it.

That evening, late at night, I had realized—from traces of ivory-yellow pus on a sheet of glossy white paper—that I had caught the disease I had suspected for some days. On finding this proof I was beset by a kind of spiritual paralysis that at first seemed to be involuntary and which prevented me from taking immediate steps about the illness. I neglected to do this, though it would have been easy enough. Nothing led me to believe that I was inflicting any kind of punishment on myself; rather, I dimly felt that the illness could be useful to me, might carry with it certain advantages of whose nature I was unaware.

As we lay in bed in the evening—before the dream—my companion, laughing, wanted to make certain I had the symptoms of the illness.

I had been expecting this illness since the previous Saturday. Having heard, at six in the evening, that the 'Sphinx' was about to be closed for good, I hurried there because I could not bear the idea of never seeing again the room where I had spent so many hours and so many evenings since it first opened, and which was for me the most wonderful place in the world.

I went to it this last time rather drunk, after lunching with some friends. At this lunch we had talked, among other things, about how interesting it would be to keep a diary and of the objections to doing so. I had an immediate desire, very unusual with me, to begin the diary at once, starting from that very moment when we were together. At this, Skira asked me to write for the next number of *Labyrinthe* the story of T's death which I had told him a little while before. I promised without any very clear notion of how to do it.

But since the dream, since the illness which takes me back to this lunch, the death of T. becomes real to me again.

Coming back from the doctor's in the afternoon, I asked myself if the mere coincidence in time of this request of Skira's and of the visit to the 'Sphinx' with its consequences, would thrust the memory of T's death on my mind with sufficient force to make me want to write about it to-day. I must say here that when I came out of the chemist's with the tubes of Thiazomides in my hand, the first thing which struck my eyes, on the threshold of the chemist's shop in the Avenue Junod, two doors from my doctor's house, was the signboard of the little café opposite: 'At the Sign of the Dream.'

As I walked along I saw T. once again during the days before he died, in the room next to mine in the little summerhouse at the bottom of the rather dilapidated garden where we were living. I saw him sunk in his bed, quiescent, his skin ivory yellow, huddled up and already strangely far away; and I saw him a little later, at three o'clock in the morning, dead, his limbs as thin as a skeleton's, sticking out, dispersed, unrelated to the body; a huge puffed-out belly, head thrown back, mouth open. No corpse had ever seemed to me so nullified; a wretched debris to be thrown like a dead cat into a ditch. Standing motionless by the couch I looked at his head: it had become a thing, a small box, measurable and meaningless. At that moment a fly approached the black hole of the mouth and slowly disappeared.

I helped to dress T. in his best, as if he were to appear at a brilliant gathering, at a party perhaps, or as if he were about to start on an important journey. By lifting and lowering the head, and moving it like some kind of object, I put on his tie. He was strangely dressed: everything looked natural and ordinary, but his shirt was sewn up at the collar and he wore no belt or braces or shoes. We covered him with a sheet and I went back to work till morning.

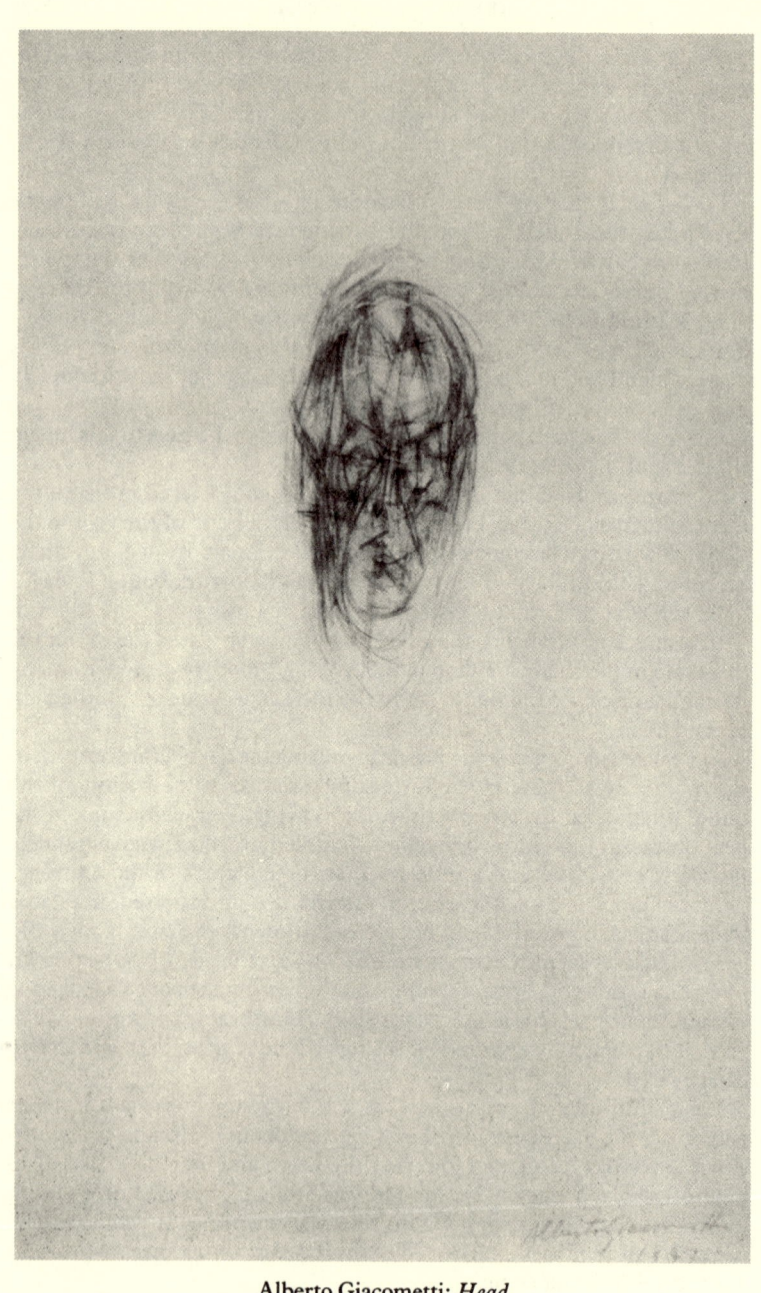

Alberto Giacometti: *Head*

The next night, on going to my room, I noticed that by some peculiar accident there was no light. A., invisible in bed, was asleep. The corpse was still in the room next door. This lack of light disquieted me. Just as I was on the point of walking, stark naked, down the black passage which passed the dead man's door and led to the bathroom, I was seized with real terror. Even while I didn't believe it, I had the vague feeling that T. was everywhere, everywhere but in the miserable corpse on the bed, the corpse which had seemed to me so inexistent; T. had no limits, and in panic fear of feeling an icy hand on my arm, I made a great effort and went down the passage, lay down in bed, and talked with A. with my eyes wide open till dawn.

I was experiencing in reverse what I had felt a few months before in the presence of living beings. At that time I had begun to see heads in the void, in the space surrounding them. When for the first time I clearly perceived the head I was looking at freeze, definitely become fixed in the moment, I shook with terror and felt a cold sweat down my back. It was no longer a living head, but an object like any other object that I was looking at—no, it was not like any other object, but like something alive and at the same time dead. I cried out with fear as if I had crossed a threshold, as if I had entered a world never seen before. All the living were dead: and this vision returned to me over and over again, in the underground, in the street, in restaurants, in the company of friends. That waiter at Lipp's became immobile, leaning over me, his mouth open, with no connection with the moment before or with the moment after, his mouth open, eyes fixed in absolute immobility. But at the same time objects as well as people were transformed—tables, chairs, clothes, streets, even trees and landscapes.

This morning when I woke up I saw my towel for the first time—a weightless towel in an immobility I had never noticed before, suspended, it seemed, in terrible silence. It had no relation to the chair with no seat to it, or to the table whose feet no longer rested on but barely touched the floor. There was no relation between objects; they were separated by measureless chasms of nothingness. I looked at the room panic stricken; a cold sweat ran down my back.

A few days after I had set down at one go what you have just read, I wanted to continue this story and work it over. I was sitting in a café in the Boulevard Barbès-Rochechouard where the legs of the prostitutes are strangely long, thin, slender.

A feeling of boredom and antagonism stopped me from re-reading what I had written. In spite of myself I began to describe the dream differently. I tried to express in a more precise and striking way what had impressed me: for instance, the size and thickness of the brown spider, the density of its hairs (it seemed to me they would be pleasant to touch), the position and exact shape of the hangings, the expected and dreaded appearance of the yellow spider, especially the shape of its scales—like flat and slippery waves—the curious jumble of its head and the acuity of its advancing right claw. I wanted to say all this in a uniquely affective manner, to make certain points hallucinatory, but without attempting to find the connection between them.

Discouraged, I gave up after a few lines.

Some black soldiers passed by in the fog—the same fog which had already filled me with unusual pleasure the day before.

There was contradiction between the affective way of expressing what I had found hallucinatory and the series of facts which I wanted to describe. I found myself confused in a mass of events, times, places, and sensations.

I tried to find a possible solution.

First of all I attempted to establish each fact by two words placed in a vertical column on the page. This came to nothing. I then drew little compartments—also vertical—which I could gradually fill up. In this way I attempted to place all the facts on the page simultaneously.

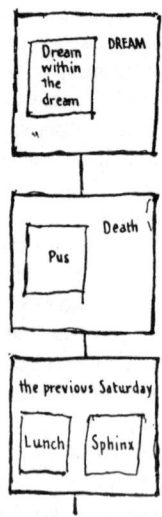

Alberto Giacometti: plans for 'The Dream, the Sphinx and the Death of T.'

Time was confused and I made a tentative effort to put everything chronologically. But always I came up against the pipe-shape form of storytelling which I find irritating. Throughout my story Time went the wrong way, from the present to the past, yet with repetitions and ramifications. In my first account, for instance, I had not found out how to introduce the lunch with R.M. at midday on the Saturday, before my visit to the doctor.

I had told my dream to R.M., but when I came to the moment when I was burying the remains, I saw myself in another field, surrounded by briars, at the edge of a forest. Pushing away the snow from my feet, digging into the hardened ground, I was burying a piece of half-eaten bread (theft of bread in my childhood). I saw myself in Venice, running, a piece of bread I wanted to get rid of clutched tightly in my hand. I roamed the whole of Venice looking for remote and deserted districts. After several futile attempts on the most obscure little bridges, on the edges of the gloomiest canals, quivering with nerves I threw the bread into the fetid water at the bend of a canal shut in by black walls. I ran away in a panic, scarcely conscious of myself. Everything has led me to describe the state I was in at that moment. Now to give an account of my journey in the Tyrol, the death of Van M. (see note), that long rainy day when, sitting alone beside the bed in the hotel bedroom, a book by Maupassant on Flaubert in my hand, I watched the head of Van M. become transformed (the nose becoming more and more accentuated, the cheeks hollower, the almost motionless mouth scarcely breathing; towards evening, while trying to make a drawing of this profile, I was suddenly overcome by the fear that he was going to die); the stay in Rome the summer before (the newspaper that fell into my hands by chance carried a notice seeking my whereabouts) the train to Pompeii, the temple of Paestum.

Also: the dimensions of the temple, the dimensions of the man who sprang up between the columns (a man appearing between the columns becomes a giant. The temple doesn't become smaller: the metrical size no longer counts. This is the reverse of what happens, for example, in St Peter's, Rome. The empty interior of this church seems small (this is very apparent in photographs). But the human beings are turned into ants. St Peter's doesn't grow bigger: it is only the metrical dimension which takes effect.)

This led to discussion of the dimension of heads, of the dimension of objects, of the affinities and differences of objects to living beings. In this way I came to what preoccupied me above all else at the moment when I was telling that story on the Saturday at midday.

Sitting in the café in the Boulevard Barbès-Rochechouard, I thought of all this and tried to find a way of putting it down. I suddenly felt that all these occurrences existed simultaneously around me. Time became horizontal and circular, was space at the same time. This I tried to draw.

Soon afterwards I left the café.

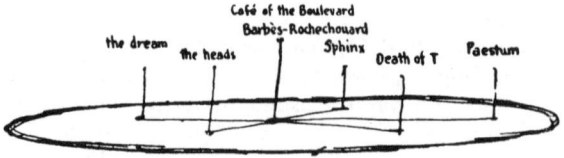

Alberto Giacometti: plans for 'The Dream, the Sphinx and the Death of T.'

This horizontal disc filled me with pleasure, and as I walked along I saw it simultaneously under two different aspects. I saw it drawn vertically on a page.

Alberto Giacometti: plans for 'The Dream, the Sphinx and the Death of T.'

But I held to the horizontal, I didn't want to lose it. I saw the design turn into an object: a disc with a radius of nearly two metres, divided by lines. Written on each division was the name, date, and place to which it corresponded. At the edge of the circle, in front of each division, rose a panel. These panels were of different sizes, and separated by empty spaces.

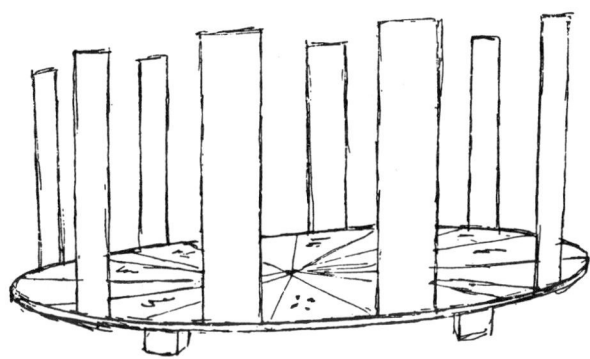

Alberto Giacometti: plans for 'The Dream, the Sphinx and the Death of T.'

On the panels was developed the story corresponding to the divisions. With strange pleasure I imagined myself walking on this disc—time—space—and reading the story before me. The freedom to begin where I liked, for instance to start off from the dream in October 1946 and, having gone all the way round, to land a few months earlier in front of the objects, in front of my towel. To find the bearings of each fact on the disc meant a great deal to me.

But the panels are still empty: I do not know the value of words or their relationships with each other well enough to be able to fill them in.

NOTE.—*The journey I made in 1921 (the death of Van M. and all the events which surrounded it) made as it were a breach in my life. Everything became changed; and this journey obsessed me continuously for a whole year. I never got tired of telling the story and often wished to write it down, but this was always impossible. Only to-day, through the dream, through the bread in the canal, has it for the first time become possible for me to mention it.*

Translated from the French by Mary Hutchinson and David Wright.

DAVID GASCOYNE

Remembering the Dead

In the mornings, the day-labourers must set to work once more, and daily tasks be newly undertaken or resumed; and they who work must disregard their usual disillusionment.

'We shall not see a culmination of these labours; our handiwork will not last long nor our success outlive us; our successors taking over what we've done will as like as not disparage it; and if we build houses, they are for strangers to live in for a little while or for the next War to destroy.

'Meanwhile we will lose ourselves with a will in what we do to-day. We will tacitly discourage those who would recall too many things or pay too much attention to the future. (All that we cannot see is very small and unimportant). We will put guilt upon them and they shall be silenced.'

And in the mornings, nevertheless, in such a year as this when rain has early in the season put an end to all hope of another extravagant Summer (since a year or two ago an unexpectedly Elysian climate did for once transform the country with such profusion and intensity of flower-hues and foliage that for the first time many millions were amazed by earth's magnificence); on wet summer mornings, when electric light has to be turned on in the offices in the City, and listlessness and resignation walk the streets, some of the workers (no-one knows how many but they may be very numerous) are disturbed by thoughts they have not thought themselves, distracted at their work as though by voices from beneath the chilly ground.

Think, ah! think how vastly they outnumber us by now, the populations of the underworld! How immemorially have they been accumulating there, and how enormous must their number be whom there are none now living to remember. Think how they too may all be working.

I think they think of us—Oh, how incalculably much more than ever we think of them! We scarcely think of them at all; we all prefer soon to forget; if we remember, it is only with regret. They think of us, they think of all of us; they think critically, no doubt, perhaps constructively, with more understanding than we have. Perhaps all day, all night, uninterruptedly.

It may be that only they fully realise that there is no other way of solving the problems of life and death than by thinking about them always.

We do not know the whole Truth; we think we know the Truth. We cannot know it, yet we must. We must seek the Truth we do not know, nor can know while we are still searchers here. Those who have neither curiosity nor doubts are the only real dead.

II

GEORGE BARKER

How to Refuse a Heavenly House

There are four lines of William Butler Yeats that make more sense on the difference between what the poet is and what the poet does than most other judgements I know on the subject.

> The intellect of man is forced to choose
> Perfection of the life or of the work
> And if it take the second, must refuse
> A heavenly mansion, raging in the dark.

I do not know whether most readers of contemporary literature are in the habit of according serious credence to the statements of poetry, or whether, like the descendants of Dr Richards at Cambridge, you dismiss such things as pseudo-statements (whatever they may be).

When Coleridge proposed that in the reading of a poem the intelligence performed a willing suspension of disbelief, he omitted to add that simultaneously an act of interpretive credence can, and often does, occur. So that an interpretive concurrence, or belief, can take place where the intelligence has elected to suspend its incredulity.

Thus it is not necessary to take these lines of Yeats as the flat statement of an ethical or artistic quandary. He is not saying merely: You must write well or live well but you can't do both. He is saying this, but he is also saying a lot more. Yeats is also defending the right of the poet to sacrifice absolutely everything and everybody, including the man or First Person Singing himself, on the altars of his own imaginative dedication. Because it is only by such extravagant offerings that the poet can persuade the powers of the air to surrender their secrets, and not always then. This of course is to say little more than that a poet has got to take writing poetry a bit seriously; for, even though this remark sounds elementary, it is in some danger, at present, of being categorically decried.

I decline to believe that a poet is by definition a man who devotes eight hours a day to the affairs of International Business Machines and then, in the evening, sits down to compose some verses on finding a green insect trapped in his typewriter. For that choice spoken of by Yeats only too truly does in fact exist. The man who spends a lot of time making sure that his nest is tolerably well feathered ought not to be surprised if he is never tempted to fly.

I am not exclusively inferring that only poets who live disreputable lives write reputable poetry. I should like to say this but I still retain a modified respect for historical facts.

Nor is it to the point that poets who appear to be living reputable lives, may, in truth, be living rather sordid lives: what goes on inside the glass houses of their heads may well be anything but proper. I recall an exquisite sentence of Rémy de Gourmont's on the matter:

> This dreary and picturesque town is licentious with so much decency that the stranger sees nothing to arouse his suspicions or curiosity.

When Arthur Rimbaud demanded that the poet should school himself in the systematic derangement of all his senses, he was claiming, at the same time, the right to forfeit even one's own intellectual and moral justification. And that was what he did. It is why the life of Rimbaud constitutes perhaps the clearest allegory of the Poetic Damnation. When he decided to become a person he did not emigrate to America (as a sensible man would have done)—he went to the Blue Mountains and started trafficking in slaves and guns.

He thought he had given up the art of poetry but instead he was practising what, until then, he had merely written. This constituted the derangement of the sixth sense.

I am aware that all this is highly speculative, for it seeks to investigate two matters neither of which is more than pretty crudely comprehended: the nature of poetry and the ethics of privacy. At such a time as these years of disgrace, with things what they so darkly are, we may, I think, allow ourselves to guess about absolute principles without being intellectually irresponsible. For even now it is not a guarantee of intellectual responsibility that you permit yourself to reflect only on physics, politics, or the functioning of your kitchen sink. When William Faulkner said: 'There are no longer any spiritual issues, there is merely the question of when you are going to be blown up'—when he said this he was guilty, to my mind, of a barely forgiveable naïvety: Will Mr Faulkner really mind very much when he is blown up? If he does, that is his spirit worrying about it. If he does not mind, that is an even rarer spiritual condition. His remark looks like the unsophistication of an intelligence that has never seriously contemplated that possibility of which a wise Frenchman said: 'It is time man learned at last to resign himself to annihilation, and even to enjoy that idea whose sweetness is incomparable.'

I ask if the poet should simply sit down and compose the obituaries of a civilization, or whisper into the ear of this wretched automation that there are other alternatives beside suicide? (It is hard to believe that the poet should stroll around the gardens of the West making petulant remarks about the young scientists who have taken the drains up again.)

There have never really been more than a couple of subjects for poetry. And here I hark back to William Butler Yeats. That noble prizewinner said that only Sex and Death were worth writing about. And I wonder what there is to say about the second, since, unlike sex, most of us possess little firsthand experience of death. This leaves us with one serious subject for poems, and if you write about sex with any penetration you find your poems banned. But it is not frivolous to suggest that some of the younger poets appear to be wandering around among the great principles of human existence with a curious Easter Island expression on their faces which might be saying: What on earth are those things for? One uses a typewriter. It has thirty-six keys. Those monstrous exaggerations are represented on none of them. Forget the things!

And it is not as though these subjects—the two great principles of existence, which Yeats called Sex and Death—have been totally exhausted, for, like lots of other troubles, they seem to recur anew with each generation. If you put Charles Baudelaire into a coffin with a young woman I don't think he would feel much out of place, but I am not so sure about some of my contemporaries.

A poet who is not a bit mad has no more right to go around claiming to be a poet than a physicist who is not a bit afraid has the right to go around claiming to be a physicist. The poem is a violation of reality in the sense that a lie is a violation of reality: it turns things upside down so that the engines of existence can be seen in operation. The natural habitation of the poem is that fata morgana which is never seen. And in much the same way as the lie and the poem are deliberate or involuntary violations of reality, so the act of madness is, also.

This is why poems are so profoundly involved with real things, rather than with abstractions or metaphysics[1]—one is very closely caught up in the nature of the phenomena one seeks to understand, or to violate, or to destroy. You only have to shoot a rabbit or a mistress to know this. For the poem is involved with reality in much the same way as a man is involved with the woman whom he can neither understand nor abandon; the poem, in this sense, is neither the effort to understand reality, nor the attempt to run away from it; but rather it is a striving to choke out of its body those disclosures it would like never to make because such disclosures must place reality a little more in one's power. Perhaps this is why the nature of things gives up even its lesser secrets only to those who

---

[1] 'A metaphysical poem, says I with my 'specs on, is a contradiction in terms'—Thomas Gray.

make audacious advances to her. With the others she is not afraid to be silent. And why should the nature of things be afraid of the violent advances of a poet?

It is because he is a bit mad, and might kill himself, like Mayakovsky, if his enthusiasms are not reciprocated. And reality wants none of her victims to escape.

At this point in making these notes I was interrupted by a copy of Robert Graves' *Clark Lectures* being thrown at me by a friend: it contained, among other things, an essay by Graves on The Integrity of the Poet. I had hoped that this distinguished madman would have something serious to give to the illumination of this subject, but if he does, it is hidden from me. Mr Graves proposes that the poet should preserve his integrity by writing novels on weekdays and poems on Sundays: but at the same time, insists, in what is, for me, the only realistic remark of his Clark Lecture, that writing poetry is a full-time occupation. Providence so favoured Robert Graves himself that he is able to perform this ambidexterous acrobatic; he can write best sellers and poems. But I suspect that if he had not wasted time on the poems, the novels would be better, or vice versa.

My point, however, is simply that this is a private solution accessible only to Robert Graves. You can count on one finger the number of poets who are also successful novelists. It does not seem to me desirable that this unlikely combination of trades should be practised by one man: they are done better by two.

For the integrity of the poet is not a financial operation, it is a spiritual condition. This is where Yeats' choice of alternatives recurs. The integrity of a poet consists in the brightness of his pineal eye as he pursues his purpose, and his purpose is to write poems. It is a matter of no concern to anyone, as we all know perfectly well, whether or not the poet expires of malnutrition in the pursuit of his poems. For if a poet is going to start behaving with prudence and circumspection, if he is going to worry about whether he can write poems and buy Georgian candlesticks at the same time, he is engaged in the wrong business.

Only a very stupid economist would spend his time writing poems, and only a very stupid poet would waste his time practising economy. Because a poet is a man who cannot, really, help himself. He has fallen in with a Clytemnestra who has no private income; there is almost no likelihood of his becoming a kept man. Nor is it of any use to persuade oneself that the art of poetry is, after all, merely a superior form of amusement, as Eliot once said it was. For the word 'amusement' is here a supremely felicitous example of Eliot's use of the pun. A Muse must amuse. Where poetry is a superior form of amusement, prose is an inferior form of proselytizing. With what a true and high seriousness Eliot in fact regards the operations of the poetic vocation is clear from a much less ambiguous remark of his. 'Anyone who has been visited by the Muse,' he said, 'is thereafter haunted.' It was in speaking about his plays to me not long ago that he said rather sadly:

'The trouble is that we don't seem to have very good ghosts now.'

The time has gone by, as I see it, when there was any sense in essaying a rational defence of writing poetry or of the vocation of a poet. Nor do I think it such a rational defence to suggest that a poet writes poems because he cannot properly do anything else. I mean that if you seek to compel a poet to do other things as well, he is even more useless than when he stews in the juice of his own poems, but without the dignity, like Johnson's walking dog. I mean that dignity which renders the word poet so unreal that you are not permitted to employ it when filling in a passport form. Society is simply not prepared to recognise that it harbours such a monstrous little homunculus in its breast. You are called writer instead. The difference between a writer and a poet is that a poet is ridiculous and a writer is not.

But this degree of the ridiculous is exactly the degree of spiritual autonomy pertaining or remaining to the poet. When Auden said that, in the company of physicists, he felt like a parson in a roomful of dukes, he was making a religious judgement as well as a social one.

The aristocracy of nuclear physics had its own king, who chose to die some years ago in America. And of the many wise things Einstein said, there is one remark that belongs to the art of poetry: 'The most beautiful thing left to us in the world,' he once wrote, 'is a sense of the mysterious.' To me this sentence is a most memorable example of the humility of a great intellect when it contemplates the imaginative remove of things. That this should have been said by a great mathematician is not, of course, as surprising as that it should be said at all.

For it does what all poems are supposed to do, it honours all the things we do not know. I believe this to be, at heart, the subject of all fine poetry, the acknowledgement of that which we cannot calculate, the praising of that which we do not understand, the honouring of all that which we do not comprehend. A poem that speaks only of matters we know—a poem which we simply and entirely understand—is a poem with the Queen of Air and Darkness left out. The poetry of a poem is like the space of a stellar system—one is really not learning much about it (although one is learning a little) from observations of the heavenly bodies. The purpose of poetry is to provide a home for the things we can observe and comprehend, but to remain, itself, merely a sort of astronomical absence, a silence awaiting a voice, a backcloth for ashes. This is why it is as easy to isolate the element of poetry in a poem as it is to remove a suitcase full of the void. For poetry subsists in the relationships of things to one another, rather than in the things themselves.

When a young man and woman meet, speak, and separate, it is verse. When they meet, speak, and depart together, it is poetry. Not very good poetry, I admit; it is fairly predictable. To make oppositions happy together, to introduce them to one another so that they find they share analogies, to encourage anomalies in mutual illuminations, this is the mechanics of poetry. It's a sort of social service for the soul; it all depends on one's relations. Thus a lucid description of the poetic process occurs in the lines:

> Distance but no space was seen
> Twixt the turtle and his queen.

This seeking of the poetic element to establish amicable communications between things estranged or alienated or separated by their natures, this is what so often looks, when it fails, like the perversity of the anarchic imagination. When it succeeds it produces poetry; when it fails it produces perversity.

Like the line:

> Sometimes on Tuesdays I am afraid of dust.

But I suggest those critics are uncharitable who shout down great failures and applaud small successes, or who cannot perceive the many large moral monuments of human mistakes. A serious poem is always an expedition into hitherto unnamed and uncategorised regions of imaginative experience: the poet who investigates such territories should be forgiven if he sometimes thinks he has seen miracles where there were only mirages. A man who is wandering about in a spiritual antarctica may find it hard to determine which visitations are visions and which are illusions and hallucinations: he ought not be judged as though he were reciting the commentary of a travelogue. A poet in the operation of composing poetry is a man caught immediately up in the working engines of reality; at any moment he may find himself being torn in pieces by this machinery.

It was Goethe who said that, if the poet in the act of composing could withdraw and watch, he would go quite mad. He is always in the position of the bacteriologist who injects himself with unknown viruses. He should be forgiven if he sometimes dies. I am speaking, of course, about those poets who know that the constant companion of the Muse is the Medusa, not those who think that she married into the British peerage.

Who was it crippled Alexander Pope and George Byron, blinded John Milton, drove Smart and Collins and Cowper and Clare etcetera out of their minds? Everyone knows the casualty list as well as I do: and the answer is the mnemonic female with the unpleasant mask. She has not left us. I write the name of Dylan Thomas, and of the young English poet William Bell who loved mountains so much he got the Matterhorn to kill him. All this is that raging in the dark of which Yeats wrote.

I need not protest that the case is imperfect; instances of confutation can of course be cited; this pair of female homicides, the Muse and the Medusa, is far too circumventive to commit a massacre when all that they want is a punitive decimation. A poet is a man in whose room the great stone statues of the Furies swing about like pendula suspended in wires. Every time he lifts his head he may get it shattered. The casualties are those who, anxious above all else to see, did look up; others were luckier, but only those statues know why. A sensible poet, you may say, will keep his head down; but if he were sensible he would not be a poet.

What I assert are the moral dimensions of poetic dedication; for there, in that feverish universe of the self-conscious spirit, every exaggeration committed by the mind comes to life, functions, operates, and is henceforth indistinguishable from forms that have always existed.

This process of symbolic creation so closely resembles those hysterical images invented by the insane that one could, with truth, call a poet a lunatic with intentions, and a lunatic a poet without intentions. I introduce again the loudmouthed figure of Arthur Rimbaud. He wrote: 'As this scepticism can no longer serve me, and as besides, I am the victim of a new sorrow—I expect to become a very spiteful madman.' For the landscape with figures of the poetic imagination, and the landscape with figures of the schizoid dichotomy, resemble each other in almost everything, except this: that the relationship between things no longer matters to the madman. To the poet this relationship of place and person, or of location and image, or of conception and communication, remains a moral one. The lunatic who inhabits this feral world achieves happiness by the simple method of disavowing any moral involvement in it; by the reverse process the poet achieves his poems.

This is why a poem without a sense of moral responsibility is really nothing more than the brilliant gibberish of a nut. And this profound and passionate moral commitment of the poem is often to be achieved only at the expense of the individual poet's spirit wandering in a waste of impersonal shame; thus the intellect of man is forced to choose perfection of the life or of the work.

ANTHONY CRONIN

Goodbye to All That: A Child's Guide to Two Decades

In the 1940s, following up new poets had become almost a specialised activity, like bird-watching; one had a feeling also that the "little magazines" of verse were read largely by people wanting to write for them; and that there was a cleavage between a bohemian, Soho-centered "poetry world" and a wider and smarter "literary world" which rather looked askance at it. The poets of the 1950s may often have an equally small audience, but it is a different one. Both the Fantasy Press and the University of Reading School of Art Press function in a university world. Most of the Fantasy pamphlets are by undergraduates; many of the new poets who have taken their degrees are university teachers. The poet has typically functioned, one may say, in three successive generations in "the great world", the bohemian world, and the academic world. And, similarly, typical new poets of the generations of the 1930s, the 1940s and the 1950s differed widely in their choice of theme, their basic moral attitudes to life, their feeling about language, about the audience. I once had the pleasure, in the Caves de France in Soho, of introducing a poet of the 1950s, Mr Donald Davie, who teaches English in Dublin, to Mr Wrey Gardiner, who edited *Poetry Quarterly* and helped to run the Grey Walls Press in the 1940s, and to Mr Randall Swingler, who has vivid memories of the political excitements of the 1930s. It was an amiable occasion, but one was aware, at the same time, very vividly, of the invisible road-blocks that hampered any real communication. Not only the poet as a type, but the concept of poetry, suffers change.

The words, my dear William, are Mr G.S. Fraser's, and may well serve as an epigraph to this letter; they have the right ring, excited and complacent at once, like a domestic fowl announcing the birth of an egg. Mr Fraser has been intimately concerned, in the two decades now over, with the earth-shaking movements he describes. It was he who proclaimed apocalypse; who thought that Mr Nicholas Moore's mind was 'more interesting than Blake's'; who compared Mr Henry Treece with Donne, Shakespeare, Chaucer, and Spenser; and who informed the world that 'the underworld of history' flowered in Mr J.F. Hendry's poetry as that of sex did in the poetry of Dylan Thomas.

Presumably it was this kind of thing, and what it led to, that Mr Fraser meant when, in the following decade, busily engaged as he then was in introducing, explaining, grouping, arranging and discovering the cosmic significance of another lot, and in the consequently fashionable practice of abusing the poor forties that he had done his bit to create, he remarked reprovingly: 'Critical standards, in the little magazines of the 1940s, almost went by the board'. Indeed they did. You will not remember, my dear William, but if you glance through those old copies of *Poetry London* in the corner, you will see all too clearly what Mr Fraser meant.

There would of course be no point in going into it now, in flogging so to speak Mr Fraser's long dead White Horseman and resurrecting the equally thoughtless tush of the fifties, were it not that we are now across the border into another decade: Mr Fraser, Mr Conquest, doubtless Mr Wain, and, even, Mr Alfred Alvarez, decadeers to a man, will be anxiously clucking about for a new notion to plague us with, like a collection of ageing ladies looking for a society in which they might meet the young. As Mr Moore remarked ruefully in the early fifties, 'the world is once more waiting for the sunrise, and by God they'll all be fanning away like billyo when it does'. There are lessons to be learnt from a glance back, dear chap, so I hope you'll bear with the boredom of it for a moment. And there are dangers worse than mere annoyance in the perpetual recurrences of the decadeers, worse than having to listen to Mr Fraser start all over again with a new set of categories like those he used in the fifties ('Academics', 'Empsonians', 'Neo-Decadents', 'Naked Sensitives', and 'Sophisticates') dangers arising out of the total dependence of certain gentlemen, unable to formulate a critical aesthetic and stick to it, on this kind of thing, which, now that we are in truth into a new decade, we might forearm ourselves to avoid. And I fear (and in future I promise you, my lad, we'll have more interesting matters to discuss) that it is necessary to go back once more into 'the underworld of history' to see what they are and to ask certain questions which did not seem to occur to anybody at the time.

The forties were, of course, dreadful; but let us see what they were, or thought they were, besides. The first thing they thought they were was a reaction. Mr Fraser was quite clear about it at the time. According to his preface to *The White Horseman* in 1941, the thirties had been too worried about 'avoiding the too blatantly "poetical".' The poets of the thirties dodged 'tackling the great things head on. . . . To write well for the [thirties] group was to write "naturally" and a style that one noticed was even taken as a mark of the bad artist.' So the apocalyptics, romantics, white horsemen or whatever they were, would be, according to Mr Fraser, 'much more definitely interested in being poets than in being persons; and (with all their devotion to living and organic experience) they are more or less resigned to losing touch with a great many of the superficial interests of common life.'

It has a familiar ring? Of course, for in this last decade we had it exactly in reverse. You will know something at least of what happened in the last decade, so I need not go into it in much detail. There was to begin with some confusion about what was afoot. The versifiers concerned were first of all lumped together by Mr Fraser in 1953 as 'Provincial Dons'. This was a factual observation and, alas, it was true. Not all the jokes made about it were well received; but since it was also perfectly true that they were all servile imitators of Mr William Empson, another label was to hand, Neo-Empsonians. Let one of them, Mr John Wain, tell us about this. '. . . No one,' he remarks sagely, 'can ever foresee what will happen in literature. After the war, there was a good deal of reconstruction to be done in the arts, and the poet who was just setting out on his life's work had a pretty hard job of selection to do. His first question was the hardest: where was help and technical guidance to come from? . . . My own answer, which certainly got plenty of support once it was voiced, was that the Empson track was the best one to repair. . . . The Empson boom that followed took me, and I think everyone, by surprise, but at least it showed that there was some sense in the suggestion that this was the handiest line to repair; certainly the mushy manner of the forties, which I thought then and think now was the nadir of English poetry, could not be kept going indefinitely. . . .'

But mere imitation of Empson was still not much in the way of a programme (nor was Mr Empson himself playing the role of figment of anybody's imagination, with his reference to 'sheer platoons of pompous young men' and his observation that though no doubt his talent was narrow, it was not so narrow as all that). However, round about this time a gushing and anonymous journalist in the *Spectator* invented the spartanly simple and exceedingly non-committal term 'The Movement'. Since a programme was needed there was always the hungry forties to abuse; it was easy enough just to reverse the terminology. What Mr Fraser had been advertising as necessary to salvation in the early forties could be turned on its head. What he had attacked then could now become the drill. And it did. You were 'to avoid tackling the great things head on'; to write 'naturally' now became a virtue, and 'a style that one noticed' once more was to be 'taken as a mark of the bad artist'. This was what Mr Conquest, whom everybody up to then had regarded as one of the 'coloured-postcards-of-Corsica-school', a minor nuisance of the time, called 'a negative determination to avoid bad principles' when he got into the act and edited an anthology for which he wrote a preface all about the poor forties (this was 1956)—though not a single versifier of the forties was mentioned (most of them were forgotten by then anyway) and the preface was buttressed with references to such well-known poets as the Id, George Orwell, and Aldous Huxley. And 'the new man', according to whichever of them wrote the thing in the *Spectator*, was 'anti-wet, sceptical, robust, ironic, prepared to be as comfortable as possible in a wicked commercial world'. Where Mr Fraser's man in 1941 was to be 'the lonely poet exploring the solitary perspectives of his own mind', the new gent was 'bored by the despair of the forties, not much interested in suffering and extremely impatient of poetic sensibility, especially poetic sensibility about "the writer and society".'

It appeared indeed (the workings of the minds of the interested parties must be explored a bit further before it becomes possible to shift the level of the discussion) that this insensate hatred of the poor old forties, by now mark you more than half a decade old, was really all that could be dredged up when a unifying principle was sought for; that just as dislike of the thirties was really about the only principle informing the poor old forties themselves, so did 'the new man', that tough but ambiguity-loving extrovert so dear to the fellow in the *Spectator*, when asked for an aesthetic to justify the entirely imaginary position he occupied, inevitably and stubbornly fall back on abuse of the previous decade. It was no wonder therefore that the cursory enquirer was left a mite baffled when he bothered to ask certain questions. What principle, for example, bound together Mr Kingsley Amis's very incoherent but vigorous anti-stuffy campaign with what can only be called Mr John Wain's pro-stuffy campaign? When Mr Amis said that Eng Lit was pretty much of a bore and that he would stand no nonsense, what did his admirers make of the ineffable dreariness and donnishness, the old maidish analysing and influence-mongering and tendency-seeking of Mr Wain, Mr Alfred Alvarez and the other contributors to *Interpretations*? What had The New Criticism in fact to do with The New Man? When Mr Conquest elegantly remarked (the phrase deserves remembering anyway) 'Some years ago Mr John Wain advocated the methods of Mr William Empson in poetry ... and soon a number of young poets were following Empsonian and similar academic principles and producing verse of a notable aridity', why did he omit to add that their number included the majority of his own contributors? As the decade wore out, other questions, of mild interest at the time, receded into the dim and distant past. Why were the novels anti-don and anti-what Mr Pound calls the learneries, when they were written by dons happily ensconced in learneries? And why, if the new man was supposed to have a job and be a respectable member of society were they apparently anti-job and in a mild way anti-society?

These questions, now of interest only to the most avid of historians, will remain as one of the minor annoyances of a literary lifetime because in fact they can have no answer. If you had asked for an answer you would have been given in all probability the usual abuse of the previous decade. What apparently bound the whole business together was a communion of service in the learneries and, for a while the fashionable imitation of a great eccentric English poet—and how ludicrous some of these imitations were the historian may discover by digging up those of Mr Alfred Alvarez. Linguistically, which was supposed to be the point, the thing had no basis at all. Leaving aside the *badness* of the writing, what linguistic principle could one possibly derive from these lines of Mr Wain's, which Mr Conquest saw fit to anthologize:

> And nature from a simple recipe—
> Rocks, water, mist, a sunlit winter's day—
> Has brewed a cup whose strength has dizzied me?

In what way did some of the best poetry of the forties, that of Auden, Graves, Betjeman, even Gascoyne, differ from the linguistic and prosodic principles that were presented as if they were epoch-making discoveries, comparable to the breech-loader, the American seat or the twelve-tone scale? The following, for instance, seem to obey such principles as were enunciated:

> That is all that I can
> Think of at this moment
> And it's time I brought these
> Verses to a close:
> Happy birthday, Johnny,
> Live beyond your income,
> Travel for enjoyment,
> Follow your own nose.

It will be seen that the verse differs from that of the group only in its excellence. Linguistically, as far as any real principle of prosody that was ever propounded is concerned, it differs not a whit. Of course the attitude that informs it is different. A member of the gang would probably have written

> Live within your income,
> Travel for employment,
> Wear the proper clothes.

And it is difficult at this space of time to see what purpose was served by language like this:

> Should poets bicycle-pump the human heart
> Or squash it flat?

Looking back now, it seems that a great deal of the nonsense that went on can be traced to the position Dylan Thomas occupied in the public eye and consciousness in the first years of the new decade. He was by then one of the few poets of the apocalyptic manner of the forties (when the place was full of people imitating, and confusing, him and Barker) still in the public eye but he was there in no uncertain fashion. When people thought of the poet they thought of Dylan Thomas, and aspects of his life were legendary. Therefore, though most of the versifiers of the time were writing non-apocalyptic English, apocalypticism continued to be abused as if it were a fighting factor; but the fight was for the public's favour, not for the prevalence of a literary style. Though Mr Conquest's document, in 1956, was still lamenting 'when a condition of this kind takes hold it sometimes lasts for decades' as far as what he elegantly called 'the general tendency' was concerned the worried air was utterly unjustified.

But why not, indeed, fight for the public's favour if it happens to be important to you to have it, even if you have to reduce your criticism to the level of 'general tendencies' and conditions 'taking hold'? Indeed yes, if there is a principle at stake. But was there? You will have noticed that I have said little about the anti-poeticism which lurked uneasily behind most of the group's activities, from Mr Wain's (or Mr Fraser's) tendency to make literature the dullest matter possible, stifling it with an embrace, so that the subject of an essay was invariably left for dead; to Mr Amis's plain lowbrow rejection of the idea of great writing, especially in the past, alleviated by an occasional admission that some masterpiece or other was 'readable'; and from Mr Larkin's poems, by far the most interesting writing to emerge, with their deliberately sad denial that there was anything in life above the level of a bank-clerk's emotions; to the common cant that 'the era of experiment' was over and that of 'consolidation' had begun, which meant the abandonment in fact of any attempt at originality of form, so that the novels of the group, such as they were, were less interesting formally than Arnold Bennett's.

I think this confused mixture of attitudes does represent a phase that the modern movement went through when it hit the learneries and the donnish consciousness in the years immediately following the war. The best modern criticism had always been hard and questioning, allowing no poetic assertion to get by without proving its relationship to experience; the modern revolution has meant a revaluation of the entire past, a revaluation from which many of the masterpieces of the past have failed to emerge; the best modern poetry is in one sense anti-poetic, the sense in which poetic means too good or too fine or too noble or simply too passionate to be true, and it has dealt with emotions which are interesting partly because they are mean. And at that time, round about the end of the war and the first years of the fifties it was very necessary to get the whole modern movement, a time of greater and more abounding originality than any other period of history, into perspective, to distinguish what made us different from the past and why our writing was different; to see when it had to be original in form and when it was simply kitsch. What the donnish consciousness *did* was to confuse all these issues on a level of suburban timidity and dreariness. The honest examination of 'literature' to see whether much of it had any value at all was abandoned in favour of a sort of lowbrow horse-play activity arising from the resentment those who were put through the learneries felt for literature in general. The examination of poems in terms of their relationship to life became, God help us, the 'interpretations' of Mr Wain and his fellow new-critical pedants. The thrust towards greater honesty to experience which distinguishes all the great writing of the century, tailed off into statements like Mr Larkin's

> Ah were I courageous enough
> To shout *Stuff Your Pension!*
> But I know, all too well that's the stuff
> That dreams are made on.

And those who couldn't break out of a job could hardly be expected to feel much necessity to break out of traditional forms of writing, or to have much interest in the question of when it was necessary to do so.

So you see, my dear William, the really terrible thing is that it was all a very, very dreary confusion of real issues, and nothing on this earth, not toothache, not rain on the back of the neck, not anything is worse than a confusion of real issues by dons, bores, pedants, explainers, introducers, prefacers and decadeers. It was in the hope that you might do your part to save us from having to go through other totally unnecessary confusions in yet another decade that this letter has been written. God bless you, my dear boy, I'm glad you decided as you did about taking English.

MICHAEL ANDREWS

Notes and Preoccupations

Making notes was a way of forestalling deliberations about distractions which presented themselves as substitute responsibility for what I was doing (for which I really felt responsibility). They are a capitulation to the anxiety to be entrenched in a certainty of any kind. If I had not made notes of them they would have stuck in my mind and would have compelled an interminable familiarisation and analysis and I should have lost my presence of mind in a preoccupation. By making a note I was able to be satisfied with at least the certainty that this was unequivocally what I had had in mind. By experience I know that a definitive speculation about the distraction was no more reassuring than the intuitive approximations I scribbled down when they occurred to me.

I

PAINTING: THE ACTIVITY—WAY OF MAKING UP MIND

Each painting formulates disposition and orientation.
To paint a live atmosphere of the way things are or ought to be. It's reassuring to know these things: right orientation, disposition, atmosphere.

Every aesthetic adjustment reflects an ethical preference.

You've materialised it, and you're now physically close to what was once in imagination.

Kind of active thinking.

I've made an alteration and I've said to myself, 'this is the way to do things' or 'you shouldn't do things like that,' and so it has seemed to be that it was a mode of behaviour that I was correcting. That's been the reality rather than anything objective.

The painting episode is a real situation imagined. Re-enacted and rehearsed until its performance is the best possible. There is nothing like it in public life except for coincidence or a game that's both wilful and conscious. It would be ridiculous to provoke the same situation again and again, revising it.

In life recurring circumstances can rarely be willed but happen by chance. You cannot force repetitions of a situation at the speed of rehearsals on a painting.

The painting episode is a rehearsal of behaviour in which I go through the motions again and again until it seems to be the best possible—I can't improve on it, conduct myself any better—do it better. The ultimate exultation one feels is that of having done something at the top of one's form. The dispiritedness is like disgust.

The activity is for me the most marvellous, elaborate, complete way of making up my mind.

Preconception: knowing what the subject is. Art: to clarify and intensify the image: to bring it into focus.

When a personality is revealed aspirations are seen to be a large part of it.

II

PREOCCUPATION AND PRESENCE OF MIND ⎧ DIAGNOSIS
⎨ AESTHETIC
⎩ REMEDIAL

I am more afraid of becoming confused than of anything else.

Preoccupation, obsession: in the very act of renouncing them forever you strive to remind yourself of the last one.

Every day there'll be problems and vague incomplete fragmentary visions—all to be fought against, resisted all the time. Each must therefore be thrust away, allowed to go. Terrible anxiety to keep things in mind in order to realise them to the full (I paint in this habit) and at the same time to get rid of them, forget them.

It's no good mentally reconstructing impressions, one must wait for them to actually recur.

Must let preoccupations go because of the impatient presence of other things which are just as important to think about.

Must just say what one thinks and trust one's intuitions and inspirations when the time comes (not before).

One must simply wonder, not puzzle or worry, over the majority of one's problems.

Keep the mind quiet, relaxed, receptively empty.

Must stop giving oneself orders and act on intuitive promptings—thus unselfconsciously, spontaneously.

'Leave your mind alone'—your mind should be a secret to you—a gradually unfolding secret.

Must actually find excitement in the flow of time—not in its important moments.

What is really important is not the situation but one's response to it, the reaction.

The expansive thing is practically always right. Never get stuck on the point.

Ethics have to do with self-consciousness, aesthetics with unself-consciousness.

Think everything once only, that's the best way to remember it.

Accept the flow and flux of things through the mind, the continual change, disappearance, and reappearance. Accept it, let it happen.

When each consequence is taken as a new situation—there are no 'conventional' consequences.

Everything is provisional, changing, reverting, needing to be done over and over again, revised, altered, reset.

III

SUBJECTS

For the sake of familiarity (which is much more valuable than strangeness) live anywhere for a long time even if you don't like the place.

I want an actual present atmosphere in my painting. I don't mind how I get it.

I'm frequently sketching the image I'm not to paint, then the right one occurs.

The inspiration more often than not only indirectly visual. The most vivid visualisation (and revised practice and appreciation) sometimes prompted by something written or spoken.

One must believe, desire, *love* (and not be embarrassed out of loving) the atmosphere one creates—that's at best.

IV

WAY OF GOING ABOUT IT

Exact approximations. In paintings get all the approximations as correct as possible.

To feel as if I am placing the brush on the place on the real thing.

I keep looking for the shape and follow up any lead I get from the painting.

Must not only paint beyond considering the painting as good or bad but beyond the stage of being aware of it as good or bad.

The image gains weight as it goes along—it snowballs; to be taken as far as it will go.

The image only reveals itself after continuous painting for long periods—actual *physical* continuity, not the thing simply borne in mind and returned to—though that *can* work.

Actual physical continuity as often as possible—continuity of activity, place, atmosphere—fanciful to imagine one can conveniently occasionally recall the trend of development.

The trouble with prolonged periods of painting: past a certain stage I begin to contract the image instead of sustaining its development.

Do it as painting (form) not as if constructing a thing.

V

APPROXIMATE PERCEPTION—CONCEPTION FORMING

All true appreciations of people are bound to be blurred (I think this goes for images too). Finding out a bit here, a bit there—it's all approximate. Everything is 'more or less' 'in my opinion.'

I start with a concept and modify it perceptually also perceptually form a concept.

The image offering the greatest complexity of sensations: e.g. the passage of time over a particular landscape.

Getting the maximum number of associations from the form, in the form.

One mustn't move so fast one doesn't see things, that they don't register. Commonplace ordinary relaxed seeing, vision.

Mysterious conventionality.

When suddenly you are out of sympathy with someone you feel your own disposition most strongly.

Poets on Poetry

HUGH MACDIARMID

Is poetry done for? Wars, the Robot Age, the collapse of civilization,
These things are distracting and annoying, it is true
—But merely as to an angler a moorhen's splashing flight
That only puts down a rising fish for a minute or two!

There lie hidden in language elements that effectively combined
Can utterly change the nature of man
Even as the recently discovered plant growth hormone
Idole-acetic acid, makes holly cuttings in two months
Develop roots that would normally take two years to grow.

I agree with a friend of mine, who is a poet and a scientist, when he says: 'If science is the differential calculus, art is the integral calculus. They are excellent separately but best taken together.'

Deeper than opinions lies the sentiment that predetermines opinion.

What subject-matter do I specially covet for poetry to-day? Many years ago I said, and I have had no occasion to change my mind, 'If I were asked to frame a test paper for literary aspirants, I would ask (1) for a poem on the fact that what is known as the 'Lorentz transformation' *looks like* the 'Einstein transformation'. When manipulated numerically both give equal numerical results, yet the meanings and the semantic aspects are different. Although Lorentz produced the 'Lorentz transformation' he did not, and *could not*, produce the revolutionary Einstein theory. (2) A short paper discussing the fact that the semantic aspects of practically all important mathematical works by different authors often involve *individual semantic presuppositions* concerning fundamentals.

Avoid reading minor poets like the plague. Asked some years later how he had managed to forge ahead so rapidly to the front rank, the mathematician Niëls Henrik Abel (of whom Hermite said: 'He has left mathematicians something to keep them busy for five hundred years') replied, 'By studying the masters, not their pupils.'

The widespread distaste for, or incomprehension of, poetry is, I think, largely due to the fact that it is taught 'backside foremost' in our schools. The great poets of the past are taught, instead of starting the pupils with contemporary poetry and then working back through the centuries and thus enabling the children to see the poets in proper perspective. As Mr George Sampson has said: 'In the schools the teachers want to begin where the great scholars ended. They set forth generalities to pupils who have no particulars. Pupils who should be acquiring some standards of value acquire instead an illusion of knowledge. The peculiar danger of a class-room course in literature is that pupils may be set up for life with third-hand or fourth-hand generalities and with a stock of details swept up by the industrious housemaids of literature, and never learn the need of wrestling in solitude with a great work of creative art. And then the students so taught will themselves become teachers and pass on a cant of literature to the young, or divert literature to a form of useful knowledge.'

A motto for poets to-day. *Hic ego barbarus sum quia non intelligor illis.* (Because they don't understand *me*, I am a barbarian.)

Justice Brandeis was right when he said: 'Ordinary men and women can grasp the essentials of any situation, no matter how involved its details, if the facts are adequately presented to them.'

Forty years ago a friend of mine said that he had 'gone scrupulously through the whole of a widely-acclaimed volume of 'Georgian Poetry', not without pleasure, and afterwards reflected with consternation that never for an instant had he the sensation of being in contact with the serious creative intelligence of a great nation.'
It would be a very rash man who ventured to assert that there has been any improvement in the four subsequent decades.

VERNON WATKINS

Natural speech may be excellent, but who will remember it unless it is allied to something artificial, to a particular order of music?

Criticism projects its high tone, its flattering responses, but of what man-made echo does the mind not weary, as it turns endlessly round the Earth?

Ambition is wholly imitative and wholly competitive until it has died.

Unredeemed ambition is the desire to survive the present. Its direction is despair.

Redeemed ambition is the willingness to die rather than accept a survival alien to present truth. Its direction is compassion.

Religious poetry is sealed like the eyes of Lazarus by a refusal to be raised except by the true God.

The fountain, what is it? What is ancient, what is fresh.

Defects of the imagination are always reflected in style.

Vagueness is an enemy of holiness; the soul of harmony continually thirsts for definition.

The epic depends on exactness of detail: the larger the theme, the more minute its organization.

The syllable is the strictest instructor. For the lyric poet what better critic than silence?

A poet need have only one enemy: his reputation.

Write for the dead, if you will not disappoint the living.

The stammerer may arrive at the truth the fluent speaker missed.

A true style cannot be learnt from contemporaries.

A fragmentary statement of truth is better than a polished falsification, for how could that live, even for a moment, beside what is eternally fresh?

What is revision except, in the interests of unity, to eliminate the evidence of words?

Suffering is a great teacher: we know nothing until we know that.

Lyrical poetry at its best is the physical body of what the imagination recognizes as truth.

The point of balance in a poem is unpredictable. Whatever weight a poet brings to it, beyond a certain point the poem writes itself.

Composition is spontaneous, but true spontaneity in poetry is nearly always a delayed thing. It is the check, the correction, the transfigured statement, that makes the poem unforgettable.

A poet, overhearing a conversation out of time, must be his time's interpreter; but how can the Muse know this, whose eyes are fixed on what is eternally fresh and continually beginning?

Critics, even unimportant ones, are bound to demonstrate their vitality, like sandhoppers.

The true critic, the true discoverer, stays in the same place.

A true poem renews itself at its close.

Art is miraculous. There is no destructive or restrictive theory of art which cannot be contradicted by a work of genius.

PATRICK KAVANAGH

Part of the Palgravian lie was that poetry was a thing written by young men and girls. Not having access to Ezra Pound who showed that the greatest poetry was written by men over thirty, it took me many years to realize that poetry dealt with the full reality of experience.

Part also of the lie was that poetry was very sad—

> Our sweetest songs are those that tell of saddest thought.

This is not true. Our sweetest songs are those that derive from that gay abandon which is the keynote of the authentic Parnassian voice. The abandon is not the riotous braggadoccio which is often associated with the poet. The true abandon and gaiety of heart spring from the sense of authority, confidence and courage of the man who is on the sacred mountain.

It is essential to consider nothing but genius; for anything less is no good. The aim of a good deal of literary and academic criticism is to raise up the mediocre, to get people to believe that the tenth-rate is in some way respectable. It takes courage not to praise the tenth-rate, for as soon as it is known by society that you are one of these mediocrity-admirers, they know that you're 'all right'—a serious traditional man deserving of a stake in the country.

Poetry is what it says. The thought shapes the language. At its purest all the didacticism is burned away, and you get that impalpable beauty which pertains to the divine—

> Absent thee from felicity awhile.

The wicked critic, instead of telling his audience to lift the child in its arms and enjoy its smiles, tells it to ask why it has eyes and what causes the smile.

One can never get away from the idea of the Audience in discussing the poet. The audience stands outside the hotch-potch of lies that is the world of journalism and politics. In London the journalist has no influence on literature. In England there has always been a traditional audience, a word-of-mouth audience. That audience cannot be bought, is uninfluenced by financial success or failure.

Great men are not concerned with whether or not their work is involved in the ephemeral. Only bad, silly writers are worried over such matters. They hope that a 'mighty theme' will save them, because they do not know that the only permanent thing is the soul, and what has happened to it.

Art McCooey, a late 18th century poet, is known for a poem he wrote on Creggan graveyard. But as is the case with so much that passes for poetry in Ireland, it is whimsical. He does not, as the true poet does, name and name and name with love the obscure places, people or events. To the poet, what is loved is worthy of love. A better poet than McCooey was Evelyn Shirley, a nineteenth century landlord from South Ulster, and he wrote no verse at all as far as is known. But in his *History of Monaghan* he names and names and names in the true poetic fashion. He recorded the history of the obscure fields, graves, forths and families, with all the Parnassian disregard for any supposed public. He had an audience no doubt, of a few of his friends.

There is only one Muse, the Comic Muse. In Tragedy there is always something of a lie. Great poetry is always comic in the profound sense. The only plays of Shakespeare which are less than comic are the alleged comedies. *King Lear* is the pure incantation of the Comic Muse. Comedy is the abundance of life.

> O, reason not the need: our basest beggars
> Are in the poorest thing superfluous:
> Allow not nature more than nature needs,
> Man's life's as cheap as beast's—

STEVIE SMITH

My Muse is like the painting of the Court Poet and His Muse in the National Gallery; she is always howling into an indifferent ear.

It is not indifference but fear. It is the fear of a man who has a nagging wife.

It is like a coarse-grained country squire who has a fanciful wife. It is like an uneasily hearty fellow who denies his phantom. These notions of the Muse are as false as the false-hearty fellow who bites his nails because of the false picture he is making. (If he were really hearty he would not know there was anybody to listen to.)

> Why does my Muse only speak when she is unhappy?
> She does not. I only listen when I am unhappy,
> When I am happy I live and despise writing
> For my Muse this cannot but be dispiriting.

This comes nearer to the truth. Here are some of the truths about poetry. She is an Angel, very strong. It is not poetry but the poet who has a feminine ending, not the Muse who is weak, but the poet. She makes a strong communication. Poetry is like a strong explosion in the sky. She makes a mushroom shape of terror and drops to the ground with a strong infection. Also she is a strong way out. The human creature is alone in his carapace. Poetry is a strong way out. The passage out that she blasts is often in splinters, covered with blood; but she can come out softly. Poetry is very light-fingered, she is like the god Hermes in my poem *The Ambassador* (she is very light-fingered). Also she is like the horse Hermes is riding, this animal is dangerous.

> Underneath the broad hat is the face of the Ambassador
> He rides on a white horse through hell looking two ways
> Doors open before him and shut when he has passed.
> He is master of the mysteries, and in the market place
> He is known. He stole the trident, the girdle,
> The sword, the sceptre, and many mechanical instruments.
> Thieves honour him. In the underworld he rides carelessly,
> Sometimes he rises into the air and flies silently.

Poetry does not like to be up to date, she refuses to be neat. ('Anglo-Saxon', wrote Gavin Bone, 'is a good language to write poetry in because it is impossible to be neat.') All the poems Poetry writes may be called, '*Heaven, a Detail*', or '*Hell, a Detail*'. (She only writes about heaven and hell.) Poetry is like the goddess Thetis who turned herself into a crab with silver feet, that Peleus sought for and held. Then in his hands she became first a fire, then a serpent, then a suffocating stench. But Peleus put sand on his hands and wrapped his body in sodden sacking and so held her through all her changes, till she became Thetis again, and so he married her, and an unhappy marriage it was. Poetry is very strong and never has any kindness at all. She is Thetis and Hermes, the Angel, the white horse and the landscape. All Poetry has to do is to make a strong communication. All the poet has to do is to listen. The poet is not an important fellow. There will always be another poet.

III

BRIAN HIGGINS

Cartons

'Try the new handy pack it will
Do more for you than any earlier sort.'
In the train, two standard men
(And I the stranded traveller who heard them)
Said how someone never sailed but built a yacht
—Clever with his hands like.

Then how these films needed extra troughs for laying
And 'the ones I dropped into the hypo—done for—
But that sort's now too obsolete to use—it's just as well.'

Wonderful these new ones. At the zoo they even show
The shadows in the corners of the cages.

3d in the slot, your change is inside the packet.

£1 on the dot and
(You think they wrench a lever for the bedroom)
3 coathangers and a three-ply dresser.

All the rooms are exactly £1 and that's quite fair
For all the rooms are exactly alike,
And so are the breakfasts for that matter.
Shall we object to:
Cinemascope and the European Cup
Turks who talk with New York accents
Irishmen in the Church of England
Gilbert Harding's indigestion?

Shall we forbid juke boxes to Basques?
Advise Franco to subsidise bullfighting?
Or shall we, being children of the Fifties,
Work towards the happy time when

The latest popular musical
Is written entirely in the notation of 'Principia Mathematica'?

Or shall we say:
The Arts are simple and difficult
Pitched between the basic response
And the visionary Philistine
Who, deliberately unhinging his mind,
Plans to flash a subliminal mutter
Right into the mind of the psychologist.
Until the emeritus professor of classics careers down the High
Shouting 'Wottallotigot'.

The successful poet both in England and France
Reviews jazz L.P.'s—but not of course just any.

D'yehearmecallinyer.

My Mother was a Burler

My mother was a burler and this is what she did
In the nineteen thirties when I was a small child;
I used to rise at seven as she went out to work
Her nine hour horror. I was just a kid
But the futility of burling and the grease in which she worked
Have stained my soul with guilt and my days with pride.
Nothing disgusts me more than slow-labouring people
One with the gradual industrial banalities,
The reiterate wheels of steel and days,
Incorporated steel and tramelled lives,
Oil and dust soaked into the fustian blue,
And muddy sandwiches of powdered meat.
O it was early when the hooter blew
And yet how glad they were when they worked late.

The smell that lingers in dark woollen mills
(And still they tramp upon the stinking bales)
Is the miasma of all human ills
(And still against the tories someone rails)

The shuttle of a burler wove my gloom,
Upon which many an aunt was crucified
And there I learned credulity of doom
And of the great Unprivileged, who died.

And there I learned (and still the lesson sticks)
There's no such thing as progress and improvement,
But only indignation at a fix,
Which is the fuse of every left-wing movement.

That most impossible of paradises,
The one on earth, with aeons to achieve it;
Though to many such a thought entices
My childhood was too dusty to believe it.

The Social Realists

Useless, they lingered on the edge of fate;
Purveying culture to midland cities,
Godless and sorry for unworking men.
Slumps they had not caused weighed down their backs.

So in symbols or in fact went North
To the rich barrenness of glacial strands
Or, apologetic for chaotic wrongs,
Vaguely tended the wounds of war-torn Spain
And fussed nervously over extremes of blood.

Cissies on horseback, they did not like the sound of bombs
(And who can blame them) when paranoic toughs
Blundered through Europe with bullying guns
And spies reported chance words of freedom.
All that they loved was questioned in closed vans
And bludgeoned by ignorant power.
Cultured professors writhed beneath jackboots
Whose undiscerning energies claimed only
The immediate animal's survival.
Later, after panic trips around the world,
Their fears were quieted and they returned
To write propaganda or help with the fire service
Which consecrated a holocaust of civilian deaths.

And in the forties they burgeoned with innocent power.

I Have No Comrades

I have no comrades
I march with clocks on my journey
I gather to speak not to tourney

In the appalling snow I would found my city

I have no comrades
I have neither hope nor doubt nor pity

I wander shouting on the hills of silence
My friends are the grey ghosts from the windy islands

I have no comrades

What do I care for the green boys and the red mark?
I wound the white paper and garble the killing stroke

I have no comrades

I have a rabble of facts pressing the sides of equations
And verbs that have licked the boots of the years with
    reiterations
I have tumble of digits and signs for the day's dues
I have answers and theorems and chequebooks and here is
    the news

I have no comrades.

The Only Need

Sad are the answers; and the answer's cold
Which runs to us unasked from stars and years.
The story which we hear when lives unfold
Gives witty meanings to our ready tears.

We spend, and need the money that we've spent;
We save, and that's the money that we burn.
God, who lingers softly with intent,
Can always steal just double what we earn.

I do not care if I should lose my mind
But only that my mind should lose its ease
And if my hope is doomed, which is to find
Ionian summers by Pelasgian seas.

Letter to a Literary Professor whom I visited with the offer of 'A Thesis Wot Scans'

I didn't know that things were so clear cut
Of course you didn't take me by surprise
Much less I you. You looked me in the eyes,
Accepted all my claims, and then said, 'But

Myself when young had much the same intent,
I got my "first" then started out to write,
Poems, plays too. Perhaps my gift was slight
Anyway it never paid my rent.

Soon I was married, taxed and overwrought
The world's stale claims bedevilled my poor Muse.
Fame or Taties, how was I to choose?
I couldn't understand it,—so I taught.

Even now I sometimes scratch my head,
For one that wins, a thousand must go down.
If you have guts you'll end up on the town'
—'Thank God I didn't have your choice,' I said.

ROBERT GRAVES
November 5th Address

I was invited to speak to you on Modern Poetry, and offered a number of dates to choose from.[1] When I saw the names of the other lecturers in the series, I chose November 5th; it suited my mood. Not because of squibs and rockets, but because of barrels of gunpowder. It would perhaps have been more fair to have warned you beforehand what I had in mind, which was to tell you a good many thoroughly unpleasant and disquieting things.

[1] *Apparently given in 1928 to the* Teachers' Union *in London, but I cannot recall the occasion. R.G.*

Let me put it to you, that you have come to this lecture because you want to know what I think of, say, Messrs Yeats, De La Mare, Masefield, Bridges, Hodgson and Wolfe, and the rest; and why it is right to admire these poets. Most of you are teachers and would like to bring back the news to the people you teach. But I find myself unable to tell you anything of the kind. Candidly, so far from having any interesting thoughts to offer on the subject, I have long ceased to admire these poets, or to think about them at all.

Well, I can at least tell you why I don't admire them. This is the 5th of November and I am making what, I hope, is my last public utterance on the subject of poetry. Why I don't admire them, and why I like to forget that they are writing, is because they are all poets who write for *us* when they write, not any particular group of *us*, but *us* as an aggregate called 'the public', and wonder anxiously whether we will like it. Now, I do not associate myself with *us*, the aggregate public, any longer; though I admit there was a time when I did, when I was pleased to be pleased as you still are. And I myself used to write to please all of you, and you were all pleased. That is how I became a well-known poet, and that is how it has come about that I am now asked to make part of this lecture series: people have not realized that it is now several years since I considered you, the aggregate public. When I write now, I write only to please one thing, and that is the sense of what the poem I am writing ought to be intrinsically, and I don't care at all whether you, the aggregate public, like it or not: and so you read nothing that I have written since about 1923. And I can read with pleasure only the sort of poems that were not written to please me as an average member of the aggregate public, but written because there was a poem to write at the time of writing. This is not being a highbrow. This is liking clean things.

I will try to convey my point of view without being hostile. Poetry, to me, is the most serious activity that I know, the most inclusive and the most truthful. It can only be written by serious people for serious people; by people with a sense of order for people with a sense of order. Serious people I would define as those whose first object in life is to be themselves and please themselves. The aggregate public is an aggregate disorder without seriousness or truth—its members are concerned only in *doing the right thing*. 'Doing the right thing' may be disguised as *Duty*, and put among the virtues; but it is really a cowardly attempt to please everyone, the aggregate of disorder, before pleasing oneself. So you wish to do the right thing by reading the right thing, which is the poetry of De La Mare, Masefield, Bridges, Hodgson, Yeats and Wolfe—the poetry that has been written by people whose first object is also to do the right thing, which means pleasing you.

When a person is doing the right thing, he or she uses a Party Voice.

You all recognise what I mean. It is the voice of the poor widow welcoming the new district-visitor who gives blankets and tracts to the poor widow. It is the voice of society girls selling flags to artisans, and of artisans buying them; of the manufacturer giving a bean-feast speech to his employees, and of the employee, deputed to speak in return, telling him that he's a jolly good fellow. Ingratiating and yet self-assertive, nervous, false. A really good person has no party voice, pitches his or her voice just the same, whoever happens to be about. There are very few really good people. And still fewer really good poets. One recognises the verse-equivalent of the party voice in ninety-nine poems out of a hundred; they are written to please you. They are not serious. They have no order except the illusion of order that they borrowed from the aggregate public—who have, as I say, no intrinsic order but are a collection of individuals wishing to shelve the responsibility of being individuals by rushing hither and thither trying to do the right thing. The result of the party voice is literature; what is provided by the lost for the lost: refreshments at an enormous party for an indeterminate number of ill-at-ease guests.

All this you, who are teachers, will find profoundly unsatisfactory. You are committed to the teaching of English literature; and in the English Literature syllabus, English Poetry occupies a very important position. Part of your job is explaining to children and young men and women, hundreds of thousands of them, what poetry they ought to admire, and why; and because it is impossible to explain why a poem is good in so many words (if it *is* good) you are forced to give all the wrong reasons. You have to explain the poem as one of the right things, which is to damn it at once. That is, you say this is a good poem because it has stood the test of time; or because it tells a noble story; or because the language is musical; or because it is by Shakespeare; or because Coleridge praised it; or because its author fought bravely for his country. Not only teachers, of course, give the wrong reasons. They merely confirm in the name of education all the wrong reasons that have been given before. And party-voice poetry of the worst kind dominates the school text-books of poetry; and, when recited, it is recited, very properly, in a caricature party voice.

Literature is, you must know, a trades union very jealous of its solidarity. As soon as a man starts writing fairly well, Literature goes after him and ropes him into membership; that is, if his name has not been put up for membership at birth. And it is the worst sort of trades union; it is a trades union with a conservative executive and headquarters in Bloomsbury. And its motto is: 'Write the right thing!'

When I read a poem by a new author, the first thing I ask myself is: '*Is this literature?*' If I decide that it is, I stop reading. What I look for is the poet who makes the least possible concession to you, the pleasable public.

Sometimes I find such a one. But it is almost always a first book, written by someone very simple and naturally independent. Then there is a second book which betrays signs of the first one's success. The third one is literature; and soon the poet is busy writing literary letters to all the other poets, reminding them of their duty to Form and Style.

Laura Riding, one of the very few poets who has not succumbed to literature, has written a book called *Contemporaries and Snobs*, in which she explains why the trades union has got more and more oppressive as this century advances. She explains that Poetry used to have an honourable place in the social scheme, but that the tasks that were once given the poet by society are now given to others. (Eulogies of Royal Princesses are written in prose biographies for the *Daily Mail*; battle ballads are written as prose histories by University Professors; and all loose sentiment of love and life is absorbed by the cinema, by variety, and by the popular novel. Religion and philosophy, natural history and astronomy have their own specialist departments.) The poet as a social prophet and teacher is out of date. He had his last fling in Victorian times, when Tennyson and Browning were advanced moral thinkers on the community's behalf; but even in this role the poet is no longer welcome.

As Laura Riding points out, this is the very best thing, really, that could have happened to poets—the being freed from old social obligations and given a holiday, at last, simply to write poetry. But the trades union leaders, the critics, would not permit it. If the poet could no longer be the philosopher, historian, or moralist of society, he had to be something—he had to be a specialist in the art of poetry and win the same respect as the mathematician or the logician.

The modern poet, then, no longer writes for the aggregate public—Yeats, Bridges, Hodgson, De La Mare, Masefield, Wolfe are old-fashioned poets—he writes for a specialist public of *littérateurs*, where the disorder is not large and shabby, but mean and arty. So if you ask me what I think of the poetry of, say, T.S. Eliot, Herbert Read, Ezra Pound, and the modernist leaders, I say what I said before: I do not like them because they are writing to please the trades unionists, and I have torn up my membership card.

At this point you'll be getting annoyed and ask: 'But, surely, a poet writes for an audience, whether it is a large one or a limited one? Surely, poetry is an art if it is not a science? Surely, the poet has to learn how to write from past masters of the art or professors of the science, before he is any good?' I cannot believe all that, however often I hear it. And I will tell you briefly what I think about poetry.

Poetry is not a science. It is an act of faith, and mountains are moved by it—for short distances, at least. The only proof of the validity of any given way of writing is that the mountain, by which I do not mean large public approval or small critical approval, but the huge impossibility of language, was moved. The mountain does not stir twice to the same way of writing, for each authentic poem has its own peculiar way of being written.

Poetry is not an art. It does not even begin as words. What happens is that there is a sudden meeting in the poet's mind of certain incognizable, unrelated and unpersonified forces; of which meeting comes a new creature—the still formless poem. The poet feels this happening at the back of his mind as an expectance, a concentration which will persist uncomfortably until it is removed. First, he objectifies it by writing it in such a way that it has a general, not merely a personal, context; then removes it as far outside himself as possible by putting it into circulation.

While he is writing he is under a hypnotic spell which, so far from limiting his normal sensibilities and powers, gives them an extraordinary enlargement. The agent of hypnotism is not an external force, or even what is called 'the unconscious mind', but the poem working itself out consciously.

Something of the enlargement of poetic composition can be shown by considering the very different state of mind when prose is being written. Prose is the science of generalised statement by suppressing as far as possible the intrinsic qualities of the words used. The prose-writer, for the convenience of those particular readers whom he addresses, uses a logical phrasing in which, though language and rhythm are artfully made to vary with the theme, he uses words for their intrinsic value only. And he could give the same message in a dozen different ways. In writing poetry, on the other hand, not only the intrinsic values but the most remote associations of every word, and the qualities and associations of these words in combination, are recognised and given a part in a supralogical scheme. Moreover, in appreciating the poem, the reader makes the same recognitions. Once written, a poem can never be translated into any other language. It is its own final meaning.

When the poet gives the poem a form in writing, and consents to accept the eccentricities and caprices of language on its behalf, and even to use an existing metrical convention (within the limits of which, however, the poem has complete personal freedom), this does not mean that he desires an audience to gratify or instruct. But, in order to do the poem justice in his choice of language and rhythm, he assumes a reader of ideal public intelligence: ideally sensitive to visual, auditory and tactile imagery, and without any literary, religious, philosophical or other bias. This reader is not identified with any actual reader, or group of readers. He is no more than the figure in the foreground of a picture, put there to give the scale. By assuming him, the poet can eliminate the irrelevant or unintelligible. In a poem nothing can be left to chance: the assumed reader is supposedly capable of recognising the main and detailed points of the poem, however delicate; but he is not left guessing at any doubtful signpost. A word in a poem may, of course, point in four or five different directions; but none of these directions are dead ends. It is possible that no reader will ever be found to understand certain poems of more than usual complexity; but this is a reflexion on public intelligence, not on poetry.

There are two familiar ways of not writing poetry. One is through fantasia; the other is through theory or imitation. The poetry of fantasia is the only sort of poetry that allows the stock analogy of poetry with dreams, because it is the product of a morbidly induced hypnotic state, which gives the mind no greater enlargement than dreams. It is fully intelligible only in a limited personal context, though the unconscious recognition by its readers of common pathological symbols occurring in it may give it wide currency. Its weaknesses are that it is not self-aware; that its parts do not tally as they should; and that it is not fully removed from the author. The only test of authenticity permitted by those who favour the poetry of fantasia is whether it seems spontaneous.

The poetry of theory or imitation goes by the name of 'Classicism'. Its first champion was Aristotle who, not suspecting the possibility of authentic poetry, could distinguish only between fantasia in verse, and prose common sense in verse. In his *Poetics*, he set himself to envisage a sort of poetry that would be prosaically awake and show no analogy with dreams. This poetry he would weed of all extravagancies and impossibilities, and confine within rational and educative limits. Poetry was, with him, no more than an intuitive imitation of how typical men think and react one upon another when variously stimulated. In practice, however, the Classical idea gets modified by conceits and deliberate ornament-borrowings from the genuine or artificially induced poetry of fantasia. Classicism is non-poetic because it recognises the public value of poetry, and can consider nothing else. The Classical poet deliberately restricts his technique to one calculated for a particular audience. He plans a poem in the fore-part of his mind, and practises with it an artificial hypnotism of the audience. He makes it the vehicle of a prose message, or a display of art. The test of the authenticity of the Classical poem is whether it can be publicly accepted as literature.

Literature is a cumulative tradition; authentic poetry is a number of unrelated events, or poems. Literature has standards which alter with each generation—a generation may be two hundred years, or thirty, or ten, according to the speed of living—and are explicable only in terms of the social and philosophic needs of each generation. Poetry has no standards and remains independent of history.

Nobody becomes an authentic poet until he has learned to like nobody's poems better than his own, yet to be indifferent to the fate of his own as soon as they are out of his way. Poetry is never written because so much good poetry has already been satisfactorily written, but because, at the moment of writing, nothing seems worth considering except the peculiar needs of the poem now to be written.

Poetry is not a morbidity but an excellence. Yet to be a poet means to be at war with society and literature, if only because society and literature demand poems written for it in a particular way, which will usually be either one or the other of the two usual ways of not writing poetry.

Little can be written initially about particular poems, unless to show that certain supposedly authentic ones are not authentic. The numerous volumes written about the fantasia of Coleridge's *Kubla Khan*, or about the literary sources of Milton's *Paradise Lost*, are only valuable as evidence against these poems. The first and last word on the subject of the authentic poem, for the reader who can dispense with a dictionary, is the poem itself. Deductions can be made from poems as to the powers and limitations of contemporary literature, and the curiosities of contemporary psychology; but such deductions cannot properly be formalised into an art of writing, or even into a means of assuming an ideal reader on the poet's behalf.

PATRICK KAVANAGH
The Flying Moment

> No man remember can lose another life than that which he now loses. The present is the same for all; what we now lose or win is just the flying moment.
>
> *Marcus Aurelius*

Some writers, whose material is 'Country life', after many years living in cities, attempt to write from the rustic vantage point. But they always go wrong. I do not write as if I were still a 'countryman' if there is such a creature. These evocations are attempts to preserve for myself so that I may live them over again, vivid moments. In this way, through love, a man may live hundreds of years. He lives with the eternal part of the self.

'What were the happiest moments in your life?' a man asked me one day. The happiest moments are those that are most vivid in the imagination. The imagination is, I think, incapable of evoking moments of sorrow.

It is a summer's day, and I am aged around twenty-two, and I am drawing my coal from the station.

There is no work as easy as manual labour: there I was, my face black, sitting on the seat-board, my legs crossed, letting the fields look at me. Ah, the fields looked at me more than I at them, and at this moment they are still staring me, and the humpy hill beyond the railway at the Beeog's lane. The house where the two yellow-faced brothers lived is roofless, but unlike most cabins of its class, the right masons must have built those walls. 'Best of bleddy walls.' Could nearly be roofed again.

I am thinking of what I heard my father say of those brothers. They spoke Irish, as did their two nieces who were alive at this time, and when one of the brothers died, the other lamented him loudly: 'Mo graer, mo graer,' he cried.

That is bad phonetics for the sound of 'my brother' in Gaelic, but what's the difference? Everyone said, however, that if he had been half as good to him when he was alive, he'd have him still.

I can see across to Harry Conlon's, on the side of the hill to Drumnanalive.

Somebody is driving a sow up the hill. I don't suppose I was ever up in that field. And it's curious how you can get a sense of travelling to strange lands, by going to some field less than a mile from your own home. And you get the feeling of returning from a long exile, when you revisit some field that you had walked through as a child.

There are several fields I long to see again. There is the corner under the Rock in our Far Field, down beside the stream, where many's the hot summer day I sat with my feet touching the cold water, and watching the violets that grew on the cool shaded bank.

There is a pad there which leads into Caffrey's field and another into Woods', and I used to go that way when I was in tow with Johnnie McCabe.

Stones were always rolling into the stream at this point, and never a week passed that I hadn't to go up there and pull them out, for this stream drained our meadow, and when it was plugged in winter, you couldn't go to Meegan's Well without being up to your arse in mud.

We were always talking about all the extra land we'd have, if a few of the cuttings were sunk a foot or so. Every few years or so, we were able to get a number of local scradins (scraping small farmers) together, to do a week's work on the drain. (Streams were always called drains.) Generally speaking, the combine tended to thin out, as each man got as far with the job as would drain his own low-lying meadows.

And that's the way it was when I was in wo (vogue) in that country.

This is a new cart I have. No danger of the shoeing coming off the wheels.

I peep over the dash-board. God! did I speak too soon? There's a shoeing there looks like shifting. Ah, no, it's all right—

'Hardy.'

'Hardy.'

A neighbour on his bicycle had caught up with me, and cycles along holding the dash-board.

'That's a bleddy good slack you're drawing, Paddy.'

'It's not slack, it's a class o' nuts. We got a bargain in it. Wi gan.'

'What are yez wastin' on it?'

'Thirty-five bob a ton.'

'That's a bleddy chape.'

'Good value all right. There's a terrible scabby field of oats—White's.'

'The worm got it. Do you know what? It looks more like a miss that stripe up the middle.'

'I wouldn't think so. Good evening, Joe.'

'Evening, lads.'

'There's a man won't be long in it, Frank. Shocking failed.'

'Shocking.'

'I must be going. I want to buy a lock of Jeyes Fluid, for we have a cow ready to calve and you never know.'

'So long. Might be seeing you the night.'

'I may be at the Cross.'

'So may I.'

The hard-stemmed wild weeds that grow on that ditch! And yet they have a curious sort of attraction for me. It's not a ditch you'd like to sit down on, but just the same it is part of your life.

Why do you remember this particular part of the road so well? I know. Because this spot, for no special reason, reminds you of yourself going with your mother to the station of a Monday morning, carrying the baskets of eggs and butter on the handlebars of the bicycle.

'And remember what I toul' you, to clane out them hen houses and whitewash the roosts. And don't forget to put the porringer on that wee calf, and not have him sucking the other calf's nabel.'

'Don't forget to bring me back *John O' London's*.'

'If I think of it. There's Mary Faley ahead of us. I don't want to catch up with her for she'd pollute a person with her oul' talk about the wonderful man Cissie got. As far as I hear the devil the much he has, a few scabby acres in the wilds of Derrafanone at the back of God's speed. Might as well be transported. And there's another thing—for God's sake will you cut them nettles at the Meada gate, for they sting the legs of me everytime I go out into the Meada. It wouldn't take you ten minutes.'

'I'll do that.'

'And you might if you have time tidy up that oul' haggard. But don't kill yourself. Don't try to take it all away in one graipful. Nothing for you only the lazy man's load. Go light and go often. Bad luck to her, she's waiting for us. Good morning, Mary. I think we have loads of time.'

'Well now, I'm not so sure. Father Gillan passed me at Little Bessy's and it can't be that early.'

'We're safe enauff', say I, the scientific man. 'The signal is not down for the up train yet. Once we get this far before the signal is down we are in bags of time.'

'Patrick, you could nearly put Mary's basket on the carrier.'

'Don't bother, sure it's not that heavy.'

'It's a nuance if you have a light basket, Mary. Give it to him and don't be killing yourself. Good people's scarce, and bad people ought to try and mind themselves. Didn't poor Micky Duffy go off very sudden? When I heard he was dead and buried I couldn't believe me ears. I met him in Carrick fair—was it two months ago or three? I think it was around April. When did we buy the drop calves, Patrick? Was it at the fair or an ordinary Thursday?'

'Ordinary Thursday.'

'The Lord save us and bless us, but it's a sudden world. But sure he has his family reared.'

I leave them at the station, where already a number of women are waiting for the train to take them to the Dundalk market, a great weekly event in that country at that time. A social event. That is one of the mistakes the price-controllers and planners make. We don't live by the guaranteed price alone. The controlled price killed all the fun. But people still manage to have a little.

The village of my native place is built around a disused graveyard. In that graveyard stands a somewhat stunted round tower. Liveliest spot in the village is that graveyard. And as I reflect, the graveyard is a living thing in the Christian tradition. Carleton wrote a weird ballad which is set in a graveyard. The chief of the McKenna clan of Trougha in north Monaghan, at the funeral of his young bride, is kissed by some fairy woman in the graveyard.

> The leech groaned loud: 'Come tell me this
>   Killeavy, O Killeavy!
> Has Sir Turlough given the fatal kiss
>   By the bonny green woods of Killeavy?'
>
> Then the fatal kiss is given, the last
>   Killeavy, O Killeavy!

> Of Sir Turlough's race and fame is past,
> His doom is sealed and his die is cast
> By the bonny green woods of Killeavy.

There is something of the banshee in this. The banshee is surely the Irish muse, a weird intangible thing. My father believed in the banshee, and he used to tell me how he stood at his door for three evenings, listening to the banshee crying for a young married woman who was dying in childbirth.

The nettles and weeds are in blossom. Somebody who may be a commercial traveller waiting for a train, is going through the graveyard, stumbling over the fallen headstones in the matted grass, reading old inscriptions. The tomb of the McMahons is here. A Protestant church stands in the graveyard beside the round tower. It is probably out of commission by now. Is there e'er a Protestant in the parish at all?

I drive round by the Civic Guards' barracks, and up past the Far House. At the door, stands a bundle of twigs and a scabbard full of Tysacks—scythes. The great maker of scythes was Tysack, though some people would swear by those Bolger made. The Bolger make was on the heavy side.

Would I ever dream of going in to have a bottle of stout?

Never such a thought in my head at that time, and look at me now.

Ah, well, times change and we change with them. Do times really change? I am not so sure. We change. Thinking back into my youth, I know I am occupying another body, with a soul that is not quite the same. I am not so innocent now. I have learned to desire, and that is unwisdom.

Up the sunny dusty road to the station. Some blackguard is after shifting the wagon down towards the stop-lock. I'll have to back in now. I tie the reins round the cross bar, and hop over the sideboard into the wagon. It's an easy wagon to fill from, for it has a smooth unpatched bottom. And the shovel I borrowed from John Parr is a powerful great shovel.

Nicely, nicely, I fill the cart. I shove the sate-board along the tail-board, so that it will make the back of the cart higher, and the coal will be in no danger of falling off going up Ednamo hill.

Far away are cities, far away. I am a young man in the depths of the world.

But I do not feel young. I feel very old.

Somebody once asked me if I was twenty-two, and I got red in the face. He said I looked twenty-two. And at a dance at Annavackey Dock someone else said I wasn't 'dog ould', and I felt he believed that I was, and wanted to console me.

Age is the worst complex I have ever had. I remember writing before I went to bed one night:

> The last year of my teens is passing to-night
> And lonely am I for . . .

I could remember the rest if I tried, but I am ashamed. The bad verse I wrote was something atrocious. Not the right kind of badness either.

Have I the courage to quote bits of those verses? One of the first was appropriately called 'The Pessimist'. I cannot remember that one. But I do remember the one I wrote in the *Dundalk Democrat*—'Lines on an Old Wooden Gate':

> Battered by time and weather, scarcely fit
> For firewood; there's not a single bit
> Of paint to hide those wrinkles and such scringes
> Tear hoarsely down the silence—rusty hinges.
> A barbed wire clasp around one withered arm
> Replaces the old latch with wanton charm,
> This gap ere long must find another sentry,
> If the cows are not to roam the open country. . . .

A whole column of that. Needless to say I got no payment, though all the neighbours said I must have got a tidy sum for it.

'The Bard used to make hapes of money writing for the Democrat,' they said.

As my imagination is levelling the coal on top of the load, trimming around the dash-boards, my present intellect is reflecting on the fact that good taste is not a natural development. The so-called simple folk, on their way out, fall into the pits of weary cliché and convention. All sorts of vulgar abbreviations, are the notes of simple folk getting 'educated'.

The key-note of simple folk is bad manners, familiarity. They intrude on one's private soul. The only tolerable simple people are those we have manufactured in our evocative memories. Of course there were some who had remarkably good natural, manners, but on the whole. . . .

Well, there's a damn good load of coal. It's getting even better at this side of the wagon. I can't have less than fifteen hundred on that cart.

I get sitting on the front-board, with my feet on the shaft, pick up the reins, and go on my way home.

It is a hot day, and the old graveyard is a-hum with bees and flies.

Aye, aye, aye! Aye indeed!

DAVID BOMBERG
The Bomberg Papers

On his death in 1957, in his 68th year, David Bomberg left behind him an accumulation of manuscripts and papers of one kind and another which altogether constitute a testament of the highest importance for those interested in the work (and in the mind behind the work) of this painter. They comprise voluminous notes for correspondence as well as drafts for proposed statements of his aesthetic and general theory of art. From the mass of these writings we have selected, with the permission of Mrs. Lilian Bomberg, those passages which had particular artistic or philosophical relevance and which taken together gave an indication of the mind of the man. In doing this we have, however, no more than dipped into the available material, which is as remarkable for its quantity as for its richness.

A subject so vast and vague as Art precludes dogmatic pronouncements as to the nature of its manifestations in the various Branches of Drawing, Painting, and Sculpture—none the less it is equally true that there can be no movement for a revaluation unless it is circumscribed with affirmations favouring one particular aspect of art at the expense of another. In this view one should accept that criticisms regarding a form of art are not absolute but rather subject to contradiction.

The saying 'the reverse is as true' is a good one regarding art. This human manifestation needs to be free from any of the spoken written ambiguities that tempt to restrict—nevertheless the contradictory statements have helped towards the comprehension of the purpose of Art though they have totally failed to define Art's actual nature. Why we draw paint or sculpt is a Mystery to-day as it was in the Italian Renaissance when artists were paid to do these things; Michelangelo referred to his life's work as a vague and vast Phantasy.

Speaking generally Art endeavours to reveal what is true and needs to be free.

All things said regarding Art are subject to contradiction.

An artist whose integrity sustains his strength to make no compromise with expediency is never degraded. His life work will resemble the integrating character of the primaries in the Spectrum. At the beginning, of the middle period, and at the end. Whether at home painting in England, Scotland or Wales or in London or Paris, in impact with the 'ists' and 'isms' or painting in Palestine, Petra, or the mountain tops of Spain or Cyprus, it will inevitably conform to the rainbow of interlacing gradations of one phase into another, regardless of what the critics think and regardless too of the standards current in taste and fashion—no one part of the work periods should be selected for preferment to the detriment of another. It is all one—and shows the way of youth to age.

I approach drawing solely for structure. I am perhaps the most unpopular artist in England—and only because I am draughtsman first and painter second.

Drawing demands a theory of approach, until good drawing becomes a habit—it denies all rules. It requires high discipline. That a manifestation so dynamic, of one of the most comprehensive and familiar of our faculties should go uncultivated in the Universities' Schools of Fine Art passes my comprehension. The virility of drawing lies in the immediate necessity to make decisions—with it departs the fears and the funk, and to that it owes its vibrant qualities.

A Draughtsman has no opinions about the wrong and the right kind of art. He registers progress by the revaluation of scale in the passage of time. The draughtsman cannot exist, unless being dead he speaks to those who have ears to hear. But living he can be useful too.

Drawing demands freedom, freedom demands liberty to expand in space—this is progress. By the extension of democracy—good draughtsmanship is—Democracy's visual sign.

The exercise of drawing from the life brings out the individuality of the [artist] in the man. When the door has been closed on the completion of an academic rendering, no matter how rendered to the resemblance of the anatomic stress and strain, it is still only saying the things you already know, it may be excellent in its representation of the form of Man in its finest, it can be a highly skilled rendering, contain and show care (?)—it is still a lifeless drawing in the light of modern art—you can teach a talented person eager to learn—but you cannot stimulate the essence of life if it is not already there.

[On the Slade 1898–1901]—the position of Draughtsmanship from that period to 1907 was to learn from John Singer Sargent that Slade Drawing was the best in the world. The tradition carried on had for its source in England Alfred Stevens, its variant was according to the temperament of each individual who was in his own inheritance a natural born Draughtsman—Hence from the life floor of the Slade were launched forth the able figure draughtsmen who performed the task of achieving what the New English Art Club had set out to do, namely to contest the notion that the sameness staleness and pretence that was the art of Great Britain in 1886 needed some blood transfusions from the younger talent at the everfilling fountain of inspiration they brought back from their visits to France—such for instance as the Barbizon School which had affinity with and was much stimulated by our able John Constable. To say that Alfred Stevens was a source is in the sense only that he was the forged link with the Central European Tradition from the early Renaissance. Alfred Stevens' work constitutes his particular fusion of opposing characteristics evinced in high Renaissance Art, namely the contributions of the three contemporaries whose work shows impact one on the other—according to the variant of his temperament. In Stevens was symbolised the united force and elegance of Michelangelo, Raphael, and Leonardo da Vinci.

Some of Lewis' colleagues who were with him partisan in a very remarkable struggle for supremacy against Royal Academy Art—which before 1911 was still the public conception of What Art Should Be in England—were Jews, some British born as it was my fate to be—I take no special pride in this (something I had nothing whatever to do with)—what however I do take pride in is being one with others of whatever derivation beyond affinity they had with other nations or races, who would in this country find in (and the United States and France) the security from persecution, the inheritance of a condition of freedom based on Tolerance observed as the Common Law of Mankind; on the Thoughts and feelings of this impulse my colleagues together went forward—irrespective of race religion education and though some of us (on our entry) may have had a proletarian environment and hard upbringing. Tough awful fruits—with a terrifying precosity—we were not discriminated against on that account—the law of the jungle at the time of our entry to the profession was Can the man draw?—or is he a Natural Born Draughtsman?

No man wants to get experience from others' experiments, he will make his own experiments. But the link is the teacher, who must be a man of great gifts if he is to be the bridge between the one who knows more and the one who knows less. Restrictions provide the rules for confining expansion.

There is inherent in the structure of moral values an integrity which performs but does not think. It will help sustain strength—the seat of which may be located in the mind; it cannot be seen but we know it is there, because it is operative. The desire for truth radiates from it. It becomes Fine Art when it is integrated in form. Not to possess it is to know you are no artist and for an artist to possess it and to sacrifice by compromise for expediency is to degrade it and the artist.[1]

The humanism of Giotto, the Father of modern painting, was transferred to his great inheritor Paul Cézanne, and as this came down the years it gathered power from Michelangelo. Cézanne's structure broke down the ineptitudes—and stifling adhesions—gathered in the eventual decline from growth to decadence of the Visual Arts of Egypt, Greece, and Rome, in the period of the culmination of their civilisations transmitted to the Italian Renaissance and inaugurated for our own time the relaxes and releases. Cézanne the precursor of our times rediscovers the earth is round and has a gravitational pull, initiates Cubism activised by Impressionism which nurtured Cézanne; therefore Cézanne is Father to me and the artists of the future. Giotto stands to Cézanne as Cézanne will stand to posterity and I who am of the line and inherit the blood stream should not be treated as a stranger in my Father's House.[1]

Cubism derives from Cézanne, it is inverted Naturalism. It provided the block moulds into which the engineers who had become Cézanne-conscious were waiting to pour ferro-concrete since 1880. To invert the

[1] These three paragraphs were recorded by Charles Spencer.

inverted is not to invent, it is clowning, and though we are prepared to applaud a man standing on his head and go on laughing we do not wish to hinder him if he believes that this is the way to save the world. There has been too much rotting and leg-pulling on the tarmac of late, both here, New York and Paris. Clowning is not comedy and this performing and pretending with ability, cleverness, and dexterity granted, has been to excess. As if to aspire to Fame's pinnacle necessitates a descent to ridicule for its consummation. Clowns are, in fact, tragedians and we wish to esteem them as such. Both French and English painting progressed to 1920, then dried up and lost the way. It is to this page of history that such contributions as I and my followers may make after me through the approach to the mass that there should be appended a footnote—and left to posterity to judge whether it was of significance or not.[1]

Good judgement is through good drawing—from the nervous system to the sensory of the brain it is the combination of eurythmics, euphony and poetry, and when the good draughtsman draws, the muses come to dance. Then the imagination is given full play, and design happens. They then become the Muses.

Experienced Artists and Architects are more convinced by painting whereas in fact the reality lies in the structure of the drawing.

To draw with integrity replaces bad habits with good, youth preserved from corruption.

The hand works at high tension and organises as it simplifies, reducing to barest essentials, stripping all irrelevant matter obstructing the rapidly forming organisation which reveals the design. This is the drawing.

Drawing flows from beginning to end with one sustained impulse—as the drawing shapes, so does its mood reveal the character in form combinations, all else is subordinated to this end on impulse.

The approach is through feeling and touch and less by sight. There are no Rules, Tastes, Styles, Fashions. Drawing is handling structure with a chariscurio [sic] force. Drawing is sculpturally conceived in the full like architecture.

Drawing in terms of speech, is to bring clauses, phrases, and their sequence, to make the sentence understood. Translated to visual form the drawing results which reveals the unknown things.

Style is ephemeral—Form is eternal.

Why British painting to-day shares with all other countries a decline is because it is so facile with its own virtuosity, trying to imitate the virtues of others, and if the artists do not feel sick it is because it has become the fashion of painting to mirror one another's complexions with the same ingredients of the 'beauty' preparations—structure has become less important.

The faith of a child to surmount the barrier of complexities existing between thought and feeling is the first factor in the making of a good drawing, painting or sculpture. Another factor is personality, both are outside the scope of a school of art to implant.

What is too vague or too vast, faith and personality will define and make absolute; in definition lies the merit of skill or the craftsman—the measure of the artist is the extent of inherited personality. There is no alternative but to accept that nature provides nourishment as much for brambles as for Cypresses and the forest is the richer for having both.

If originality exists in Drawing, Painting, and Sculpture it will be found in Treatment—namely the idiom, which is the total experience to formulate a satisfying way of integrating with integrity—Form, Personality, and Content.—teaching consists in stimulating integrity.

Of the durable factors that go to make a good Drawing, Painting, Sculpture, some can be described while others cannot. Hence the floundering of judgement regarding merit on one's own work or that of others. In a manner of speaking best is for a work to go through the Furnace and be Fired, should it survive it may wear. Among the discernible factors, immediately discernible for endurance, is definition—be the inspiration of the artist vague, the forms nonetheless that are to convey and define the human element of thought and feeling, whether in abstract or in natural form, must be clear. In this matter of Clarity the Florentines of the 15th and 16th centuries are our masters—is it not by definition that we test our sincerity? A work which has no design cannot come into the category of Fine Art—and by design is meant not only line, colour and mass but the purposeful functioning of all parts to form the unity, in short an Organic Whole.

Among factors which cannot be described is Personality—the factors that form the character of the personality of an innovator and an originator in the approach to the art of Drawing, Painting, and Sculpture displays a quite different [   ][1] to that of an artist who is a craftsman first and originator second. To acknowledge the vast difference is sufficient—to analyse it impossible.

Cézanne and Pissarro are examples of two good artists with wholly different personalities—where Cézanne inaugurated the New Era in the interpretation of nature, Pissarro brought the European Tradition in the imitation of appearances to its ultimate conclusion. The personality of Van Gogh is that of an originator; that of Renoir of a fine craftsman first.

The character of Personality in the artist alone determines what it is, by inspiration, intuition, or instinct, and also what measure of success. Visual form cannot be described by words that are not contradictory. The Symbol, The Spirit, are compressed in the design

---

[1] Word omitted in MS.

with Line, Light Colour and Mass to the sum total of the Personality. This is the work of Art.

In the harvest after the Industrial Revolution was nurtured an exclusiveness regarding Art and Artists. Art was respectable and artists gentlemen, there were retaining fees, private patronage, and palaces for studios—all this is past; to-day the most able of artists are cut off completely from the rest of the community; no Church, no State, public or private employment—not unlike Cézanne, Van Gogh, Rembrandt in old age.

Many of the most serious threats to the liberty of art come not from the reactionaries or the sterile Academic Tradition or Conditions of Art in a State but from the activities of private individuals not born for the profession but for organising opposition to those that have been, and form for themselves one man organisations and legislate in Art Polemic a principle for the crowd composed of individuals; the core of intolerance in the distorted notions of freedom of art.

On the note 'Leonardo da Vinci' I went forward in the experience of my teachers—men with the integrity of surgeons—never resorting to a poultice.

On this note I shall add in conclusion that the world of Art is as much a jungle as the Hyena inhabited swamps of Burma Africa and the Amazon. Hunters and Hunted acquire Fame as Killers. With indifference they rip out one another's guts. The Vultures who bare the Kill, and those who submerge and drown to kill are still our Professional Colleagues. There is no difference to ourselves, Claws Fangs Tusks are the requisites for defence, together with the Strategic mind and the ugly looking Wolf Knife for those with a free hand.

The imputations daily in the press that the reason the English cubists painted cubisticly was incompetence, though damaging to ourselves we regarded as the natural public prejudice against any change in the art forms of the day. It seemed to me preferable to the calculated indifference of the polite gentlemanly critics—seen revived to-day the Pestilence of 1912–14 has become the naturally honoured art form of 1956–57 due to inadequate understanding giving fishmongers insufficiently qualified to distinguish 'Sprats' or stale Fish from Salt Herrings, the option to confuse reputations built on Creative able Draughtsmanship. Where the Crazy fishmonger would have his knuckles rapped in holding forth on the circulation of the blood the Crazy Art Director goes scot free. I submit it would take as many years of a physician's life to study in practice and theory—to realise and experiment with the nature of the nervous system; before he was able to make a positive pronouncement regarding one aspect of the Study the physician would be ready for retirement from Practice. The study of draughtsmanship is no less dense yet fools jump in where angels fear to tread. Like Monet I have entered my

66th year. I feel as he did when taking up chalk—the immensity of nature contained in the volume and mass of one small form and should I direct my sight to the Mountains I, like Monet, feel humbled—that any artist gifted with genius should presume he could solve—with the limited means at his disposal—the problem of the magnitude contained in the Billions of tons of living rock.

Is it only a rumour that £30,000 was paid by England for a painting located as it is said behind the Studio Stove after Cézanne's death and now in our National Gallery—La Vieille au Chapelet—the type of selecting committee of artists that rejected Manet from the Salon d'Autumn exists in artist associations in England to-day rejecting work of originality and innovation on grounds beyond scope of comprehension.

To correct this in their country the Société de l'École Française have federated groups of exhibitors founded 1945—the 1954 exhibition in the Palais des Beaux Arts comprised 15 groups of approx. 7 to 20 members. Could not the Arts Council of Great Britain put into action a similar scheme so that not only the work of popularly approved British artists comes before the public, but those of the less known and whose art is less popular.

I have often tried to find the reason for spontaneous acceptance of one kind of Drawing, Painting, or Sculpture and an equally immediate rejection of another—and whether this judgement is the result of practice and experience or whether it is intuitive.

Fortunately the reasons given for acceptance of one particular kind of Drawing, Painting, or Sculpture over another are so contradictory that it has even been impossible to frame upon these submissions a standard of judgement—we may say that a Drawing is good when it tells us something we do not know, reveals some aspect of truth with which we have hitherto been unacquainted with and very good when its convincing execution brings acceptance of its reality; but will this continue to hold its power once truth is revealed?

If Michelangelo in his day had been asked to expound on the Character of his Art there would have been no long-winded philosophical dissertation in which words like Inspiration, Symbolism, Spiritual, would be used. His reply would be essentially Practical, workmanlike and dealing with Craftsman's Problems—yet of all Personalities among artists working in the light of his own inspiration, and one who has more than any other integrated Symbolism and Naturalism with a vitality and power never before known, and whose Spirituality brought to fruition a unity out of the dead Cultures of Hellenism and Byzantinism, and gave the force of reality that will endure for all time—this unique man would speak the most banal commonplaces. We will follow his example and learn to refrain from explanation when we come together.

ANDRÉ MASSON
Dissonances

DECEMBER 1959

I am illustrating, from Rimbaud, *Une Saison en Enfer*.

	Original mud
	Gold
	Blood
	Ancestral lust
ELEMENTS	To be thrown under the hooves of horses
OF	To flay animals
INSPIRATION	Immeasurably large hands (century for hands)
	Love, essential to be reinvented—the impossible.
	Purity?—flouted.
	Ferocious cripples back from tropical countries
	To wander through splendid cities
	(Meanwhile, poetry, very quickly, and then: 'burn for me all this filth . . .')

I am illustrating Rimbaud and trying to *see* him. He wrote this revealing phrase: 'par délicatesse j'ai perdu ma vie'. That is to say: For a sensitive being a certain experience can be the cause of infernal and constant suffering, whereas for so many brutes ludicrous or sinister it may only provoke passing discomfort or even undisguised *merriment*. This is the real inequality.

Rimbaud (at the dawn of his day) was defeated by the revelation of a terrifying reality. He killed the poet in himself, trained himself to be insensitive. To be as hard as iron, as the stones of a sierra.

Simultaneously with *Une Saison en Enfer* I am working on a set of prints which may make up a book and whose guiding thread is this thought in the manner of Chamfort: For savouring the felicities of love there are no palates delicate enough; in this matter gluttons are legion. Here is something that does not take me far from Rimbaud!

TAO

The heavens are no longer above you. For how could one call such emptiness, such absence the heavens? But three drops of music will put you back in the saddle, ready to leap over spaces red and black.

ZEN

The world of sensation we imagine we experience—it is there—yet always it eludes us. The 'real' passes and the possible comes. Lethargic abundance without truce or rest.

In a fissure of alternation—in pure time—to insert oneself; to find an awakening. (A sudden illumination. The non-mental.)

Long repressed, the thought and mysticism of Asia: Tao, Zen, Tantrism, have since the beginning of the century, taken possession of the best minds in the West; while Asiatics were prostrating themselves before Western 'ideas', which, as we know well, are often destructive, or out of date or rightly abandoned.

Listen to what is living in you. Do not allow yourself to be carried away only by what lives outside yourself: this is the profound advice of the most ancient Asia.

DELIVERANCE THROUGH EXCESS

That truth should be the delirium of a confraternity in which there is not one member who is not intoxicated is a proposition to which few artists would not subscribe. But how many understand that this much sought after madness must by a supreme operation become 'a translucent and simple repose'?

It was in America, in exile, that my painting achieved complete awareness of its virtue; that it began to look at me, as Paul Klee used to say of his own painting.

Happening to re-read a criticism of my work, I found that I was accused of complicity with Chaos. I can hardly disagree with this as for me Chaos is not the pre-world of the classicists but the melting pot of creation. Chaos included in the Cosmos as Paradise in Hell.

Since Impressionism the adherents of *drawn-painting* have added nothing to their reprobation of *painted-painting*. 'Their picture is no more than a palette' they say. This sometimes happens but it also happens that a drawn-picture is less than a palette.

Real modern draughtsmanship no longer consists in outlining or signifying a form, but is the consummation of a gesture or a leap forward. This conclusion may bring to view an unforeseen 'figure' or it may remain a mere scribble.

DREAM-EATERS

We, the very first surrealists, were, although unaware of it, in agreement with Burne-Jones' definition of a picture as the dream of something which has never existed and never will exist, seen in a light superior to any which has ever shone, in a country that nobody can define or remember . . . (I quote from memory and imperfectly) while all other painters followed, Maurice Denis' dictum on the fundamentally material character of a picture: 'a flat surface covered with colours assembled in a certain order.'

Art is impossible without unquenched passions or without the misery of profound dissatisfaction. It is strange that it should be the most wretched frustration which is transformed into wealth and the most abysmal emptiness into fulfilment and delight.

IN EROTICIS

Between the last two wars there were in Paris certain original prostitutes of a singular reputation. One of them on summer nights used to wear a fur coat that she would throw open before the late passer-by. (Is it necessary to add that underneath the coat she was clad only in her nakedness?) She used to appear at the Tuileries or near the Rue de Rivoli. She once exhibited herself to my eyes near the statue of Joan of Arc that stands on the little Place des Pyramides. The conjunction of a tart with her dark sex and prominent breasts, in close proximity to an arcaded street (in the manner of Chirico), at the feet of an effigy of The Maid, and an evocation of the Pyramids, suggested a film sequence of an eminently surrealist character.

He has seen his success becoming confirmed, why attempt to surpass himself?

Worldly success, in art, inevitably results in setting a boundary; Fortune's favourite if he is clear-sighted then becomes aware of his misfortune.

If you are seeking the un-limitable climb on to your own head; your neighbour's can be of no use to you.

BAD INTENTIONS

A coldly calculating art laying claim to *pure plasticity*—in fact: rudimentary, is inferior.

An art of unreason, fundamentally very reasoned, is no better. Far from these stratagems there shines on the peaks the harmony of the being in accord with life in its original state, the sense of form emerging—the latent image. Symbols of anguish or desire.

Not to put one's trust in the 'taste' of '*avant-garde*' groups. Especially if one is oneself very *advanced*.

James Joyce—the surrealism then in vogue left him cold; he liked the Symbolists when everyone had to be *for* Lautréamont; he was mad about *bel-canto* when Bach alone, or Stravinsky . . . And he had in his library the works of Sacher Masoch whereas a 'lion' at that time felt obliged to place on the shelves allotted to 'curious' books only those of the Marquis de Sade.

TAOIST MEDITATION

Every powerful or exquisite work finds itself at first consigned to the aristocratic pleasure of displeasing, so runs the accepted formula. But even to displease is to offer oneself to the crowd.
Only solitude is divine, and the withdrawal from others reassuring.

LEAP, TRAJECTORY, AND DEATH

The destiny of Jackson Pollock—his life and work has an *emblematic* value.
Starting with a feverish 'figuration' (in my eyes something fraternal or filial) he rushes into the most absolute act of painting: virgin forests of the unconscious, labyrinths of automatism. But in the last period of his flashing life, out of these wild interlacings there surged up again vestiges of human and animal form. Desperately, like a forgotten Andromeda the *Image* beckons to him once more.

Thus in his rapid career, Pollock sums up the situation of painting since 1940: at first restricted and surrealist figuration, then non-figuration, and finally the intuition of a figuration which would, 'have no truck with anything that ever was', inserted into painting that is freer than ever.

I have often noticed it in the course of my work: the proliferation of signs or the exacerbation of details are occasionally the result less of a desire for expansion than of an impotent fury in the face of inaccessible purity.

GENIUS AND DISTANCE

The fate of Odilon Redon makes one reflect. It is never, or hardly ever, the originality of an artist that is perceived during his lifetime. What is recognised is his skill—let us say what is taken to be skill at a given moment. Thus skill is as a rule highly praised, while what is extraordinary passes unperceived. The explanation in part of the cruel fate

meted out to Cézanne, Van Gogh, Gauguin, Munch, and many others.

These painters disdained for their 'clumsiness' were not *cunning*; but were untamed, isolated, mysterious. Their own world and not that of other people gravitated around their genius. Their inner light only appeared later; and Redon's star is still veiled, obscured by the mist of rejection.

Pictorial creation joined to lyrical effusion, metaphysical thought to symbol—all this together. Thus the future picture if there is occasion for it.

It took me long years of admiring attraction to grasp fully that the art of Turner (in its extremes) is a vision of *motion* so forceful that it annihilates every kind of spatial preoccupation.

The very notion of classicism was dominated by spatial conceptions: a divine sense of space (Perugino, Raphael) and no less firmly by a will towards timelessness. Baroque art and following it all the aspects of the various Romanticisms (Turner-Blake-Delacroix) were embraced by the great serpent of which Hofmansthal speaks: devouring Time.

The transmutation of time into space is no doubt the final temptation of a means of expression that wishes to survive.

But time having become space, this very mutation, is generator of forms mechanically hardened and cold; or sometimes on the contrary these forms (then said to be non-formal) are astutely liquefied: tempestuous amorphousness in an atmosphere of exacerbated crisis, for which there may be no other issue than the death of painting in the form in which it has been known for thousands of years.

MISURINA

La chaleur de l'aigle
La verdeur du torrent
Dolomites du desire
Cristaux ensanglantés.

Translated by Jane Bussy and Mary Hutchinson

DAVID WRIGHT
Adam at Evening

The falling sun stands on a hill
And shall for quarter of an hour
Before I see the darkness come
To lapse for us the labouring farm.
The long shafts range (against the night
To which a half-lost globe conforms)
As, once, before the Eden gate,
Those hostile and obedient arms.

In the garden where I was made
Ran through the original grass
The alert novelties, hoofed or pawed,
Unprofitable and harmless.
There was nothing to use or fear,
All things existed in their praise.
Each bird its phœnix broke the air,
And fiery imagos flew and strummed.

Last of the inaugural park,
Last bestowed, fatally endowed,
The Friday that the spirit breathed
Choice to the dust of his image,
Between the dumb and bursting trees
The singing speechless birds and beasts,
Able to name and half to create
I walked articulate and proud.

The leaflit concepts moved between
The minted light and primal shade
As the first things for the first time
Obeyed their delight and obeyed
The nature that had created them.
A blackbird on a thornless thorn
Whistled to its marvellous world,
A world where nothing had been born.

The pomegranate to my hand
Bowed, and a berry from its spray.
To all things I returned a name:
Substantives hovering to my tongue
Became them. They in turn became

More than they were. Fish, water, bees,
The dolphin antelopes that leapt,
Or moon and stars as they came out,

Existed also as my poem.
Was a spiritual pride
Conceived in this creating hour
That, rearing at the flanks of Eve,
As a scotched angel, spoke to her?
Then the gambler lost his throw,
Then the consequence began
That can not be ended now.

The smoulder of a grounded sun
Burns under conglomerate shade,
Invites the falling dark to fall
Which, smoking from a bloodless east,
Blots out my stead. Goodbye the light,
Let darkness shelter man and beast.
The valley fills its pool with night.
My children sleep below the hill.

IV

EZRA POUND

Conversations in Courtship

Made from a literal rendering into Italian by
Boris de Rachewiltz of an ancient Egyptian text
(papyrus of 1200 B.C. or thereabouts).[1]

HE SAYS:
Darling, you only, there is no duplicate,
More lovely than all other womanhood,
    Luminous, perfect,
A star coming over the sky-line at new year,
    a good year,
Splendid in colours
    with allure in the eye's turn.
Her lips are enchantment,
    her neck the right length
        and her breasts a marvel;
Her hair lapislazuli in its glitter,
    her arms more splendid than gold.
Her fingers make me see petals,
    the lotus' are like that.
Her flanks are modelled as should be,
    her legs beyond all other beauty.
Noble her walking
        (vera incessu)
My heart would be a slave should she enfold me.
Every neck turns—that is her fault—
    to look at her.
Fortune's who can utterly embrace her;
    he would stand first among all young lovers.
Deo mi par esse
    Every eye keeps following her
        even after she has stepped out of range,
A single goddess,
    uniquely.

---

[1] Boris de Rachewiltz, *Liriche Amorose degli Antichi Egiziani*, Scheiwiller, Milano, 1957.

SHE SAYS:
His voice unquiets my heart,
    It's the voice's fault if I suffer.
My mother's neighbour!
        But I can't go see him,
    Ought she to enrage me?

MOTHER:
Oh stop talking about that fellow,
    the mere thought of him is revolting.

SHE:
I am made prisoner 'cause I love him.

MOTHER:
But he's a mere kid with no brains.

SHE:
So am I, I am just like him
    and he don't know I want to put my arms round him.
      THAT would make mama talk . . .

May the golden goddess make fate,
    and make him my destiny.

Come to where I can see you.
    My father and mother will then be happy
      Because everyone likes to throw parties for you
        And they would get to doing it too.

SHE SAYS:
I wanted to come out here where it's lovely
    and get some rest,
Now I meet Mehy in his carriage
    with a gang of other young fellows,
      How can I turn back?

Can I walk in front of him
    as if it did not matter?
Oh, the river is the only way to get by
    and I can't walk on the water.
      My soul you are all in a muddle.
If I walk in front of him my secret will show,
    I'll blurt out my secrets; say:
                Yours!

And he will mention my name and
> hand me over to just any one of them
> > who merely wants a good time.

SHE SAYS:
My heart runs out if I think how I love him,
> I can't just act like anyone else.
It, my heart, is all out of place
> It won't let me choose a dress
> > or hide back of my fan.
I can't put on my eye make-up
> > > > or pick a perfume.
'Don't stop, come into the house.'
> That's what my heart said, one time,
And does, every time I think of my beloved.
> Don't play the fool with me, oh heart,
> > Why *are* you such an idiot?
Sit quiet! keep calm
> and he'll come to you.
And my alertness won't let people say:
> This girl is unhinged with love.
When you remember him
> stand firm and be solid,
> > don't escape me.

HE SAYS:
I adore the gold-gleaming Goddess,
> Hathor the dominant,
> > and I praise her.
I exalt the Lady of Heaven,
> I give thanks to the Patron.
She hears my invocation
> and has fated me to my lady,
Who has come here, herself, to find me.
> What felicity came in with her!
I rise exultant
> in hilarity
> > and triumph when I have said:
> > > > Now,

And behold her.
> Look at it!
> > The young fellows fall at her feet.
Love is breathed into them.

I make vows to my Goddess,
>   because she has given me this girl for my own.
I have been praying three days,
>   calling her name.
For five days she has abandoned me.

SHE SAYS:
I went to his house, and the door was open.
>   My beloved was at his ma's side
>   with brothers and sisters about him.
Everybody who passes has sympathy for him,
>   an excellent boy, none like him,
>   a friend of rare quality.
He looked at me when I passed
>   and my heart was in jubilee.
If my mother knew what I am thinking
>   she would go to him at once.

O Goddess of Golden Light,
>   put that thought into her,
>   Then I could visit him
And put my arms round him while people were looking
And not weep because of the crowd,
>   But would be glad that they knew it
>   and that you know me.
What a feast I would make to my Goddess,
>   My heart revolts at the thought of exit,
If I could see my darling tonight,
>   dreaming is loveliness.

HE SAYS:
Yesterday. Seven days and I have not seen her.
>   My malady increases;
>   limbs heavy!
>   I know not myself any more.
High priest is no medicine, exorcism is useless:
>   a disease beyond recognition.

I said: she will make me live,
>   her name will rouse me,
Her messages are the life of my heart
>   coming and going.
My beloved is the best of medicine,
>   more than all pharmacopia.
My health is in her coming,
>   I shall be cured at the sight of her.

Let her open my eyes
    and my limbs are alive again;
Let her speak and my strength returns.
Embracing her will drive out my malady.
    Seven days and
            she has abandoned me.

C. H. SISSON

Money

I was led into captivity by the bitch business
Not in love but in what seemed a physical necessity
And now I cannot even watch the spring
The itch for subsistence having become responsibility.

Money the she-devil approaches under many veils
Tactful at first, calling herself beauty
Rip off that disguise, she proposes paternal solicitude
Assuming the dishonest face of duty.

Suddenly you are in bed with a screeching tear-sheet
This is money at last without her night-dress
Clutching you against her fallen udders and sharp bones
In an unscrupulous and deserved embrace.

Moriturus

The carcase that awaits the undertaker
But will not give up its small voice lies
Hollow and grim upon the bed.

What stirs in it is hardly life but a morosity
Which when this skipped as a child was already under the lids
Rebellious and parting from the flesh.

What drunken fury in adolescence pretended
Merely to possess the flesh and drove onwards
The blind soul to issue in the lap of Venus?

The hope of fatherhood, watching the babe sucking
(Ah, he will grow, hurled headlong into the tomb!)
Gives way to a tenderness spilt into amnesia.

The last chat of corruption reasonable as a syllogism
The image of God is clear, his love wordless
Untie my ligaments, let my bones disperse.

Sparrows Seen from an Office

You should not bicker while the sparrows fall
In chasing pairs from underneath the eaves
And yet you should not let this enraged fool
Win what he will because you fear his grief.

About your table three or four who beg
Bully or trade because those are the passions
Strong enough in them to hide all other lack
Sent to corrupt your heart or try your patience.

If you are gentle, it is because you are weak
If bold, it is the courage of a clown
And your smart enemies and you both seek
Ratiocination without love or reason.

O fell like lust, birds of morality
O sparrows, sparrows, sparrows whom none regards
Where men inhabit, look in here and see
The fury and cupidity of the heart.

Ightham Woods

The few syllables of a horse's scuffle at the edge of the road
Reach me in the green light of the beeches
Les seuls vrais plaisirs
Selon moy
Are those of one patch between the feet and the throat.
Possibly, but the beeches
And that half clop on the gravel
Indicate a world into which I can dissolve.

Family Fortunes

I

I was born in Bristol, and it is possible
To live harshly in that city

Quiet voices possess it, but the boy
Torn from the womb, cowers

Under a ceiling of cloud. Tramcars
Crash by or enter the mind

A barred room bore him, the backyard
Smooth as a snake-skin, yielded nothing

In the fringes of the town parsley and honey-suckle
Drenched the hedges.

II

My mother was born in West Kington
Where ford and bridge cross the river together

John Worlock farmed there, my grandfather
Within sight of the square church-tower

The rounded cart-horses shone like metal
My mother remembered their fine ribbons.

She lies in the north now where the hills
Are pale green, and I

Whose hand never steadied a plough
Wish I had finished my long journey.

III

South of the march parts my father
Lies also, and the fell town

That cradles him now sheltered also
His first unconsciousness

He walked from farm to farm with a kit of tools
From clock to clock, and at the end

Only they spoke to him, he
Having tuned his youth to their hammers.

IV

I had two sisters, one I cannot speak of
For she died a child, and the sky was blue that day

The other lived to meet blindness
Groping upon the stairs, not admitting she could not see

Felled at last under a surgeon's hammer
Then left to rot, surgically

And I have a brother who, being alive
Does not need to be put in a poem.

V

Pity if you will
The old man maddened by Eros

Close at his back
One who can spring on him like a leopard

It rejoices him above all
That there is still flesh to tear

He is not pursued
But reaches out ecstatically into the darkness.

Epictetus

I want to die creditably and with permission
Or I would long since have ended my days
The moon rises and the vast elms
Stand black at the edge of the haze.

Whether I live or die there is no I
Only the multifarious skelter of nature
Nothing except pride in this crowd
Marks out the rational (as they call him) creature.

CRAIGIE AITCHISON
Fragments from a Conversation

I don't think I know the reasons for lots of the things I do in painting, but I have an idea about why I do not do certain things. It is a case of trying all the time to get the picture *right*.

There are lots of variations in the way I get a painting done. I get a bit of help from showing pictures to certain people, ones I think I have finished, or I might show an unfinished one to somebody, asking him all about it. I am doing a certain bit, concentrating, say, on doing an arm from a model, when someone sees it, he might say he does not like a certain shape, perhaps not the arm, but the shape that the arm is making to its left, and then I might see that through concentrating on the arm so much, an unconsidered thing had happened. I was painting irises and I thought for one reason or another that the picture needed part of an iris higher up, I put it in that way, and thought it was all right. For about a year I had it this way, looking at it off and on, often wondering if it was really right, suddenly someone came in and I showed the picture to him, he said immediately, you have ruined the picture with that one iris, when he went away I painted it out quickly, but was ready to put it in again if he was wrong. I had found him a help, in the way that looking at a picture through a mirror is sometimes a help.

It's got to be a shape but an iris as well, the two things at once. I hate when a flower turns into just a shape, that is what had happened, there, and yet it has to be a shape when all is said and done. But then if the shape is right, the whole painting will have taken on a life of its own, and then the shape will be completely forgotten, but it will still be there for anybody who wants to look at it for itself alone. I find in painting that it becomes a flower first, very quickly, then it goes into a shape then back into a flower, if it does not go back, then it's useless and the picture is terrible.

Sometimes, of course, it does not alter from the first flower, but this is rare, and so far, in painting I have found that the pictures I have altered the most have been better.

I just want to get it right, I have no idea what right is until I get it that way, then I know like a flash; but I know when it is *wrong*. Sometimes, of course, I am taken in for ages, then the whole painting goes wrong for a time, until I suddenly see what has happened, I expect everybody is the same. I put in something I want, and as soon as it is in, I know immediately if it is to stay or come out, but sometimes I am not so certain, but still

I have to decide the same day, because the paint will dry overnight, and then I would have to paint over it with thick paint which I can't use, then the picture would be hopeless, not all *tight*.

Because of altering so much, I have tried painting on thick dark grounds, for I could then paint with more confidence because of the feeling that I could alter without difficulty and there was not the rush to decide on things the same day, but I lost the tension painting like this, *as the act of painting no longer seemed urgent*, and any pictures I did this way were no use.

Sometimes in the course of rubbing out something, I arrive at the conclusion I have been seeking. Once when painting Adam and Eve I suddenly realized when taking out the figure of Adam, that I liked the leg, and so I decided that I would re-paint it alone, it was sufficient to indicate what I wanted, the very idea that I once had, of painting the whole figure in again, seemed completely unnecessary and *wrong*.

I have several times painted the garden at home for itself, but more often I use it for other pictures—the proportions—where the grass ends, and the wall begins; in three crucifixion paintings I have the cross cutting through the garden wall. If I was not there I would take from wherever else I was, if I liked the place enough.

I don't learn much from my paintings, by this I mean, I do not feel one picture helps the other much, they might teach me something technically, or I might learn to have a bit more patience, wait till the first arm dries, once I have decided it is right, for to paint into it when it is wet, muddles it, apart from that I do not associate one picture with another, though all the pictures I have got at home, I associate together if they have been done at the same time. I have only once done a series of paintings, by this I mean that the pictures have been connected. I did a very gloomy picture of a moor with telegraph poles, then I did from memory a very bright picture, it was of butterflies in a red and orange landscape, then afterwards I painted a very dark purple landscape, for by then I was against the bright picture. I disliked each one when I finished it, but liked them all in the end. They should have been all one picture really, I do not like remembering them separately, and one seen without the other loses its force.

There is somebody I know who talks about getting an 'equivalent in paint', I feel I understand what he means by this. If you are painting say flowers, and leaves, you mix up some white (your equivalent) for the flower and place it in one brush stroke on the canvas, if it looks right then it is all you need. Always I find I start meaning to paint a whole thing, say a flower, and then I find that maybe two strokes of the same or different colours and the whole thing seems to be there, and so I stop, the thought of continuing putting anything else in is just ridiculous, it would never occur to me, but if I make it occur to myself just for a 'commonsense' reason, *I am then absolutely certain that I could never put another piece of paint down.*

I always do five or six pictures at the same time, if I was doing only one at a time, days would go by and I would not know what to do to it, but I might be doing five and not know what to do to any of them. I don't sit and think about the pictures, I just think maybe as the years go on you'll get better at knowing what you want, and there will not be this wait.

The paintings I have been able to do quickly and easily have been of no use, so I am quite pleased the more difficult it is, and although I do not like altering, this seems to be what I do most, and what turns out for the best, it is also best when I have great difficulty in deciding, when there is no difficulty I am usually on the wrong track.

I'm suspicious if the whole picture comes right ever, I don't really expect to get more than one bit or 'The Bit' right, but it would be marvellous if one day all of it got right with equal intensity. I *never* change the first bit, because if it is not there after the first day I know there is no point in continuing that canvas, for I have tried doing so, it is simply that I have not been sufficiently interested in what I set out to paint. There is always one bit that has got to be good enough to stay for ever, and if the picture is to be painted at all, it has to get there immediately. I won't ever turn against the bit, *once I have accepted* it, the bit that made me start the picture and *continue* with it. I have an idea how I want the whole painting, and do it in very quickly, hoping I will get it the way I want it in my head, then suddenly I realize it is not going to work, but one bit I have got, and so for a time I go on with my original intentions, simply to convince myself that they will not work. I put things in almost *perversely* very quickly in, but often quicker out, hoping something will come of them. Then comes a long wait. I have got to revise, but there is always that bit and it is now just a case of making the most of it. I think I have given up the bit that I like once or twice, I have tried to make a whole different picture from it but this has always failed. I have one picture I have thought worth continuing with for five years because it has this bit in it, but I just can't, somehow or another what I have got there refuses to be married with anything else, and yet it is not sufficient by itself. It is a question of deciding day after day about everything, for everything on the canvas must be considered equally, for it will all be seen. I like when I have made a big decision—to cover a whole area with a colour, it is all right then until it is finished, then I go through the whole process of deciding whether I want it that way or not.

Painting from a model I find very different to painting without somebody there. If there was a nude model posing in front of me, I could paint away for some weeks completely unaware that I had not put in part of a leg for instance, I wouldn't notice, for what I am doing there is a visual activity and it would never occur to me to paint something I did not see *to such an extent* that I wanted to paint it. It is different in a picture from the imagination; when I imagine for the purpose of doing say a crucifixion, and this is different from an entirely imaginative picture, I imagine a normal person with all his limbs until I know I don't want them all; so that the first time I paint the figure in I will put in everything, later I might take a foot out, if I find it is not needed, or I might lengthen a leg. It's enough that I have tried them in and I can then go on with complete conviction that it does not want them that way. They might ultimately come back and an arm might have to go out, or nothing might have to happen at all after that. It is always just a case of trying to arrive at a suitable form to convey what is wanted in the picture.

ANTHONY CRONIN

A Question of Modernity

I

The last fifty years have been the period of a literary revolution as important as any which has ever taken place in the English language. Paradoxically this seems to have been easier to recognise when it was first taking place, say forty to fifty years ago, than it is today. The nature of the modern achievement was then of course often misconstrued. The revolution was partly a return to principles which had been forgotten or ignored. Nonetheless there is a sense in which the modern revolution, that is to say, in English, the work of Pound, Eliot and Joyce and the later work of Yeats, though it is in some of its aspects traditional—it has more in common with the traditions of good writing that it has with those of bad—is in fact revolutionary, a completely new thing. The emphasis on the traditions which they shared with others which these great writers very properly insisted on has tended to obscure this. And of course these writers were individuals, seeking to come to terms with their individual dilemmas and attempting to make their writing serve their individual purposes. We must naturally treat them as individuals: Yeats's mind was very different from Joyce's; his problems as a man were different and the integrations which he sought in belief and non-belief and in the practice of literature itself were different. The critic should certainly respect the individuality and the individual vision of every writer he deals with, but for certain purposes which are also important he must try to see what they have in common. There is a type of criticism which seizes on the individual situation of the writer at the expense of the comment he himself makes on it, the literature he creates which is of value to us all, however different our circumstances; and there is a type of criticism which seizes on the public pre-occupation of the writer at the expense of the universal truth which it leads him to express—which seizes on the machinery of circumstance, belief and creation in the wrong way. Mr Eliot's religion; Joyce's lack of it; Mr Pound's economics; Yeats's astrology—these have been grist to a thousand irrelevantly pounding Professorial mills. Yeats is a great writer whether we understand or care anything about his astrology or not. It is arguable that the kind of mind which does care, cares less about poetry and the truths it contains than a concern with Yeats suggests that it should. Of course Yeats has his own vision of the world, and it differs from Eliot's or Joyce's. Of course the emotions communicated in his verse are different from those expressed in Eliot's. Yet there is an important sense in which all three are modern writers with a characteristically modern approach to the emotions which they do convey. There is a characteristic 'modernity', however difficult it may be to define. Different as all these progenitors of the modern movement may be they yet have this thing in common. It is important for us to recognise what it is if we are to understand our own situation: what has been done and what needs to be done. And of course a great deal of the difficulty in recognising it arises from our own confusions about what we are in fact doing.

II

Oddly enough Pound's precept preceded anybody's practice, including his own. It may have been Yeats's volume of 1910, *The Green Helmet*, published when he was forty-five, that first showed him as the poet who as Pound said 'stripped English poetry of its perdamnable rhetoric' and 'made our poetic idiom a thing pliable, a speech without inversions', but at forty-five Yeats was still some way from becoming the great modern poet we know. In those years Pound believed that prose had become a superior instrument. Quoting Stendhal, who had objected that 'la poésie, avec ses comparisons obligées, sa mythologic que ne croit pas le poète, sa dignité de style à la Louis XIV, et tout l'attirail de ses ornements appelés poétiques, est bien au dessous de la prose dès qu'il s'agit de donner une idée claire et précise des mouvements du coeur; or, dans ce genre, on n'émeut que par la clarté', Pound demanded a poetry that should come as close as prose to being the 'instrument of a precise psychology', that 'could be carried as a communication between intelligent men.'

In the writers of the duo-cento and early tre-cento we find a precise psychology
... if we cannot get back to these things; if the serious artist cannot attain this
precision in verse, then he must either take to prose or give up his claim to being a
serious artist. . . . As for Stendhal's stricture, if we can have a poetry that comes
as close as prose, pour donner and une idée claire et precise, let us have it, 'E di
venire a ciò io studio quanto posso . . . che la mia vita per alquanti anni duri'. . . .
And if we cannot attain to such a poetry, for God's sake let us shut up . . . let us
acknowledge that our art is out of date and out of fashion.

Only Gautier, Corbière, Laforgue and Rimbaud, Pound believed, redeemed poetry from Stendhal's condemnation; and the only immediately preceding poet whom England could offer who had attempted a precise description of a diverse and realistic psychology in verse was Robert Browning.

What is interesting here is to remember that poetry was not then looked upon as 'the instrument of precise psychology'. As early as 1900, Joyce, writing about Ibsen, had praised him for choosing 'average lives in their uncompromising truth for the groundwork of all his later plays. He has abandoned the verse form and never sought to embellish his work after the conventional fashion'. This was Joyce's first published article and he was a very young man when he wrote it but what is interesting is that association of the idea of verse with the idea of embellishment. It had not occurred to Joyce at the age of eighteen that poetry could give as cool and unadorned an account of the movements of the heart as he was finding in the prose of Flaubert.

Pound prophesied in 1911 that modern poetry would be:

harder and saner . . . its force will lie in its truth, its interpretative power (of
course poetic force always does rest there); I mean it will not try to seem forcible
by rhetorical din and luxurious riot. We will have fewer painted adjectives
impeding the shock and stroke of it. At least for myself, I want it so, austere
direct, free from emotional slither.

This idea of poetry as an exact instrument of communication is part of the general statement of aesthetic which Pound's early essays make. Thus:

By good art I mean art that bears true witness. I mean art that is most precise.
You can be wholly precise in representing a vagueness. You can be wholly a liar
in pretending that the particular vagueness was precise in its outline.

And:

In proportion as his work is exact, i.e., true to human consciousness and the
nature of man, as it is exact in formulation of desire, so is it durable and so is it
'useful'. I mean it maintains the precision and clarity of thought, not merely for
the benefit of a few dilettantes and 'lovers of literature', but maintains the health
of thought outside literary circles and in non-literary existence.

Literature to Pound was a means of communication. It was valuable because precise poetic communication improved the level everywhere; because it provided data about the nature of man sounder than that of the 'generalising psychologists'; and because this flow of communication between men 'does incite humanity to continue living; it eases the mind of strain, and feeds it, I mean definitely as nutrition of impulse'.

There was of course more to be said about the art of poetry than simply this, and very well Pound said it, but this idea underlay all his discussions of the matter for many years:

> You wish to communicate an idea and its concomitant emotions, or an emotion and its concomitant ideas, or a sensation and its derivative emotions, or an impression that is emotive etc., etc., etc. You begin with the yeowl and the bark, and you develop into the dance and into music and into music with words, and finally into words with music, and finally into words with a vague adumbration of music, words suggestive of music, words measured, or words in a rhythm that preserves some accurate trait of the emotive impression, or of the sheer character of the fostering or parental emotion.

And it accounted, in some measure at least, for his interest in Pre-Elizabethan English, in the poetry of Provence and in Dante:

> I cannot too often repeat that there was a profound psychological knowledge in medieval Provence, however Gothic its expression; that men, concentrating on certain validities, attaining an exact and diversified terminology, have there displayed considerable penetration; that this was carried into early Italian poetry; and faded from it when metaphor became decorative instead of interpretative; and that the age of Aquinas would not have tolerated sloppy expression of psychology concurrent with exact expression of mysticism.

Now some of these statements were, in the nature of things, prophecies, since there was at the time no modern poetry in English at least to support them, neither Pound's nor anybody else's. Joyce had published a book of poems in 1907, but there is no evidence that Pound was aware of the fact, nor indeed any reason why he should have been. All the poems in it had been written by 1902, at a time when Joyce like many others believed that poetry was not a fitting instrument for the expression of a great many of the emotions and states of mind that interested him. If the musical element, always most delicate and often charming, was inspired by the great song-writers whom he admired, the influence of Ben Jonson is hardly present in the language. It indeed is often so conventional that everything is invisible, words, objects and situations, and it often requires a huge effort of concentration to remember that these poems are superficially supposed to be about human situations and to discover what they are. All the faults of the diction of the day are present, including 'poetic' inversion to get at the rhymes. Nothing could be less analytical than these poems of a conventional passion and desire. Joyce in fact just did not realise that poetry was anything other than a sort of garland, a crown for life. If he had realised that earlier the great genius for honesty that went into prose might have gone into poetry. But in 1902 it is obvious that Joyce's mind was working on the same lines as Pound's; that although, unlike Pound, he did not believe that poetry might be other than an instrument for the vague, musical expression of passionate, noble or rapturously melancholic emotions, he did agree that the best instrument for the expression of a precise psychology had been, since Flaubert, prose. Pound himself had been publishing poetry since 1908, but at the time when some of these statements were made his precept had outrun his capacity to practise what he preached. It was not the first time that precept had outrun practice, for poetry, which depends for its force on its 'interpretative power', its wisdom, is not, as was also commonly believed before Pound came on the scene, a young man's game. John Keats, the worst possible example the Palgravians whom Pound vanquished could have picked to illustrate their conception of a necessary causative connection between adolescence and poetry, may well in fact stand as an example of enormous critical perception as yet unallied when he died with poetic power. But if some of these statements at the time they were made were mere prophecy, or the expression of a wish, they were not to remain so for long. In 1914, when he had 'come close on fortynine', Yeats published *Responsibilities* and modern poetry had begun. One of the qualities that distinguishes *Responsibilities* from its predecessors is in fact the 'clarity and precision' with which 'the movements of the heart' are presented; the poems are becoming among other things 'the instruments of a precise psychology'. The verse itself follows the trend towards austerity and directness that was first clearly visible in *The Green Helmet*; the poems are 'harder' and by the standards of commonsense that we have a right to apply to any poem 'saner'; there is now hardly any 'slither'. And the psychology is exact; the movements of the heart are precisely stated:

> The exorbitant dreams of beggary
> That idleness had borne to pride.

And:

> Now all the truth is out
> Be secret and take defeat
> From any brazen throat,
> For how can you compete
> Being honour bred, with one
> Who were it proved he lies,
> Were neither shamed in his own
> Nor in another's eyes.

A process had begun that was to culminate in the wonderful emotional and psychological exactitude of the later poems.

It is also, among other things, this psychological and emotional clarity and exactitude that distinguishes the poems contained in *Lustra*, published in 1917, from those contained in Pound's earlier volumes; and it is certainly, among other things, this psychological precision, this startling exactness in examining and communicating the emotion that makes *The Love Song of J. Alfred Prufrock*, which appeared in the following year, such a landmark.

> ... And time yet for a hundred indecisions
> And for a hundred visions and revisions,
> Before the taking of a toast and tea.
>
> I have seen the moment of my greatness flicker,
> And I have seen the eternal footman hold my coat and snicker,
> And in short, I was afraid.

But of course, this in itself would not have created a poetry that we could specifically speak of as modern. There is psychological precision in Shakespeare, in Donne, in Johnson and Pope, Crabbe and Wordsworth, Browning and others (Pound would have been, it is true, more rigorous than this); though there is not I suggest, or not to any extent worth bothering about, whatever their merits, in Swinburne, Tennyson and Shelley. Every poet worth the name is, in Pound's sense, a true recorder, though we should be eternally grateful to Pound for pointing this out, for bad poetry is always otiose with lies of one kind or another and the truth was not in 1910 and is rarely, if ever, looked upon as the touchstone.

Was there then anything else? Make it new, Pound had said; and he had also said: 'the man who first decides certain things are poetry has a great advantage over all who follow him and who accede in his opinion. Gautier did decide that certain things were worth making into poems, whereas the Parnassians only acceded in other men's opinions about subject matter'. If psychological exactitude, though highly uncommon since the death of Samuel Johnson, LL.D., was still not altogether new, was there, in the verse of these first great modern poets anything else, which was?

III

In Frank Budgen's sane and admirable book, *James Joyce and the Making of Ulysses* there are two highly revealing stories about Joyce's aesthetic:

> I asked him if he did not think Dostoevsky a supremely great writer.
> 'No,' said Joyce bluntly. 'Rousseau, confessing to stealing silver spoons he had

really stolen, is much more interesting than one of Dostoevsky's people confessing to an unreal murder'.

The other concerns a lady novelist who called on him to ask his opinion of a book she was writing:

'She told me she had already shown it to the porter of the hotel where she stays. So I said to her: "What did your hotel porter think of your work?" She said: "He objected to a scene in my novel where my hero goes out into the forest, finds a locket of the girl he loves, picks it up and kisses it passionately". "But", I said, "that seems to me a very pleasing and touching incident. What did your hotel porter find wrong with it?" And then she tells me he said: "It's all right for the hero to find the locket and to pick it up and kiss it, but before he kissed it you should have made him wipe the dirt off it with his coat sleeve." '

According to Budgen, Joyce continued: 'I told her (and I meant it too) to go back to that hotel porter and always to take his advice. "That man", I said, "is a critical genius. There is nothing I can tell you that he can't tell you." '

Here, in a nutshell, is a statement of Joyce's own achievement. *Ulysses* is in fact a more accurate description of the texture of life, real life, than had hitherto been achieved. It is not simply that Joyce mentioned a great many matters about which other writers had kept silent; though he did, and that was an achievement of some importance too. It is that a more accurate representation of the nature of human feeling has been achieved. We do not feel as lyrically or dramatically as literature taken as a full human record would lead one to believe. Our emotions are more complex, more impeded, more desultory than that. The Joyce who wrote *Ulysses* and who told that story to Frank Budgen is recognisably the same Joyce who, according to his brother, as a very young man made up his mind that 'most artists, even the greatest, belied the life they knew, and offered the world a make-believe. Literature, he said, was a parody of life. He declared bitterly that he believed in only two things, a woman's love of her child and a man's love of lies, of lies of all possible kinds; and he was determined that his spiritual experience should not be a make-believe.' And he is the same man of whom Stanislaus also wrote:

The poetry of noble sentiments, of romantic music, and the dramatic passions, with a dominant love theme, which culture offered him as a truer poetic insight into the universal problems of human life, did not fit in with life as he knew it. That life was admittedly debased, but he suspected that a less debased life might have its secrets, too, and in any case the life he did not know did not interest him.

Life is more humiliating; we are meaner; reality is more mundane than most writers in the past have cared to recognise or at least succeeded in suggesting. I do not mean that *Ulysses* is not a hopeful and indeed a triumphant book, because in fact it is; or that Joyce was suggesting that our feelings and experiences are less worth bothering about than literature would lead one to believe, for he is not. It is simply that a new dimension of irony, self-knowledge, analysis and complexity has been added which any honest examination of experience must take account of. And when we look again at Eliot's work and at the later work of Yeats we find that they have discovered and are exploring this new dimension also. And perhaps more important still, a whole range of emotions and feelings, apparently, by the old standard, trivial and unworthy has been discovered to have dramatic and indeed lyrical possibilities and intensities which were never previously explored. More people might agree that this is true of Eliot; but it is also true of Yeats in his later work. He too has, in Pound's phrase, 'decided that certain things are poetry'. Over and over again in the later poems he takes account of failures and mysteries which a lyric poet, of the kind he began as, would have ignored as not being fit material for verse.

> Things said or done long years ago,
> Or things I did not do or say
> But thought that I might say or do,
> Weigh me down, and not a day
> But something is recalled,
> My conscience or my vanity appalled.

This is the modern achievement, specifically: a return of psychological precision and a gain in honesty, complexity, wholeness. Mr Eliot's work has other things to offer and so has Yeats'; but they share this much with each other and with Joyce. And this, and not the introduction of urban imagery, or a concern with the outcome of the Spanish Civil War or whatever, is the distinguishing characteristic of the best modern poetry as compared to most of the poetry of the past. The fact was obscured by the social preoccupations of the thirties and by much else that has happened; but what distinguishes *Prufrock* from any poem that preceded it and most of the good poems written since from the poetry of other times is its inclusiveness: things about which humanity in general had long kept almost silent and poets wholly so, have now found their place, with other emotions, other experiences in verse as material for poetry. Of course there are exceptions: in art at least there is nothing new under the sun. There are passages in Shakespeare which have exactly this 'modern' note:

> Wishing me like to one more rich in hope
> Featured like him, like him with friends possessed,
> Desiring this man's art and that man's scope,
> With what I most enjoy contented least.

There are hints here and there in others: in Crabbe and in Mangan for example; but it is nonetheless true that the range of emotion expressed in poetry has been enormously extended in our time; and that the admission that our feelings are interpenetrative, confused and less pure than poetry had hitherto suggested is a modern achievement. And a modern gain. To succeed at last in calling a spade a spade; to extend the recorded area of human experience; to identify new emotions;—if that has been done the modern movement has been a great one, even if, as a critic has recently been saying, it has produced no emotional, no philosophical synthesis as did the Romantic Movement. The primary virtue of literature is honesty; its primary purpose is to record. It is not simply that Mr Eliot succeeded in bringing the modern world into poetry, or Joyce a sort of 20th-century urban experience; it is that emotions which have always existed, experiences which man has always had, have at last been brought within the scope of poetry; and far from being at the end of a great period it may be true that we are still at the beginning of one; for there is no limit now except the perennial one (and alas the most important one), our power over words, to the range of human experience that we may succeed in bringing into poetry. However that may be, in the honesty, the courage and the daring of its art at least, the 20th century can, if in nothing else, take pride. Albeit it is not only a question of 'deciding certain things are poetry' but of proving that they are in the hands of a poet.

IV

For it is now pertinent to ask whether the 'poetic' has, then, been abolished altogether. And with it, the poet? If all emotions are fitting subject for poetry, provided they are precisely described, premise an insurance salesman, or a stockbroker, or even a provincial don, with if it can be premised, the proper verbal equipment, let him set down his experience of the world as he sees it, and is the result poetry?

The point surely is that the honesty of which one speaks is the honesty of the poet. The gentlemen one has just premised will give as partial and therefore misleading view of the nature of human experience as any romantic adolescent. Attitudes of cowardice, dishonesty, weakness, failures of emotion, of sympathy, of decision are fitting subjects for poetry in the hands of a poet. For it is a question of poetry, not of the confessional impulse of a limited man. The primary virtue is honesty we have agreed, but honesty accompanied by the insights of a poet and honesty also to the courage and freedom which are a part of the poetic spirit. For the poet in the end is not simply an ordinary man with an ordinary man's emotions; we do ask insights from him that are of interest; we ask for an apprehension of life, its possibilities and its failures on a level rather higher than that common, one supposes, in suburbia:

> I detest my room,
> Its specially chosen junk,
> The good books, the good bed,
> And my life, in perfect order . . .

Even Leopold Bloom is in the end more than an unsuccessful salesman who keeps out of trouble and masturbates; by the end of *Ulysses* this shabby man is in fact a moral hero. And when we speak of the honesty, the complexity, in a word the truth that is characteristic of great modern poetry, we must remember that if it were not part of something we describe for whatever reason as poetry, it would have nothing but a casebook interest. The lines quoted (from Mr Philip Larkin) are honest it is true, but of what interest is the honesty?

One does not ask for heightened emotions or faked insights. One does not ask for a moral, a tag, or a message of hope. And it is not simply a question of a verbal 'beauty' accompanying and redeeming the sense or even of the imagery that the poem evokes. It is a question of the poet's depth of awareness and the extent of his sensibility, of the poem's giving us

> both a new world
> And the old made explicit; understood
> In the completion of its partial ecstasy
> The resolution of its partial horror.

It is in fact, to use Pound's phrase again, a question of the poem's 'interpretative power'. We have perhaps no right to ask that a poem should redeem or console; it would certainly be wrong in most cases for a poet to do violence to his experience in an attempt to wring anything, more particularly a mistaken notion of poetry, from it; but we have every right to declare that the interest of the revelation depends not only on the honesty but on the quality of what is revealed. That the poet should go as deep as he can is an excellent thing, but the value of his work will depend on the distance he has to travel before his honesty and his accuracy can encompass the range of his feeling. There is no 'emotional slither' in this:

> I am content to follow to its source
> Every event in action or in thought;
> Measure the lot; forgive myself the lot!
> When such as I cast out remorse
> So great a sweetness flows into the breast
> We must laugh and we must sing,
> We are blest by everything,
> Everything we look upon is blest.

PATRICK SWIFT

The Painter in the Press

It is tempting but neither useful nor desirable to regard art criticism as merely a pornocracy in the world of painting. It may be this; but it can be something more.

It is not an accident that *Histoire de la Peinture en Italie* remains readable; as Cézanne found it, who read it many times, or Baudelaire, who borrowed from it. This pleasant and incisive book provides us with an example of a kind of critical writing which is illuminating, instructive, and wholly delectable. And its importance does not depend on the validity of Stendhal's comparative judgements. It is an eccentric personal work full of specific observations and we get the sensation of being in the presence of a temperament and an intelligence[1] excited by pictures. This is an exciting experience. It is a personal matter.

And the art of painting is itself an intensely personal activity. It may be labouring the obvious to say so but it is too little recognised in art journalism now that a picture is a unique and private event in the life of the painter: an object made by a man alone with a blank canvas. I have not yet come across the painter who has achieved the discipline of being able to make pictures on top of a bus. On the contrary the pattern is almost always the same—Delacroix remote in the Place Furstemberg, Rembrandt turning the canvases to the wall—moments of purest intuition in silence and stillness about the nature of the man who paints and the world he experiences. It is astonishing to think of Renoir or Cézanne painting for an audience in old age. But this was the reward of years of high moral discipline and even old age does not always bring it. One has only to think of the ageing Rembrandt and the face which looks out at us in the last terrible paintings.

A real painting is something which happens to the painter once in a given minute; it is unique in that it will never happen again and in this sense is an impossible object. It is judged by the painter simply as a success or failure without qualification. And it is something which happens in life not in art: a picture which was merely the product of art would not be very interesting and and could tell us nothing we were not already aware of.

The old saying, 'what you don't know can't hurt you' expresses the opposite idea to that which animates the painter before his canvas. It is precisely what he does not know which may destroy him. (Though of course the meaning of the adage really depends on the quality of the

---

[1] In the stricter meaning of this word—a spiritual being capable of choice.

deception). One thinks of the demented Goya, the mad old Seraphine locked in religious frenzy, the sophisticated and gentle Soutine caught in the furious machinery of creation.

Pictures made in this sense and this kind of awareness are difficult to categorise in any systematic manner. Yet the notion that there is a special public obligation to classify these perverse objects so illogically the product of unique occasions animates art criticism and in fact constitutes the reason for the dullness which pervades it.

An analysis which attempts to arrange and evaluate the mass of work being done at any moment must have pretentions to objectivity. A point of view which makes simple judgements about the success or failure of individual pictures without qualification and experienced specifically is subjective.

The idea of objectivity in the evaluation of pictures introduces the concept of rational and scientific assessment.

There are some sciences involved in the making and in the study of pictures, but the art itself is finally not a science and will not submit to scientific regimentation because its life depends on the degree to which it is inhabited by mystery, speaks to us of the unknown. It is simply an avoidance of the interesting difficulty to subject the inexplicable to the process of rational explanation. For since the real pleasures of painting and the reality of its meaning exist in the part of its structure which cannot be explained, all suggestions and pretensions at explanation must lead us away from the area of greatest interest. This is to say that such analysis as purports to lay bare the machinery which makes a painting work—makes it a good painting—not only leaves out the most important factor, the element of mystery, but actively denies the reality which is the justification for the art at all.

The subject I want to examine is diffuse. Further it flows along like a wash in the wake of the whole picture-making business (a term it is only too possible to use about painting now). However I incline to believe that certain useful distinctions can be made. There are certain broad categories and divisions in the types of critical writing about the painter in the press at the present time. These divisions are sectarian and philosophic (if this is not too vague a term) and there is a common factor from which none of the writers on art is totally free: the element of scientific pretention.

I will propose three broad categories of critic: I. the socially conscious whose attitude is pragmatic and more or less that of the Marxist materialist or a form of idealism which is a corruption of this. II. The Formal purist, which may be regarded as the latest manifestation of the *fin de siècle* 'art for art's sake', sometimes with an expressionistic extension incongruously tagged on. III. The popular expounder and explainer of an undenominational theory of art perhaps deriving from Berenson but anyhow frankly addressed to the neophyte middlebrow.

I do not wish to be invidious but for the sake of clarity shall suggest three representative figures: Class I: Mr John Berger. Class II: Mr Allan Bowness. Class III: Mr Eric Newton.

All of these kinds of critics while pursuing different ends employ a method which is essentially the same. It is a form of analysis which emphasises the historical and the technical using a stylised vocabulary with scientific and philosophic overtones.

It would be too much to say that these characteristics are deeply rooted in any logical structure held firmly by any individual. The nearest thing to a logically held view is that of the Marxist, it is the most simple and therefore in practice produces the most satisfactory journalism. Which is to say a form of comment more or less making sense. The difficulty for the critic of this order would seem to be that living in a free society he cannot be sure that the painters he espouses will toe the party line. Thus Mr Berger had the unhappy experience of fostering a group of 'Social Realists' none of whom, five years later, could be thus classified. Mr Berger's sad announcement of his failure to sustain the 'movement' which he claimed at one time was 'winning on all fronts and taking international prizes everywhere' is a remarkable document for the insights it provides into a form of egotism peculiar to the critic of art. But the truth is one can only have such a safe art as Mr Berger would like if one has the system to enforce the compliance of the painter. For the notion of art as a social function of man is tenable only if there is a definite constriction of purpose and range on the part of the painter—as the Communists rightly recognise. It requires a particular kind of political coercion to ensure this constriction.

The notion behind art as a social service, an instrument of political advancement with a message of hope for the betterment of Man, when examined in its central implications is paradoxically seen to be much the same as that which animates the Purist view. In the first instance it is the concept of art as a function and a product of Hope which will act as a social therapy on a broad scale, and in the second it is the idea of art as a psychological agent acting as a personal therapy. The extension of this personal efficacy of art into the realm of public affairs leads to such vague pious claims as:

Our artists have often been violent or destructive inconsiderate (sic) and impatient, but in general they have been aware of a moral issue facing our whole civilisation.

With the unlikely and pretentious conclusion:

To present a clear and distinct visual image of sensuous experience—that has always been the aim of these artists, and the rich treasury of icons they have created is the basis upon which any possible civilisation of the future will be built.

The unnecessary introduction of the word icon gives the clue to the basic character of thought that has led the Formal purist so far from his initial assumptions about the freedom and autonomy of the artistic activity etc. In spite of all the jargon about 'form and gesture', 'pure harmony' and 'the beauty of the incidental and the accidental' the justification of art depends, as with the social realist, on its validity as an instrument of salvation. So the religious implications of the term icon are very apt in the context even though the form of art referred to is abstract (the character of an abstract image, religious or otherwise, strikes me as being unimaginable).

This idea of art as an instrument of salvation, social or psychological, is so widespread and has become such common currency in all forms of critical writing that it may be foolhardy to attempt to throw doubt on it.

Nevertheless it may be remarked that this idea devolves finally on the extent to which the activity is a function of hope. Hope for a better life, a better civilisation or whatever term one wishes to use; meaning anyhow some far off desired perfection of life; implying that art is animated by a pious aspiration for this state. The virtue of hope becomes the animating principle of art. But the virtue of hope has only a serious position within the eschatology of true religion. To the man who prays it is the supreme virtue.

Art on the other hand speaks to us of resignation and rejoicing in reality, and does so through a transformation of our experience of the world into an order wherein all facts become joyous; the more terrible the material the greater the artistic triumph. This has nothing at all to do with 'a constant awareness of the problems of our time' or any other vague public concern. It is a transformation that is mysterious, personal and ethical.[1] And the moral effect of art is only interesting when considered in the particular. For it is always the reality of the particular that provides the occasion and the spring of art—it is always

> those particular trees
> That caught you in their mysteries

or the experience of some loved object. Not that the matter rests here. It is the transcendent imagination working on this material that releases the

---

[1] An ethos is a difficult thing that cannot be formulated and codified; it is one of those creative irrationalities upon which real progress is based. It demands the whole man and not just a differentiated function.—Jung.

mysterious energies which move and speak of deepest existence. It may even be possible to argue philosophically that all those loose and imprecise worries of the Commonweal—about which surely Dr Johnson was right when he said that no man lay awake at night on their account—can be validly if vaguely related to the particular thus found; but to do so is to drag in the irrelevent and the unnecessary. It is to obscure the area of true excitement.

What is most common then with both the critic who sees art as a social mechanism, and the critic who views it as a pure and esoteric activity free from constraint of any kind—this usually means free from the discipline of the object—is the tendency to elevate (or degrade, if one happens to be a humanist) the activity into a surrogate for religion. In doing so they involve categoric prohibitions inimicable to the spirit of art which is the spirit of real freedom.

I state the case more or less in philosophic terms taking the attitudes as relevant to some degree: but in the end they are not relevant at all. This is my real objection.

That the mass of art criticism should have drifted so far from the reality of painting that no one any longer wishes to speak of enjoying pictures[1] may not however have its root cause in the mental attitudes of the critics at all. It may well be that the difficulty is endemic in the manner of analysis rather than in any philosophy of the art.

The manner of analysis most often used may be distinguished by its two main characteristics: the historical and the technical.

Historically the view may be that of the progress-monger for whom the value of any work is determinable by its relation to a supposed historical progression in a certain direction. The idea that art is a progression and that one man takes up where the last left off is a basic to nearly all critical writing about painting. Even the popular explainer who confines his argument to the elucidation of the past presumes to say that there could be no Massacio without a Giotto etc. It is more pernicious when the argument is involved in the evaluation of contemporary work. Pictures are labelled 'avant garde' 'reactionary' or more dubious labels still, and all serious standards of judgement or enjoyment go by the board. Nor are

---

[1] Instead one speaks of understanding—
' "Understanding" is something that people more respectable than myself assure me that they burn to apply to everything. If they look, for example, at a picture, and are in danger of feeling pleasure from it, they either declare that "they don't understand it" or they apply their understandings to some object which, but for their assurances to the contrary, I should have suspected wasn't the picture: in either case, it seems, they feel the better for having avoided submitting to the indignity of pleasure.'
—A review in *The New English Weekly*, July 28, 1949.

the exponents of this method always frank about the weapons they use. For the notion of progress in the arts, (either spiritually or artistically) has been discredited by many respectable intellects (Kierkegaard and Baudelaire above all, both of whom encountered the idea when it first reared itself in its present form in Europe). The more self-aware (Sir H. Read for example) accommodate the difficulty by acknowledging the fallacy of the argument and then proceeding to use it rigorously: presuming, one supposes, that the reader's dialectical capacity may be relied upon to perform the necessary suspension of logical thought.

Also part of this category, but strictly an extension of it, is the obsession with derivation, and the premium on any obvious kind of originality which follows from this. Discoveries made by such methods are of doubtful validity if evaluation of particular pictures is the aim, and this is so even in their own terms, i.e. historically.

The co-existence at one moment of two such painters as Ingres and Delacroix, or the odd derivations that started great painters such as Cézanne (from Delacroix himself at the beginning) or Van Gogh (from Mauve at one point) on their path towards a shocking individuality incline me to doubt the usefulness of these criteria when applied to contemporary painting. That is to say in the judgement of paintings at the time when they are made.

The historical view with its doubtful presumption of understanding laws of time and development leads to the pedantic and the dry side of the study of painting, but is really less irrational and remote than the technical element in critical analysis.

Technical criticism of painting is a very dubious activity if the aim is evaluation and not merely identification or the examination of masterwork by painters themselves.

In this case the critic undertakes to explain through an analysis of the paint, the structure, and the physical character of the work the reasons for its success or failure. This is very tiresome because it is the one realm in which the writer can have only the most incomplete kind of knowledge. For even the painter himself cannot be fully aware of the way in which the picture gets made: there is a wide area of the unpredictable in the act of pushing paint about in the definition of an image. It is hopeless to present vague guesses and intuitions expressed in what's called 'studio jargon' as if such information were in some way scientific and explanatory.

This misuse of a technical terminology is perhaps the chief fault in the prevailing vocabulary of art criticism. Most culpable are those critics who champion abstract painting. Here the reason for resorting to such language is, however, understandable. When there is no specific image and so no direct reference to our experience of the world of objects it becomes necessary to explain in terms other than human the meaning of the work which itself is merely paint spread on a flat surface without the dimension of illusion.

Then the pattern of analysis falls into two parts, a dimorphic monstrosity, composed of specious technical description and philosophical justification. As for instance in this sentence:

A world in whose purist, light-filled regions, the relief of a dab of white pigment on a flat ground constitutes an event; a sophisticated world of reference of nuances of exquisitely pleasing pure light only slightly modulated of forms bathed and dissolved in light; at once decorative and painterly, seeking towards an integration of surface and image—to become not pictures but paintings.

This, as those who read art criticism regularly will remark, is by no means an extreme example—it is very venial. Yet it has the characteristic opacity and pretentiousness of tone. It is the jaded, vague, and abstruse quality which tires in this sort of writing. A paradoxical aspect of it is that while its chief characteristic is a tendency towards abstract language and esoteric phraseology its subject is supremely committed to the concrete and the real. And oddly enough this is truer still if the subject be itself abstract, i.e. non-figurative painting. For the very basis of the concept of non-figurative art lies in the notion that the picture itself becomes pure object, the idea of illusion is sacrificed to the desire for direct sensual apprehension of the concrete reality of the material and the gesture that constitute the picture. Admittedly of late there has been a tendency to equivocate about this kind of purity which is the only respectable element in a form of art otherwise clearly nothing more than decoration. An attempt to define the non-figurative as somehow capable of being considered as image or icon. This is intellectually disgraceful as well as unconvincing. For the desire to get direct experience of the sensual reality of the image, to recreate and transform reality as we live it into an image which will bring tangibly before us the living mystery, may be the keynote of the sensibility of our time. Mr Robert Graves may even be right when he suggests that the aesthetic that underlies modern English poetry derives from French painting. So that a form of writing about an art above all sensitive to the concrete simple realities which is itself ambiguous, obscure, and abstruse, is particularly unfortunate, paradoxical, and in the end comic.

There are ambiguities in the art of painting but they are the ambiguities of a fine precision: the discovered fact of the image containing at the same time the reverberations of the unknown, the truly mysterious. In the kind of art criticism I speak of the ambiguities are those of immediate opaqueness of language and the reverberations are those of the obvious and the commonplace or of nothing.

I would take this further and add that painting is itself precise in its ideas. In the sense that the image is the idea in its purest form[1] and the sad unhappy muddle created by bogus methodical criticism is unjustifiable in terms of this logic.

The pedants and explainers of art (I am aware there are exceptions) have dominated art journalism so that the notion of an alternative form of comment has virtually been lost. As early as 1855 the disastrous direction that art criticism was to take had been clearly seen by Charles Baudelaire. It must now be regarded as one of the gloomiest and most discouraging of activities.

These are depressing reflections. Further it is difficult to envisage the sort of shift in sensibility which might redeem the situation taking place easily or quickly. This is not the fault of the art critics who are sincere men. It is the simple result of the trap they occupy and which was constructed in all its monstrous ramifications over the last hundred years. The problem is how to get back to that freshness, the innocent experience of the reanimated idea as it is embodied in the true painting; how to speak of this experience without claptrap about public historical or technical significance etc.

I believe that a reorientation is necessary. That certain facts must be accounted for and some vigorous redefinition pursued. Not formal or scientific definition, but that clarity about the nature of the experience of art which will bring back a note of immediacy and personal gaiety into the effort to articulate the sensations produced by good pictures.

The interesting thing is what happens in the specific picture: its precision in terms of the sensations it produces—the illusion it creates and the effect of this illusion on the psychology opposed to it.

General philosophical and technical information however interesting in itself is secondary to this reality.

Certain illuminations may be possible; chiefly about the mind of the man who made the picture. Thus it is revealing to learn that Soutine made no formal preparation for his painting and occupied himself with desultory reading in the poets and philosophers when he was not caught up in the actual fury of picture-making. Such illuminations, even when they consist of small factual information, may reveal to us a morality of approach which might otherwise remain beyond us and ignorance of which might make it the more difficult to share the more secret levels of the picture's existence.

In this respect the words of painters themselves are always of value— I except the specious technical language by which certain superficial painters attempt to create a professional mystique.

---

[1] The image is a principle of our knowledge. It is that from which our intellectual activity begins, not as a passing stimulus but as an enduring foundation.
—S. Thomas Aquinas, Opusc XVI.

Apart from this there remains that kind of criticism which is most serious and most desirable. This is the exploration of the experience of the picture when this is treated simply as experience in life and not as Art. Proust, Baudelaire, perhaps Jean Genet on Rembrandt, Artaud on Van Gogh, provide examples of this kind of writing about painting.

The evaluation of a picture in this sense is implicit in the moral character revealed in the articulation of an experience which at once tells us of the work and of its human situation. The question of comparative rightness is irrelevant.

It would be sheer quixoticism to expect this sort of writing in the press (no one seriously expects to open his morning paper and find himself confronted with the spectacle of a creative intelligence at work). Nevertheless we are entitled to look for something less remote and less tiring than the average criticism meted out.

The severe judgements so often passed by painters on critics are not without reason. For the painter finding what for him is a collection of unique objects treated as a vague and general expression of personality is merely logical in concluding that he is in the hands of shifty men:

Mr.—'s exhibition is not quite convincing and must be regarded as transitional. He's proceeded from his earlier nervous lines and bland washes towards more solid forms.

Is the art of painting such a dull matter as this implies? We know it is not; this is merely a man writing without emotion about something which has evoked no feeling.

If critics wrote only about what they loved, if they spoke only of what moved them deeply one presumes that this could not be written. That automatically art criticism would become more amusing. Even the castigation of what one dislikes is only interesting when done in terms of the things one loves. This sort of partiality would endow the activity with a dignity that mistaken ideas of objective fairmindedness can never give it. For it is important to be clear about the area of one's commitment and one's love.

What I would advocate is a form of subjective writing about art which would eschew the dry impersonal notion that the picture had an existence outside our experience of it: that there was some absolute formula whereby its value could be estimated. Whether this formula was one of human and social progress or one of aesthetic qualities. The passionate voice of a man speaking clearly of the things he loved and castigating that which threatened their existence or the justice of their survival would not be as boring as the tentative excursions into comparative judgement which form the basis of nearly all critical writing now.

But the reader most likely sees by now the ground I wish to occupy which is exactly that of a famous dictum voiced unheeded in 1846:

To be just, that is to say to justify its existence, criticism should be partial, passionate, and political, that is to say written from an exclusive point of view, but a point of view that opens up the widest horizons.

V

C. H. SISSON

The Profession of Letters
or Down with Culture

If you go round the busts in the Library of English Literature and interrogate them as to their standing in the profession of letters, you will get some strange answers. Most of these thoughtful brows will have got through their own careers without the help of the *Shorter Oxford Dictionary*—which might account for their being confused—but we who have that advantage over them may turn and read:

Profession. II: The occupation which one professes to be skilled in and to follow.

The innuendo of 'which one *professes* to be skilled in' certainly needs a gloss, and one may read further:

a. A vocation in which a professed knowledge [the same innuendo] of some department of learning is used in its application to the affairs of others, or in the practice of an art founded upon it.

'Applied *spec.*', the dictionary goes on, 'to the three learned professions of divinity, law and medicine.' The distinction between knowledge (a professed knowledge) applied to the affairs of others or in the practice of an art founded upon it well bears reflecting upon in relation to divinity, law and medicine. It is luminous in relation to the profession of letters. But the *Shorter Oxford* goes on to a sordid but important point:

b. In wider sense: Any calling or occupation by which a person habitually earns his living. 1576.

It must be admitted that, when we talk of the profession of letters, it is this not indefinite meaning which is generally uppermost in our minds. In this we resemble those who discuss a similar problem in the pages of *The Hairdressers' Journal*. There is almost no occupation which is not at the moment giving itself a diploma, forming an institute, and calling itself a profession, as a powerful argument for increasing its financial winnings.

Mr Allen Tate—not, one would have thought, a notable humourist (or even humorist) but undoubtedly a man of letters—gives an account of the

Profession of Letters[1] which is not wide of that of *The Hairdressers' Journal*:

> In a French village where I was unknown I was able to use a letter of credit without identification upon my word that I was a man of letters. The French have no illusions. . . .

That 'the French have no illusions' is one of the sweetest of Anglo-Saxon illusions, but we may believe that this village banker, or perhaps he was a grocer and *Monsieur le maire* as well, had none about Mr Tate. The cut of his American clothes, their excellent condition perhaps (though I merely speculate), enabled this shrewd man to see at a glance that here was someone substantial enough to be trusted with money. And what superlative delicacy he showed in hinting, as he handed over the francs, that he could do this convenient thing because he acknowledged Mr Tate's standing as a man of letters! The scene does honour to the land of France, but proves nothing, I think, about the profession of letters. Mr Tate goes on, as if claiming kinship with some daring characters:

> we are not asked to believe that all French writers are respectable. The generation of Rimbaud and Verlaine was notoriously dissolute.

This seems to tell against the general argument. The point Mr Tate is trying to establish is that in France 'a sufficient number of the best writers find a public large enough to sustain them as a class'. It is all rather obscure. If that is what Mr Tate's village banker thought, it must have been that he thought that Monsieur Tate was sustained by his public in a pretty concrete way. Alternatively he might be supposed to have thought (as a Frenchman, with no illusions but a generous heart): Monsieur Tate may be notoriously dissolute, like Rimbaud and Verlaine, but for the honour of letters I will cash his cheque.

Although his anecdote is inconsequential, Mr Tate's objective is quite clear. It is that of Sir Alan Herbert. He wants the writer to make plenty of money. The mention of Sir Alan Herbert somehow makes this high objective seem less serious. Mr Tate, of course, does not put the matter so coarsely. He talks of writers becoming 'an independent class'. Sir Alan Herbert's products have made him independent all right, one supposes. It would not be difficult to name better writers who have not done so well. Mr Tate is sensitive about the 'piratical commercialism of plutocracy', but to talk of establishing writers as 'an independent class', necessarily supported by their writings, is to confuse two problems—one, putting up the price of printers' fodder and the other—of quite another order of seriousness—the promotion of good writing. Is there any connection between the two?

[1] 'The Profession of Letters in the South', in *The Man of Letters in the Modern World*.

One may pardon the professional writer, who happens to be a good one, for thinking there is. No doubt it is to the advantage of 'all who care about letters' (a small number, one sometimes thinks) that the good writers should get a good price for their writing, thus simplifying for them the purchase of bread and beer, and the bringing up of their families. But as one may read in Southey on *The Uneducated Poets*:

The mediocres have long been a numerous and increasing race, and they must necessarily multiply with the progress of civilisation.

This necessary increase is the most striking evidence we have of the progress of civilisation since Southey's day and, so far as there is a profession of letters, it must consist mainly of this numerous race. So it is not to be wondered at if those who care about letters feel a little limp at the prospect of encouraging it to increase yet more. One can sympathise, of course, with the 'professional's' indignation against the 'amateur' (using both terms in the financial sense).

There are too many ladies and gentlemen

says Mr Tate bluntly, but this feeling has nothing to do with the health of letters. It is the understandable resentment of the regular soldier who sees a war-time entrant become a major in a year, or of the hairdresser who watches the deplorable growth of home perms—resentments which, alas, have nothing to do with martial capacity or with skill in the art of dressing hair. Mr Tate points a finger at Congreve who

frivolously gave up the honour of his profession when Voltaire asked to see the great dramatist and got the answer that Mr. Congreve was no scribbler but a man of fashion.

A piece of snobbery, or an educative reply to the overweening Voltaire, as you look at it. But Congreve might well not think himself obliged to parade as a man of letters on the strength of having written some plays. Even in Pope, a little later,—and he was surely a professional of letters, as we conceive it—we find a similar, almost insane self-congratulation that he is not a damned scribbler who has left his father's counter, or other virtuous occupation, to take up the making of rhymes.

> I left no calling for this idle trade,
> No duty broke, no father disobey'd.

Pope had Dryden behind him—another undoubted professional—but he lived still at the very beginning of our conception of a profession of letters. What is left to us of the seventeenth century shows us few names of that kind. There was, generally speaking, no living for the writer as such. There were gentlemen, above the necessity of earning a living, or earning it in some way other than by writing, like Milton or Marvell. There were the clergy, who produced masterpieces in the course of their proper vocations. They were professional strictly in the sense of the dictionary definition, using

professed knowledge of some department of learning . . . in its application to the affairs of others.

—which the dictionary intends of their divinity but which was true, in their case, of their letters as well. They used letters for what could not have been so well done without: the preparation of sermons and books of devotion. *The Golden Grove* and *Holy Living and Holy Dying* exhibit talents which a secular Jeremy Taylor, in the twentieth century, might have spent his life hawking round the publishers. Lesser men than Taylor conceived that they were using their learning (which was how they tended to think of their gifts) if they employed it in similar works, which at that time were accounted useful even if they do not now seem to us beautiful. A George Herbert could live as a country parson, and his divine poems be published only after his death. Henry Vaughan the Silurist was a physician, but Sir Thomas Browne's works, if not his own, will indicate the little space there was between a 'professed knowledge' of humane letters and the practice of medicine as then conceived.

It is in relation to the seventeenth century that Coleridge invented the notion of a 'clerisy'—a body of learned men remote in conception or practice from the hairdressers' idea of a profession—whose identity with the priesthood of the English Church was 'no more than a blessed accident'. A society which can support a body of literate men, and make social use of their literacy, is no doubt in a healthier way than one whose literates can remain alive only by keeping themselves in a constant state of effusion and selling what comes out to make work for printers. It is not that there is not or should not be writing for which no social use has yet been thought of. Many literary productions of high value are of this kind. But to mould a class on the pattern of genius is asking for trouble, both because it deprives the ordinary social world of injections of talent which it needs for its health and because it must result in the mediocres entertaining fantastic notions of their own artistic performance. You can see in any gallery the work of uncertain painters who would have been admirable interior decorators or needle-women. If you go back to the Elizabethan age you have a class of men making their livings by writing plays—or by a combination of writing and acting—and we think of them as *writers*, but really they made plays, something that the guffawing public had a use for, as the long-faced or merely serious-minded public had for sermons. The *man of letters* of Elizabeth's age is Edmund Spenser, and one has only to look at *The Faerie Queene* to see how much less satisfactory that was. Of course the useless poet is needed, or rather the poet whose usefulness is not for all to see, but one does not imagine that Wyatt would have written better if he had spent anxious hours pleasing booksellers instead of going on diplomatic missions for Henry VIII.

The profession of letters as we know it grew up in the 18th and 19th centuries, and one would not seek to deny the notable examples of identity between professional success and literary achievement. The world of patronage, with the beastly Chesterfield turning Samuel Johnson from his door, was also the world in which the bookseller Richardson invented the contents of three-volume wonders, but there is no equation between literary and professional success then or at any subsequent time. What happened, notably in France but also, in more subdued fashion, in England, was a growth in the pretensions of writers, so that even men incapable of regulating their own private affairs did not hesitate to recommend themselves as practical guides to whole nations. Perhaps the Congreve who tried to freeze out Voltaire had some intimation of pretensions to come. Rousseau, whose gift was for revealing the odd kinks of his own mind, with such marvellous clarity that he became practically the inventor of the modern notion of personality, cut a grossly over-sized figure as a political philosopher and, the very type of the silly man of genius, played a rôle, which has been variously estimated but which was certainly important, in the French Revolution. Even so sober a man as Matthew Arnold—an inspector of schools, think of that!—tried to set up the man of letters as a sort of religious regulator. It was a plausible enough half truth in an age over which Tennyson and Browning brooded as sages on the strength of ideas which were certainly more half-baked than Arnold's. Since then serious attempts have been made to bring the writer back to his proper rôle, and Ezra Pound and T.S. Eliot have both fought stout battles in that behalf. But in the thirties the delusion of grandeur broke out again, in the persons of young poets then near-communist, who at any rate seemed to claim a clarity of political insight on the grounds that they were poets, though their politics are seen in retrospect—even by those who did not see them so at the time—as only the vulgar fashion of the age. It was certainly no 'department of learning' peculiar to them that these young gentlemen were using 'in its application to others'. The heavens rang with the manifestoes of poets and artists in those days but they were, politically, no wiser than anyone else's.

The truth is that the existence of a 'profession of letters' has no necessary connection with the health of letters. It is a social form, inevitable in our age but not the more desirable for that. Characteristically, it is the product of the 18th and 19th centuries and, more particularly, of the swelling movement of industrialization which, like a great cow-catcher, has pushed a mass of printed material before it. An industrial civilisation needs literate people, to read the instructions on the packet and the figures on the dial. Literature does not need them so badly; indeed, it may well be that it needs a reservoir of illiterates, who mould and re-mould speech without reading, and it has still to be proven that literature can be long sustained in a welter of reading matter. We are supposed to be anxious about the future of arts courses in universities, but do they or the professional critic contribute more to the hardening or the softening of language? A deficiency of purpose eats away at these institutions. The poet has a purpose, not the grand one of reforming the world or improving its politics, but the limited one of making a poem. He, if you like, is practising 'an art founded upon' knowledge of 'some department of learning'. But the mass of critics, impresarios and purveyors who make up the bulk of 'the profession of letters' are using their 'professed knowledge . . . in its application to others', and being neither lawyers, nor divines, nor doctors they really do not know how to apply it. They maintain cultural standards, perhaps, but you can search me as to what that means. An appalling poem in the *Times Literary Supplement* for 9 December, 1960 at once gives the atmosphere and illustrates the manner:

> But the guilt's there, just the same. We oughtn't to
> Be sitting round, just talking. I've a line
> To shoot and you've a lecture. Off we go,
> Relieved that we're no longer wasting time.

GEORGE BARKER
III Roman Odes

I
A Shower in Rome

The rain flickering here on this lonely day
      Over the brown roofs of Rome
Calls to my mind I am not so far away
      From my own house and home.
But then I hear the old clay within me cry
      Every man is in Coventry
And to the dirt his day is exiled from
      Must sometime come.

Patrick Swift: detail from *Portrait of George Barker*

Patrick Swift: detail from *Portrait of C. H. Sisson*

Patrick Swift: detail from *Portrait of David Wright*

Patrick Swift: detail from *Portrait of Patrick Kavanagh*

David Bomberg: *Self-portrait*

Michael Andrews: *The Gardener*

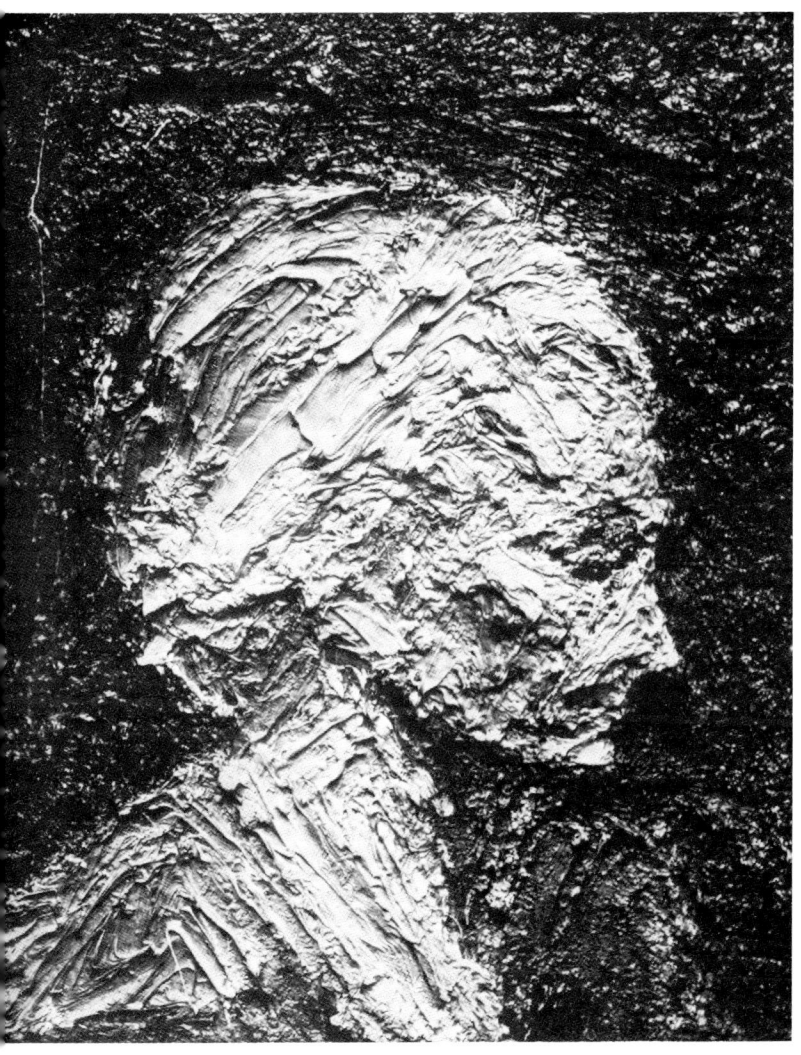

Frank Auerbach: *Head of E. O. W.*

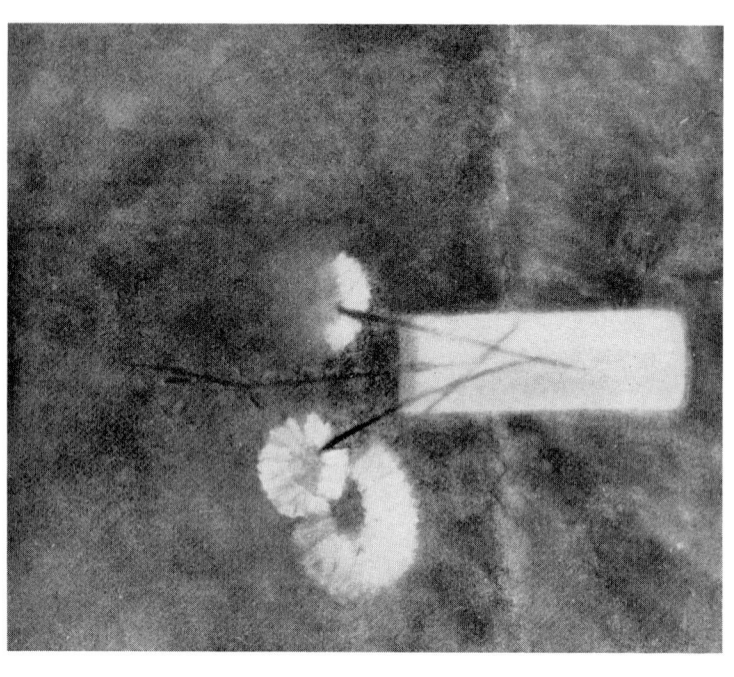

Craigie Aitchison: *Chrysanthemums*

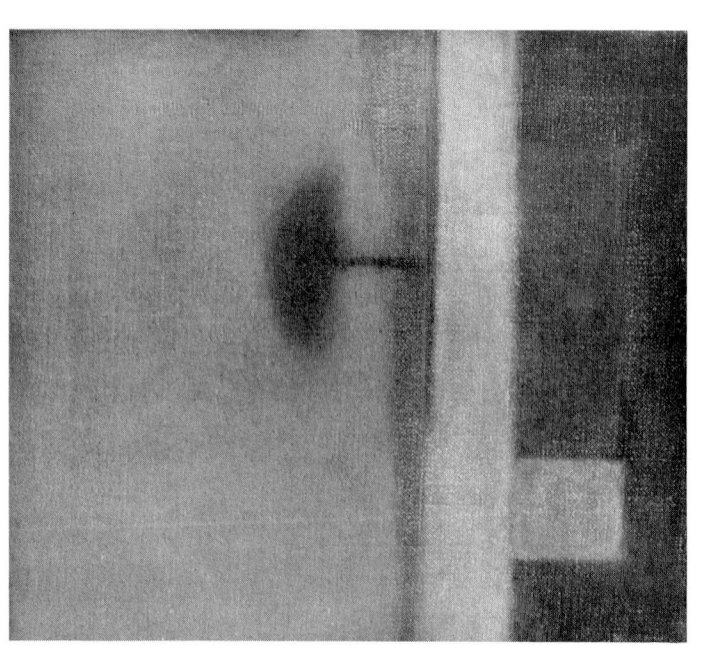

Craigie Aitchison: *Tree and Wall Landscape*

The shower veers westward to Ostia
        Like a plane trailing
A trembling net of rain, and on the far
        Landscape toiling
Armies of cloud climb and fall and are
        Gone. At once the air
Sunbursts with radiance like a shattered ceiling
        Dazzling everywhere.

Everywhere save here in the vaults of love
        Where no sun can
Delve to the blood-filled urn. In this living grave
        Of the unhouselled man
Only a gnashing of silence can penetrate
        From those also immured
In their open tombs. Deep in its fate
        Bone howls to be heard.

Nevertheless above, like birds with rain,
        The larks of circumstance
Draw off those lifelong shrouds and, once again,
        I feel the spirit dance
Up from its unholy cave, and regain
        That delight once
Unhaunted by the bell and clappered presence
        Of a lost innocence.

So bright in pits the triumph of the Tarquin
        Regales the smiling dead
Just as though human delight could win
        Life instead
Back from the damp tomb and the last bed.
        Sexual joy within
Those muddy tenements lifts up its head
        And begins, for ever, again.

And caged in rock beside the Capitol
        Padding her twenty-foot track
The mother of Rome, loping up and back,
        Smiles as the kids howl
Proudly: Lupe! at that imperial
        Bitch on the prowl—

The pride of a creature that has never died
    Crowns her, and her whole pack.

A bed of roses and a wreath of bay
    Birds of a shower, bear
Down to the tarnished demigods of clay—
    Triumph is here
To ornament with the trophies and regalia
    Of our crossed victories,
Or to degrade, as with a snivelling shower,
    Its eternal glories.

II

A Visit to Lake Albano

Why is this lake so sacred? It is sacred
    Because it is still.
Such a stillness is holy, for, unlike a river,
    Or even the sea
Those huge mythologies endemic overhead
    May, without a lie,
Behold themselves here as they truly believe
    The gods to be.
Shown in the drowning heavens of Albano
    Would they rather
Die in its deeper altitudes than the sky?
    Sometimes a feather
From them descends onto the evening surface
    To take upon
Itself the curve and veer of that faint sail
    Leaning for haven
Over Albano. Or a small fish may rise
    Seeking to leap
Into the mackerel patterning of their wings
    And dying eyes.
Holy Albano, I have seen the low storm
    Saunter more slowly
Over your font and prism, as its form
    Immersed in so
Lucid a peace, received a christening grace:
    Or perhaps more
Slowly moved over not to vex that still face
    With a sudden shower.
    Birds in your air

Loiter like visiting hierophants who hope
        To steal from the place
Some miraculous touch. So I, too, this day
        Having further come
And for as brief a slaking at this lake
        Of laving expiation,
Having a little refreshed in your lustration
        What may be saved
Of jaded nature, I, too, take away
        From your holy springs
The evanescent absolution of water.

III

A Sparrow's Feather

There was that empty birdcage in the garden.
        And in it, to amuse myself, I had hung
pseudo-oriental birds constructed of
        glass and tin bits and paper, that squeaked sadly
as the wind sometimes disturbed them. Suspended
        in melancholy non-existence they sang
of things that had never happened, and never
        could in that cage of artificial existence.
The twittering of these instruments in lamentation
        over their absent lives resembled elegies
torn from a falling harp, till the cage filled with
        engineered regret like moonshining cobwebs,
as these constructions grieved over not existing.
        The children fed them with flowers. A sudden gust
and without sound lifelessly one would die,
        scattered in scraps like debris. The wire doors
always hung open, against their improbable
        transfiguration into, say, chaffinches
or even more colourful birds. Myself I found
        the whole game charming, let alone the children.
And then, one morning—I do not record a
        matter of cosmic proportions, I assure you,
not an event to flutter the Volscian doyecotes—
        there, askew among those mechanical images
like a lost soul electing to die in Rome,
        its feverish eye transfixed, both wings fractured,
lay—on my word, Catullus—a young sparrow.
        Not long for this world, so heavily breathing

>   one might have supposed this cage his destination
>   after labouring past seas and from skies
> whence he had flown, death not being known there.
>   Of course, there was nothing to do. The children
> brought breadcrumbs, brought water, brought tears in their eyes
>   perhaps to restore him, that shivering panic
> of useless feathers, that tongue-tied little gossip,
>   that lying flyer. So there, among its gods,
> that moaned and whistled in a little wind,
>   flapping their paper anatomies like windmills,
> wheeling and bowing dutifully to the
>   divine intervention of a child's forefinger,
> there, at rest and at peace amongst its monstrous
>   idols, the little bird died. And, for my part,
> I hope the whole unimportant affair is
>   quickly forgotten. The analogies are too trite.

C. H. SISSON

Natural History

I

I can remember, in my young age, sitting at the table in the breakfast room, trying to make a poem about sleigh bells while my mother made the Christmas cake. I have no doubt that she was more successful than I was, and that my despair was justified. In adolescence I often knew in advance—sometimes the day before—when a poem was coming on, and I had not to think about it in case I should spoil it. It may be that that prohibition was no more than the superstitions which have always readily attached themselves to pregnancy, but there is probably something in the nature of poetry which makes it necessary to avoid conscious premeditation. The beginnings of poetry are hopelessly imitative, and it is difficult to see how the gathering burden could unload itself in rhymes which were nothing but John Drinkwater or Robert Louis Stevenson. But that was how the ecstasy in the coal-house ended when, later, I pressed my heart against the edge of the table and wrote the lines which appeared in the Children's Corner of the *Bristol Observer*.

It is no doubt a sense of the inadequacy of the vehicle that makes one discard one's models with fury one after the other. John Drinkwater gave way to Rupert Brooke, Rupert Brooke to Edith Sitwell and to Dante Gabriel Rossetti. Finally John Drinkwater and Robert Louis Stevenson had to be got out of the house, it shamed me so to see them on the shelves. Need I say that it was the first intimations of sexual love, as for Beatrice, which filled out my sequence of sonnets in the manner of the House of Life? It could be said that that represented a progress, for the model was at least a little nearer what I had to put into it.

At this time, naturally, Thomas Stearns Eliot put in a grave appearance and bade me desist from these excesses. I was about seventeen. Shortly afterwards, I was pounded by Pound. I had my *Weltanschauung* adjusted by T.E. Hulme. Public schoolboys invited me to admire the working classes. From all this I never recovered. At intervals for the next year or two I wrote poems which 'showed awareness'—that would have been the expression. For about a year (*circa* 1932) I must have been contemporary. How I got over this is mysterious, but it was not all done by literature. I was struck down by an appalling adolescent grief, as is not uncommon. Rene Béhaine identifies the very moment when he left behind him 'le sens du bonheur et le pouvoir d'être heureux.'[1] It was something of that kind.

At the same time, my learning grew. Do not be alarmed, ignorant reader, it was never very great. But were not Thomas Stearns Eliot and Ezra Pound learned? And, although I have not told you, I had been—oh, on a much more modest scale than those two thought indispensable—a not unlearned boy. For in the Rossetti period I had already read through the *Britannia's Pastoral* of William Browne of Tavistock, Robert Greene, the *Hero and Leander* of Christopher Marlowe, besides many other poets recommended or unrecommended in schools. I read them aloud in the lavatory in those days. But now the obligation to acquire culture became grave. I advanced through the seventeenth century looking for strange creatures, but more especially for those who had earned a mention in the works of my masters. I too could evaluate poets then. I despaired of being a poet myself (I was despairing of everything at that time, you will remember). I believe I must have aspired to be an educated man. So I gave up the exercise of verse.

This was in the year of our Lord nineteen hundred and thirty-four, and the twentieth of my age. The muse took her leave of me in Berlin, at a time, appropriately enough, when I was supposed to be writing a thesis on the translation of poetry, though no such work was ever produced by me. Instead, I gawped at marching columns of young men in jack-boots, at blond prostitutes in the Kurfürstendamm, at paintings by Klee which could still be seen at the Kronprinzenpalais, at anything that could be gawped at, and at four o'clock in the morning lectured on a particularly

---

[1] The reference is to be found on pp. 132-3 of *Avec les yeux de l'esprit*, which is Volume VI of the *Histoire d'une Société*—surely one of the best books of the century.

abstruse sentence from *Ulysses* in the waiting room of the Friedrichsstrasse station. It would not repay you to follow me to Prague, Nuremberg, Munich or the several other cities I honoured at that time. My pre-occupations were political, and when I reached Freiburg I was looking for books by Léon Daudet.

I do not wish to say more about these days than will indicate what I was up to while the Muse's back was turned. The next year I was in Paris, a passionate reader of the *Action française* and of everything of Maurras I could lay my hands on, from the *Enquête sur la monarchie* to the *Conseil de Dante*, partly because I had already had the left-wing part of my education, and partly led on by the seductions of his prose. Everyone had had enough of educating me by then: it was the public authorities that did it, though they were less free with their money then than now. The young will have heard, and their elders will have learned more forcibly, that in those days you either fought your way to a job or rotted on the dole. I already knew about having no money. And I was acquainted with no-one who could conceivably help me to a job. So I became a civil servant. You had only to pass an examination and they could not refuse you, even if you said (as I did at the interview) that you chose the civil service because it was remote from everything that interested you.

It was remote. Most of my contemporaries struck me as rather Oxfordy young men and, meaning to be friendly, everyone asked me what college I came from and of course I came from none. I was put into a room with a man of experience who was doing things about unemployment insurance. I had read Kafka so I understood all this perfectly, but the working of the civil service was a mystery to me. It was possible to read bits of the *Decline and Fall of the Roman Empire* in between times. I acquired habits of diligence, however, though not the applause of the more influential of my betters.

My first article appeared in *The New English Weekly* in 1937. It was called 'Charles Maurras and the Idea of a Patriot King'—with allusion to Bolingbroke. Others followed. In 1939 I wrote for a review called *Purpose* a long essay which asserted

> that the distinction between public sentiments and private perceptions is fundamentally the same as the distinction between good writing and bad. If this in fact is so [the essay went on] it may be said that bad writing is writing which expresses the politically manoeuvrable sentiments and is therefore part of the system of force which is government. Good writing alone may be described as independent of government, and one has intellectual liberty just so far as one has the capacity to distinguish between valid work and invalid.

It was an assertion which did honour to the Muses, but the one we are talking about did not visit me during these years except to say

Here lies a civil servant. He was civil
To everyone, and servant to the devil.

It was only in the immense, prison-like leisure of a troopship moving southwards through tropical waters, that a few lines were squeezed out, to define my condition.

It did not occur to me to amuse the boredom and oppression of military life by continuing this exercise. I kept an intermittent note-book, and three or four times during this exile the lines broke up, and stresses and rhythms took charge, I like to believe because of an involuntary concentration of attention. I had sweated for months and years for those poems: not in the writing of them, but literally sweated, travelled vast distances, protected my bread and jam from the kite-hawks. If I had set out to provoke myself to poetry it would not have been in that way.

My most deliberate attempt at writing at this time—to keep my wits alive and vent my spleen—was the translation of some of the political poems of Heine.[1] The value of such performances is that they provide technical exercise without conscious meddling with the writer's own experience. After the war I had the good fortune to be asked to translate some stories of Supervielle, which loosened the muscles of my prose and gave me hints as to how I might use it for narrative and imagination. I did so use it, and when the muse of verse rhythms popped up again—it was not until the nineteen-fifties—it was to pre-figure in twenty lines what became a long work in prose. I do not mean that these verses were any sort of a deliberate sketch of the prose work, but when I had written that work I could see that it had been pre-figured. The twenty lines with which I resumed my writing of verse had been ground out, much as the lines on a troopship had been, without wilfulness and out of an accumulated pressure. The springs went so deep that I had only to get up at six every morning for a year and put a bucket into the same well to draw up my sixty thousand words of prose.

From that time the practice of verse has been intermittent but has never been intermitted for immense periods, although 'on voit le style d'un homme qui a toujours commencé à écrire, et qui n'a jamais écrit.' That was said of a man of affairs—of Richelieu and his *Testament politique*—by Montesquieu[2] and, because scale does not matter I may be forgiven for thinking that I know what is meant. The pressure of affairs, by which one earns one's living, is at a barely tolerable emnity with the needs of the writer, yet it may not be wholly unproductive. Certainly the conduct of affairs is, by the standards of the writer or artist, for the most part a frivolous business. There is more genuine difficulty in the ordering of

[1] Versions and Perversions of Heine (Gaberbocchus Press), 1955.
[2] In the *Cahiers*.

material, the simplification of complex problems, than the writer who has been spared these horrors is apt to give the man of affairs credit for. But ideas are frowsy by the time they come to be used for action. The language of business is stale. It is the mechanical faculties of memory and logic which have most play in it. The men are vivid, however. This is the world, and the gamut of the classical moralist—ambition, fear, dissimulation—is not to be exhausted without some experience of it.

One should not write more poetry than one must, and some formula has to be found for passing the time between poems. The conduct of affairs is one, though probably not the best. While one is seeing this world, what worlds is one not seeing! But at least these avocations prevent one from thinking of oneself as a poet, which for most writers of verse must be salutary. The annihilating pressure of work seems an enemy, but so many times of idleness, as a student and in the army, have produced nothing that one cannot say with certainty that relief from this treadmill would produce more, though I think it would. The writing of poetry is a matter of personal economy, but it cannot be treated as such, for one does not know what one wants to discover. One can only go on living, and be grateful for this bye-product if it comes. It may be just pleasure, or it may be the truth peeping out. 'Un homme qui écrit bien'—to quote Montesquieu again—'n'écrit pas comme on a écrit, mais comme il écrit, et c'est souvent en parlant mal qu'il parle bien.'

II

The poet has problems which you can call technical, if you like the word, but when he is at work all his problems are one, which is to keep what he is saying within the limits of the perceptible. The words of most of the communications which pass between people cannot be seen, smelt, or tasted; they can barely be heard. They are (what is called) understood, by which is meant that they have certain practical effects, as the turning of switches or the movement of gear levers. It is this skeleton language which is used, almost exclusively, in the conduct of business, so that you have the absurd spectacle of people—fine figures of men, perhaps, well dressed and otherwise covered—talking to one another as if they were constructions of wire, watching for answers on a number of dials and occasionaly blowing one another's fuses. The ordinary document of business has no existence apart from the use of the moment. It *does* a particular job: it establishes certain very limited connections, but try to look at it apart from that particular purpose and you will see what is meant by saying that it has no existence. The poem exists less contingently, and you could make an esthetic theory (no doubt someone has) on the basis that the more the poem succeeds in living independently of time and place the better it is. But that would be tautological like most esthetic theories. The point is that the poem exists as a natural object exists, so that you can look at it, hear it, smell it, as you can wind, waves or trees, without asking why you are doing so. The poet literally feels his way forward, and when the moment comes when he is no longer touching something he has either finished his poem or is left with a broken piece in his hands.

Perceptible literary objects come in all kinds of shapes, and the work of a particular writer, taken chronologically, is likely to show a series of shapes related in the same way as the shapes you might expect to see emerging one after another from a painter's studio. The changes in the series pass for being the poet's development, but how does it look to him and why does he pass from one point to another in the series? He is not ordinarily thinking of developing (to give the professors something to write about). He is thinking—so far as he can be described as thinking of anything apart from the subject-matter—of making a poem which will not be the same as the last one. The development of the series is in one sense the result of a negative rather than a positive effort. If the familiar presents itself as he feels his way through the poem, he discards it, knowing that it would not be part of the poem, but would be a 'soft' bit. What, through its familiarity, can no longer be attended to, is of no use for his purposes. The unfamiliarity ought to be continuous but it is not absolute. Unfamiliarity is a relative thing. It is related to what is familiar; there is a background of expectedness to all that is unexpected. The poet may change things, but he starts from somewhere.

In the matter of verse forms, where he starts from may be more or less firmly dictated. The volumes of Johnson's poems show how obsessive a form can be. They also show what variety can be produced within a single form and how the attention flags if nothing new comes up. The difficulties of the twentieth century are not those of the eighteenth. We are not too narrowly dictated to but, like our architects, have now such a variety of possibilities that we can easily think ourselves original when we have not attended enough even to familiarise ourselves with a pattern that we could depart from.

It is an absurdity to try to be original. You might as well try to be beautiful or intelligent. But the complementary process of ridding yourself of obsessive influences can possibly be assisted by some conscious effort. A young man, however, cannot shrink back at the first touch of an alien hand. He has to live through his Eliot, his Yeats or whatever it may be. For a time he must wear fashionable clothes. Then he must discard them, and be prepared to find, not merely that he is naked, but that under those clothes he simply was not there at all. Those who are simply not there at all do not hesitate to fill the poetry pages of respected journals, or even whole volumes, but silence is better. (Tarr went round persuading his friends to give up art.) Indeed silence is an admirable thing, nearer to poetry than the chatter of literary apes.

Because of the negative aspects of unfamiliarity, the fact that what is new is recognized by being different from something that is known, people may have difficulty in distinguishing a genuine variation from a mere copy of the theme. There is no sure way of making the distinction except by being able to do so. Some people can look and listen but more, it seems, can not. It is generally claimed that this is difficult only for contemporary work and that anyone can tell that *The Splendid Shilling* or *Cyder, a Poem* are superior (in their modest way) to most Miltonic blank verse of the eighteenth century but I think this phenomenon must be due to some other process.

The idea of the poet as a maker of novelties sets some puzzles. Is the difference that must exist between one poem and another by the same hand, of the same kind as that which must exist between the work of different poets? I do not know whether it was the same Anon who wrote *The Oakerman* and *Tom o' Bedlam*,

>   From the Rugged Ile of Orkney
>   Where the Redshanke walkes the Marish

and

>   I know more than Apollo,
>   For oft when he lies sleeping.

I find it hard to believe that it was not, but I do not see how one can say that it could not have been one man picking up another man's tune and making his own variation on it. This is easier, perhaps, at times when there are less tunes to be heard than in our day when we are deafened by polyphonies and on every hand the libraries give up their dead.

One readily thinks of the poet's problems as being that of learning to speak with his voice, but there is a lot of metaphysics as well as history behind this apparently innocent view. It raises all sorts of questions as to what this self is which is said to have a voice of its own. When I think of bits of writing which echo in the mind as *personal*, it is often of bits which are more obviously of another time and place than of another person. Thus it is England still climbing out of the Middle Ages which speaks in this from *The Life of Lord Herbert of Cherbury*, written by himself:

> And certainly since in my mother's womb this Plastica or Formatrix which formed my eyes, ears, and other senses, did not intend them for that dark and noisome place, but as being conscious of a better life, made them as fitting organs to apprehend and perceive those things which should occur in this world: so I believe since my coming into this world my soul hath formed or produced certain

faculties which are almost as useless for this life, as the above-named senses were for the mother's womb; and those faculties are Hope, Faith, Love and Joy.

And it is the sixteenth century—though seen under the modus of action rather than of philosophy—which speaks in these verses of Sir Walter Raleigh:

> Although to give the lie,
>   deserves no less then stabbing,
> Stab at thee he that will.

But probably it makes sense to say that these authors sound real because they are telling the truth, as it seems to them, which is the only form of truth anyone can tell, except inadvertently.

As a piece of technical advice to the writer: Tell the truth and hope for the best is, however, inadequate. Some good writers have been quite extraordinary liars, along certain lines, as for example Ford Madox Ford. The truth is interesting if you can tell it, but the writer will feel a need to simplify his problems by abridging it in some way. What is not so good is putting in phoney bits. This also everybody does more or less, but the better writers less. The advice one might give—if any advice were of any use—might be to write about something about which you have some truth to tell. For the poet the truth is what he can perceive. This is the point at which the technical problems and the problems of subject-matter become the same. But is rhythm a part of the truth? It seems odd to say so. One feels for the subject, and if one finds it one finds the words. But the rhythm? The fact is that you cannot find the words without the rhythm, and what you might call your words, in a borrowed rhythm, would not be your words. So evading other people's rhythm is part of finding your own words, though you might help yourself by a preliminary decision to use or eschew certain forms, as the Pound of *Mauberley* and the Eliot of *Sweeney among the Nightingales* are said to have opted—with what reservations the products show—for the metric of the Bay State Hymn Book because free verse 'had gone far enough', or as one might decide that it is too dangerous to attempt satire in pentameters of Dryden, Pope or Crabbe.

To know when one has some truth to tell is in a way the whole tact of the poet—a sort of slyness he has to use within his own mind. Rilke talks about 'Tausende von Liebesnächten' going to the making of a single line, and the poet's choice of a subject is no doubt related to his physiology and to the succession of his outward circumstances. One imagines that Shakespeare could turn anything to account because his receiving apparatus was as nearly perfect as could be, but most writers can manage only a few scratchings on the limited subject-matters of which, amidst the general obscurity of their lives, they manage to apprehend something more or less concretely. Why their gropings should sometimes succeed and sometimes not is about as explicable as why love and liking turn up how and when they do. Though I could not find a subject-matter by saying: That has been much in my experience, looking at my poems after the event I recognise that many of them are the small visible pinnacles of apperceptive ice-bergs.

III

When Charles I saw some of Denham's poems he advised him

that when men are young, and have little else to do, they might vent the overflowings of their Fancy that way, but when they were thought fit for more serious Employments, if they still persisted in that course, it would look, as if they minded not the way to any better.[1]

'Whereupon', says Denham, 'I stood corrected as long as I had the honour to wait on him.' In some sense poetry is secondary, a series of glimpses on a journey, which you would not have had if you had taken another journey. Nonetheless, most of the business of life is trivial by comparison. The stockbroker, the business man, the civil servant, the commentator, and such-like figures of the popular imagination, are generally easily replaced by other despatch cases with the same contents. We are more like one another than we care to think, so that is less derogatory than one might suppose. But what the poet does is not to be replaced by the work of anyone else, and the capacity to produce even a few bits of poetry is incomparably rarer than mere ability to transact business. As to whether that makes the poet incomparably more valuable than the man of affairs I know nothing, but it is hardly for the disciples of the price mechanism to say that it does not, unless they maintain that no-one wants the stuff anyhow.

GEOFFREY HILL

Annunciations

I

The Word has been abroad, is back, with a tanned look
From its subsistence in the stiffening-mire.
Cleansing has become killing, the reward

[1] The Epistle Dedicatory, in Denham's Poems.

Touchable, overt, clean to the touch.
Now at a distance from the steam of beasts
The loathly neckings and fat shook spawn
(Each specimen-jar fed with delicate spawn)
The searchers with the curers sit at meat
And are satisfied. Such precious things put down
And the flesh eased through turbulence the soul
Purples itself; each eye squats full and mild
While all who attend to fiddle or to harp
For betterment, flavour their decent mouths
With gobbets of the sweetest sacrifice.

II

O Love, subject of the mere diurnal grind,
Forever being pledged to be redeemed,
Expose yourself for charity; be assured.
The body is but husk and excrement.
Enter these deaths according to the law,
O visited women, possessed sons. Foreign lusts
Infringe our restraints; the changeable
Soldiery have their goings-out and comings-in
Dying in abundance. Choicest beasts
Suffuse the gutters with their colourful blood.
Our God scatters corruption. Priests, martyrs,
Parade to this imperious theme: 'O Love,
You know what pains succeed; be vigilant; strive
To recognise the damned among your friends.'

JOHN McGAHERN

The End or the Beginning of Love

EPISODES FROM A NOVEL

It was fearful to lie there in the night, the moonlight on the scarred brass bells that hung from the railing at the foot of the bed, and wait for Mahoney to come home. Tonight again, he would have to pretend to Mahoney that he was asleep.

There were few distractions to allay the pure anxiety of waiting: count the thirty-two boards across the ceiling, listen to the clock beat on the mantelpiece, examine your conscience. 'As each night's sleep can be your last, the very sleep of death, never go to sleep with a mortal sin on your soul. Go carefully back over every action of the day. Say your Act of Perfect Contrition. Let these be your last thoughts at night,' the priest had said at the Catechism Class. But to pretend to Mahoney that he was asleep when he was wide awake was to lie. It used to be stolen sugar and apples, now it was lies. Lies, lies, lies. He had lied eight times that day. But how could he have saved himself if he hadn't lied? You had to lie continually to get safely through any day.

The heavy bolting of the door warned him that Mahoney was in the house. His boots sounded on the cement of the hallway. He heard him hang up his great coat on the back of the door, and in the silence he must have been drinking his mug of barley water beside the fire. He came very softly up the stairs.

'Are you asleep, Francie?' he called.

The boy lay rigid in the bed. It took all his resolution not to answer. One word and he would no longer have to lie there, apprehensive and afraid. But he could not bear to talk with his father. He heard the scrape of a belt buckle against the railing of the bed, the soft plump of coat and trousers and pullover being thrown in a heap on the floor. He wound the clock and brought it close up to the moonlit window to set the alarm for the morning. Then he asked quite suddenly, 'Are you sleepin' yet, Francie?'

Had he betrayed himself?—stirred, or opened his eyes to watch him wind the green clock. Now it was too late to speak. He heard him fumble through the heap of clothes for his matches. Then a match cracked and flared. It was shaded above his face. His lids lit up like bright red curtains, the heat was on his face, and he could sense his father's eyes searching him from above. With a choked cry he turned sideways and covered his face. When he lifted his hands the flame had burned down the black char of matchwood to his father's fingers.

'You were quick to wake?' he said, his face ugly with suspicion.

'I was sleepin'—and I felt something,' he managed to lie desperately. Then he no longer cared. He shivered with the terror of having been blind under the burning match. A cold sweat was on his forehead.

'Did you want me for something?' he cried. All Mahoney's sureness disappeared. He was afraid he had frightened the boy out of his sleep. He didn't know how to answer him.

'No—I didn't want you for anything. I just thought you might be awake. I wanted to see if you were sleepin' yet.'

He climbed awkwardly into the bed, his feet as cold as clay, and he touched Francie's hair with his hand.

'We're too cooped up in ourselves here. We must dress up for the town wan of these days. We'll ate our dinner in the Royal Hotel!'

He spoke quickly, restless with this sudden excitement. 'You'd like to go to town, wouldn't you?'

'Aye. It'd be nice to go to town.'

'Every family has their differences. Things don't all the time run smooth. But we're not supposed to be down here for sport, are we? But to earn the bread be the sweat of our brows! But that's not what counts, shure it's not?'

'No. That's not what counts.'

'It's aisy for anybody to lose their temper—it's only natural. But no matter what happens you know your father loves you?'

'I know that.'

'And you love yer father?'

'Yes. I do.'

Mahoney seemed afraid of silence and sleep. He wanted to talk and talk but it was impossible to go on against Francie's cold resentment, who hated these midnight hearteasings, these strivings to be understood that could continue far into the morning. But when his father finally turned on his side with the hopeless, 'It's time for us to sleep now', it brought him little release.

The moon had climbed and the room was in total darkness. A bat screeched once or twice about the eaves but there was no other sound but the clock's ticking. What it is to lie all night beside some one we loathe, the imagination its own king in the silence and darkness, raising a hundred figures, out of the touch of bare flesh or a muttering, more repulsive than the dying leper! Francie lay far out on his own side of the bed. He shrank away from his father, and tried to avoid being touched as he moved in his sleep. He was soon stripped except for the cold linen sheet that he held by its edge. Mahoney gathered the now loose blankets about him in a ball as he slept. A few fainthearted tugs showed that they were firmly wedged beneath him, and to edge them out would run the risk of waking him. As he stiffened with the night's cold Francie drew in from the edge of the bed but he still couldn't bring himself to snuggle into his father's sleeping warmth. He lay beneath the sheet, trying to find each of the twenty-eight knots under the brown varnish on the ceiling, while the coming day that he was longing for made the figures on the face of the five-shilling alarm clock easier and easier to read.

II

Between the lone ash trees, their branches pale as human limbs in the rain, Francie and Josie picked the potatoes. The long rows of the potatoes stretched ahead of them to the stone wall, washed clean on top by the rain and gleaming white and pink and candleyellow against the black acres of clay. The boy and girl worked without any hope of picking them all. Their clothes were leaden with rain. The wind numbed the side of the face turned towards it and great lumps of clay gathered on their boots, held together by clay and dead stalks.

Yet Mahoney did not leave off. He dug close to the stone wall, muttering and striking savagely at the ridge with his spade. He slashed earth and potatoes together, doing far more harm than good, his hair limp with rain, and the eyes alive with venom.

'He's out to spite us, he'll never leave off,' Josie said, and it was less than a half-hour from pitch night when he gave up. He threw the spade in the furrow and blundered towards them across the muddy ridges.

'Give me that bucket in the name of Jasus,' he shouted at Francie. 'The bloody spuds'll not pick themselves. Such bastards——'

He heaped fistfuls of mud carelessly in with the potatoes. He was in far too great a rush. The bucket overturned and scattered his picking back on the ridge. Then he cursed, and kicked the bucket from him in a mad fit of temper. 'If you'd stopped from school we'd be in none of this pissin' mess. Christ tonight! Nothing right. Nothing right. Nothing ever done right. Now do you see!' he raved.

They were in dread of him, his blue cotton shirt plastered to his body under the army braces, so that he looked half-naked. They seemed wet and miserable as he glared at them through the night and rain. He became aware of the cold and lashing rain: 'I'll get me death out of this! Such bastards of childer!' he raged and hurried towards the house.

They were glad to see him disappear. They continued to fill the buckets but the gloom of night was thickening rapidly. They could barely see their way. When Francie found himself walking on the potatoes he stopped.

'We're only trampin' them into the ground, Jo.'

'But there'll be murder if we leave them here for the night?'

'We haven't cats' eyes,' he told her. She looked so small and pinched, drudging up the ridges with her bucket. They could pick no more. But the potato pit had still to be covered. Then they would have to face Mahoney in the house.

'As I was goin' to the fair of Athy I met nine men and their nine wives. How many were goin' to the fair of Athy?' Francie riddled her, trying hopelessly to kick away the oppression of wind and rain, their fear of Mahoney.

'Only the one,' she answered rightly. He saw how wan her smile was in the wet dusk. She had probably read it in *Ireland's Own*. All their riddles and jokes were as outdated, as familiar and useless as the old calendars that still hung in the kitchen to take the bare look off the walls. They soon tidied the face of the pit. It looked marvellous and strange in the last glimmers of light, the long pyramid sloping palely upwards to a fine edge, the potatoes along the sides washed white and gleaming like blobs of flesh through the rain. Josie hunkered down in the sheltery side of the pit when Francie went to the haystacks for a backload of rushes. He was startled to find her laughing to herself when he got back.

'O God, O God, such bastards of childer!' she started to mimic her father.

'It's in the County Home ye'll all finish up! In the dale coffin of the pauper! WILful waste is WOEful want,' he continued on. They roared laughing. He loosened the rope about the backload of rushes. She helped him scatter the fresh green rushes over the bare potatoes. She went with him to the haystacks for the second load. When they had the pit covered they went together towards the house.

It was a dark night. The wind had risen, sweeping walls of rain across the fields. Some of the last leaves fell lightly against them as they came through the orchard. Mahoney had the lamp lit and they made straight for the yellow tunnel it made into the night, the brilliants of the raindrops flashing through it. They had lost their courage coming through the fields. Josie was afraid and would not go in until Francie promised to face Mahoney first.

He was sitting in his dry clothes in the kitchen. He had put turf and sticks on the fire and it was blazing up the chimney. The traces of an eaten meal were on the table. He was far more tired than angry, but he had to assert himself in some way when Francie stood doggedly in the kitchen, his hair and clothes dripping water.

'Did you pick them all?' he demanded.

'No.' The sullen answer came back, thick with anger. But his father had worn himself out too much to fly into his rages. He began to nag.

'Aye, an' they'll be in a grand state if the frost comes.'

'I never saw frost and rain together.'

'Shut that up now,' Mahoney warned. 'Frost and rain! Who cares about frost and rain! If you had to stop from school there'd be no talk of frost and rain. And did ye cover up the pit itself?'

'We did—with the rushes.'

'Aye, and I suppose ye'll be expectin' a leather medal for that much.' Mahoney jeered. Francie cursed under his breath as he turned away to take off his wet clothes. Mahoney continued to nag wearily on when Josie came down from changing in her room. Squalls of rain broke against the window pane and beat overhead on the slates: when the nagging stopped and they sat uneasily silent together in the kitchen, they could hear the overflow from the tar barrels spill out on the flagstones of the street.

III

Mahoney was waiting for Francie outside the chapel. He was fingering the lost rosary beads that hung on the crosses of the gate.

'It's surprisin' they never manage to lose themselves,' he remarked, and they laughed together, the intimacy of Confession still about them. Ideally confession is made to God, which means nothing to the senses, it is no more than a sophistical balm for pride; the real need is to confess sensually to another man, a need as old as original sin, as emotionally intimate as the act of hatred or of love. It is the effort required to make confession and a sense of the priest's understanding of the individual guilt that satisfies; even the theatrical effects, the naked blood-daubed Jesus on the cross above the curtained grille, stand out in the memory of the ritual; and the idea of God is yet farther away than the ritual. The lonely and ignorant never realise that sin is as common as flesh. For them it is always the first sin and through confession they are always beginning—as if they were beginning life again with their first innocence. And in some measure Francie and his father walked in the joy of this beginning, having shared the fear and shame of confession and the relief of forgiveness. They felt closer to each other, the pain of their essential loneliness at rest until the next sin, the next hurt, the next failure. It was then that Mahoney asked what never came up between them:

'What are you goin' to do when you lave school?'

'I don't know, it'll all depend on the exams,' Francie answered with new readiness.

'Exams!' Mahoney hooted. 'Be the acres of names that appear these days in the 'papers every clown in the country will soon have passed and qualified for something or other. But where's the jobs comin' outa? That's the question! All qualified to ate wan another if you ask me!'

'I might go on for a priest,' Francie said apprehensively. His father's mood changed. It became quiet, not without some cunning and bitterness. He hadn't said more than a few words when Francie regretted having spoken. He cursed the false feeling of intimacy that had betrayed him.

'It's a hard life but a good wan,' his father began. 'It or a doctor's is all there's respect for in this country and a doctor isn't for the like of us. We're not rotten enough with money and ignorance! But a priest's a good clane life and you don't have bostoons tryin' to sit on you like in the police. Begod we'd have grate times when you'd be ordained. I'd sell out the place here. And I could come an' answer the door for you and not have them annoyin' you about every mouse that went astray on them . . . .'

When Francie walked alone with himself and made no response,

Mahoney's excitement trailed away. The eagerness went out of his walk as if he had been broken by his years of toil. He lifted his hand to touch Francie's shoulder and then let it fall hopelessly again. His heart was heavy with failure. In his own strange way he loved his son desperately.

IV

A wet and a windy May
Fills the barns full of hay.

That was their hope, but hardly a cloud appeared in the May sky, and at night white frost scorched the apple blossoms. Only scutch grass greened the cemented clay of the potato ridges; the young oats was stunted; grass was no stronger in the fenced-off meadows than in the pastures. Then the weather broke late in June. Now they fought to get home enough dry turf to see them through the winter and to keep the weeds from choking the root crops. The sudden rain after draught brought up a lush unhealthy growth of grass: it was infested with worms, bringing sickness among the cattle.

'It'll tighten up to keep from starvin', never mind pay rent and rates,' Mahoney railed and when the plastic factory closed down in Cloone and Maura came home she was given the starvation welcome: 'Another belly to fill, another back to put clothes on.'

It was decided that it was now Josie's turn to go out into life. She was afraid to go. The little dark haired girl, with the tiny hands and darting quick eyes, had become a common drudge about the house since failing the County Scholarship. She took none of the young girl's pride in her appearance. A faded yellow scarf was always over the lovely head of hair that had grown dull and wiry for want of care. She cried by the window the first day a job was mentioned. She was so broken that she could only see the same drudgery and despair in everything; and what she knew was less to be feared than what she didn't know. Only the indignant and disgusted destroy themselves; they have still hope in something; real despair will want to drag on living—for left to herself the girl would have stayed at home.

It was Mahoney who did everything for her. He picked out the ads and wrote the applications. He loved this work. He would change into his new clothes before he sat down before the glaring Tilly lamp to write. He had Smith's shilling dictionary always at his elbow and an old copy of *Famous Love Letters*, with forget-me-nots and small red roses on the cover, that had belonged to his wife's youth. And he knew nothing about the dusty formulas that were the currency for all such applications. He searched and searched these stilted love letters of celebrities for the lofty words and phrasing that he loved:

Dear Sir or Madam,

I beg most humbly for the position you so graciously offered in that paragon of newspapers, *The Irish Independent*. I am in most excellent health, having being reared in a part of the country renowned for its beautiful woods, waters and benificient climate. I come from a most respectable family. I attend regularly to my religious duties and am forced to say the rosary each night.

If you allow me the great pleasure of being your employee, I most sincerely promise that I shall cherish your most dearly beloved interests as my own and shall serve you, if you so wish it, to the bitter end.

      I Am,
      Your Most Humble Applicant,
      Josephine Mahoney.

He took unbelievable pride in these compositions. A dissenting murmur infuriated him.

'I see nothing wrong with it! Its grammar and syntax is perfect. That paragon of newspapers! How could that be said better?'

'These people only want some one to work. What do they care whether this part of the country is beautiful or not?'

'Jasus, the intelligence some people have! Has climate nowthin' got to do with health? They don't want her stinkin' with T.B. do they?'

'You didn't mention what age she is?'

'The whole bloody country can't be as thick as the people of this house. Don't they know that she's not a child in the cradle or a dodderin' auld fool if she's lukin' for a job? You can't just go and insult people's intelligence like that. They don't want things spelled out for them.'

He would have his way. But when not an offer came back even he lost heart; and in the end it was Father Gerald who got a place for her in a 'hardware and general merchandise' shop near his curacy. Mahoney was sick of it all by the time the priest came to take Josie away. 'She's very young to be goin' out on her own in the world. Twenty years ago I little thought a girl of mine would be a shop girl, a door-mat for the whole country,' he brooded.

There wasn't much preparation for the priest's coming. The front room was dusted and swept, the grey calico covers taken off the armchairs. Maura trekked to the village for a fruit cake and the sacred blue china set was unwrapped out of the linen sheets in the bottom of the press. A fire of sticks blazed in the room from early morning. The girls had a shining cloth, bleached white as snow on the tussocks in the frost, over the table. But even towards the night, with the lamp-light and the friendly hissing of fresh wood on the fire, it was as cold and lifeless as every good example.

Father Gerald came at six. He sipped his tea and tried to make conversation with Mahoney. Neither of them spoke a word in his own voice. It was as if the conventions of the china and fruit cake had made them as perfect and lifeless as the poor room; and, besides, they had an instinctive dislike of each other. The weather, crops and cattle, the luck of Ireland in having the Catholic Faith to stand up against the Communists were shuttled back and forth for two hours of crucifying boredom. Then the priest asked Francie to walk over the fields with him for the night air: it would give Josie time to get herself ready.

The winter's night was too cold for strolling and the fields were rough with frozen hoofmarks. Father Gerald wasted no time in coming to the purpose of the walk. He wanted to speak alone with Francie.

'Do you still think about the priesthood?'

'Yes, Father,' Francie replied, hesitant and afraid to be so definite.

'I guessed as much. It was a great pity you were never sent to the Diocesan Seminary at the proper time. Then you would have gone naturally on to Maynooth. Your father, of course, wouldn't ask for help.'

'But there's the Mission Colleges, Father. . . .'

'Yes, of course! Any Tom-Dick-and-Harry can go there. But do not worry, only work at your books, and when the time comes we may be able to find a vacant place for you in Maynooth. After all, we are cousins—not a little thing. If we cannot help our own, who can we help?' the priest smiled in the darkness. He seemed frail and tall, his overcoat turned up over his roman collar. They walked back in the shelter of the thorn hedge that skirted the plantation of evergreens, fir and dark yew trees. 'But do not worry, Francie; only work at your books. And Josie will be all right,' he said before they went into the house.

Josie's cases were strapped at the door and they left immediately. Mahoney was surly and silent. Not until he stooped to kiss the girl goodbye did he soften. He could smell the brilliantine that damped down her black hair.

'We'll write, girl. We'll write,' was all he could mutter. She was pale and frightened, not fully able to believe that she was leaving, and she could make him no answer. They opened the green gates for the car. For a minute they watched the headlights fumble into the hills, and then they were gone.

Mahoney was restless about the kitchen when they came in, pacing about. He collected the bits of twine that were scattered about the house and put them together in an empty tea box on the mantelpiece, complaining all the time that nothing was ever kept tidy. Then he went out for the boards that had been got from the mill to put a new floor in the cart. He laid one across three chairs and looked for the red-handled plane.

He had to screw out the blade to sharpen it, and wet the black hone with bicycle oil. When he was savage in himself he had a fierce need to do things.

He was soon in his shirtsleeves in the warm kitchen. He drove the plane furiously over and back along the board, holding it steady with one knee, the long white shavings scattering on the cement. His face was wet with sweat when he stopped to get his breath again. He did not finish them. He got tired and stood them on their ends in the corner.

'Sweep up the shavin's. They'll do for kindlin',' he ordered as he put on his coat.

Then he pulled the old Morris car seat that he had fixed into a wooden frame up to the fire. He found the small playing board which he rested across the arms of the chair, and the pack of cards. There was soon nothing but his playing; the ruffling of the deck, the sharp boxing together; as he dealt them out on the board nothing but the flicking of the old cards of patience, not even the whisper of the yellow cat stretching in the ashes. The King of Diamonds for the Ace, Eight of Clubs for the Nine, the Seven for the Eight; slow dealing of the cards, three by three, red and black, the Queen of Hearts to fit; turn the cards again, from shuffle to shuffle till no move is left, nothing will fit nothing; or then all the cards suddenly and magically leaping for their ordered places, once in every three or four hundred dealings of the slow patience of the lighthouse.

But Mahoney was too ill at ease to lose himself on this slow tide of chance. He let the board fall, and he flung the pack back among the newspapers on the window sill.

'What was your cousin talkin' about?' he demanded.

'Not much,' Francie told him.

'Not much! But Jasus he must have been talkin' about something? He was hardly walkin' for the good of his health on a night that'd perish the hide on a monkey.'

'He said about being a priest,' Francie admitted, but reluctant to confide in him at all.

'And what did he say about that? Has everything to be dragged outa you be the hair of the head?'

'He said he'd help me. He said that there was no cause for worry. And that nothing could be done till after the exams.'

'He'd buy the calf when he was reared a bullock?'

'No—he didn't mean that,' Francie protested, annoyed and excited now. 'He said he might be able to get me into Maynooth.'

'Maynooth, no less! Doesn't it take money to get into Maynooth?'

'It does.'

'And who's goin' to do the payin'?'

'He didn't say.'

'Believe me, he didn't. Not on his nanny! And what did he say about Josie?' the father asked with cunning casualness.

'He said nothing.'

'I suppose he thinks I should have brought ye all up to be lords and ladies, educated in the height of fashion, not to be shop girls,' he accused wildly. There was a desperation in his stabbing questions, the frustration of knowing that he had been talked about in his absence. He had been discussed and judged when he was helpless. Nothing he could ever do or say again would entirely displace this idea of him that had been shared.

'I suppose he thinks I didn't do right be ye,' he shouted.

'He didn't say what he thought,' Francie said.

'No. I'm sure he didn't say what he thought. He's too clever by far for that.' His face was heated, the lines of the mouth moving, his eyes tired and hunted. He brought up his old boots that were wet from driving the cows through the rushes and put them by the fire. The heat was bad for the leather but he had to have them dry for the morning. Then he took off his light Sunday boots and stood on the cement in his stockinged feet. The red flames of the fire gave as much light as the small glass lamp on the sill. Everything was still and calm in the late hour except the aging man.

'It's not what he says counts: it's what he thinks,' he shouted. 'Don't listen to what they say if you ever want to get on in this world, find out what they think; what's goin' on in those numbskulls of theirs, that's what'll get you on.'

'Think what you say, but don't say what you think,' he shouted angrily. 'Then you have some chance! But what do I care what they think? They can think themselves into the Sligo madhouse for all I care; think till they burst, burst I tell you!'

This ranting exhausted him. He seemed as he often did now, suddenly tired and old. Mechanically he combed his fingers through his hair.

'I've a splittin' pain in me head,' he said. 'Say yeer own prayers tonight. I'm in no form for givin' them out. Go to yeer bed soon and don't forget to quench the lamp.' The whisper of his heavy wool socks was loud in the stillness of the kitchen as he walked across the cement to the door. Over and over again Francie heard him mutter the same words as if they held some hidden poetry or magic:

'Think what you say, but don't say what you think. Think, say; say, think. Think what you say, but don't say what you think.'

DANNIE ABSE

The Magician

Off stage, the Great Illusionist owns bad teeth,
cheats at cards, beats his second wife, is lewd;
before studying his art he qualified
      as obsessional liar, petty thief.

Transformed by glamorous paraphernalia—
tall top hat, made up face, four smoking spotlights—
only fellow magicians can sense beneath
      that glossy surface a human failure.

Ready with unseen wires, luminous paint,
with drums and ceremony he fills the stage,
rich twice nightly in his full regalia.
      Two extras planted in the audience faint.

Allezup! Closes his eyes, seemingly bored,
and astutely fakes a vulgar miracle,
mutters and reclines to become fakir, saint,
      on a hotbed of nails, swallows a sword.

For encore will saw a seedy blonde in half
a music spirals to a shrill crescendo;
now hacks through wood, skin, vertebrae, spinal cord,
      and all except the gods applaud and laugh.

Lord, red blood oozes from the long black box,
oh hocus pocus, oh abracadabra,
whilst, in trumped up panic, manager and staff
      race breathlessly on stage, undo the locks.

Patrons prefer bisected blondes to disappear.
Relieved, commercial men and their average wives
now salaciously prepare for further shocks,
      eagerly yearn to see what they most fear.

Now and then, something he cannot understand
happens—atavistic powers stray unleashed,
a raving voice he hardly thought to hear,
      the ventriloquist's dummy out of hand.

In the box a vision of himself—and on
those masochistic nails fresh genuine blood,
within his white glove a decomposing hand
    and, unimaginably, his own face gone.

Quite disturbed, the disconnected audience boo.
What cheek! This charlatan believes his magic:
not luminous paint across the darkness shone
    when happily, for once, his lies came true.

Or so it seemed. Oh what overbearing pride
if no longer fake but Great Illusionist;
yet, as phoney critics pierce him through and through,
    he begs for mercy and is justified.

Off stage, that Great Illusionist owns bad teeth,
cheats at cards, beats his second wife, is lewd;
before studying his art he qualified
    as obsessional liar, petty thief.

ANTHONY CRONIN
Getting Wurred In

There was nobody in the office, so I sat down and read some letters. I had a clear vision of what Prunshios McGonaghy would be like from the tweedy, marxist novels about peasants and fishermen I remembered, and when eventually there were footsteps on the stairs and the door was thrust open he was exactly as I had imagined him: a huge, grey, lean and fevered man, dressed all in black like an Irish politician of the old school. He came into the tiny office like a man about to address a meeting in a draughty hall, a meeting of insubordinate supporters, a man who was late, earnest and angry, his hands thrust in the pockets of his long, black frieze coat; took off the wide-brimmed, black hat which is the standard uniform of the patriotic man of letters in Ireland, and flung himself into a chair, abandoning his air of stern haste for one of tired greatness, weariness and contempt.

'Good morning,' I said.

'Good morning be dommed. What the hell is the motter with all you young men?'

I found no reply. There was so much the matter with me and so much of it unbelievable: troubles of the heart and of conscience, ills of the flesh, the poverty of the grave.

He pulled open two or three drawers, swept some papers impatiently to the floor, retrieved what I recognised immediately from its awful condition as my manuscript and flung it on the desk. 'I don't feel the fresh wund of your mind blowing through this,' he said.

'The fresh what?' I ventured in unaffected anxiety.

'The fresh wund. The fresh, free gale of your mind is not blowing in this. It's not forward looking.' He glared at me. 'Are you wurred in?' he demanded.

'Wurred what?' I said, though I meant it the other way round.

'Wurred in—wurred in to life. None of you young fellas are wurred in to life. Where do you live?'

I told him. In a converted tool-shed at the bottom of somebody's garden, in company with a floating population who begged in the same pub and who, whatever else they were, were certainly not wurred in.

He snorted, 'Tick, tick,' he said. 'How do you expect to know anything about the movements of the dialoctic in a place like that? It's appalling, nothing short of appalling. If it were the slums now.. . . .' He snapped his jaws shut. 'Get out of there immediately,' he said 'and get a room in a slum.'

'But,' I said innocently, 'It is a slum.'

'It's the wrong kind of slum,' he roared. 'Ye'll not have yer finger on the pulse of the people in a place like that.'

I tried to explain that I actually spent very little time in the place, what with begging in the pub, reading in the National Library and other activities.

'Matter a domm,' he shouted. 'It's as plain as the nose on yer face that yer not . . .' He sought for a metaphor. I was to realise in time that his stock was limited. His eye fell on the telephone. He picked it up, base and all, and held it aloft. 'Yer not wurred in,' he declared triumphantly. At that instant, held up at arm's length as it was, the instrument began to ring. He slammed it down on the desk and scowled at it ferociously; then, making no effort to answer it, he picked up his patriotic hat and strode impatiently to the door, gesturing me to follow.

'We'll talk in the coffay' he declared, glaring at the telephone, 'about being wurred in.'

In the coffay, a monstrous, gilded place over a cinema, he was a changed man, flirting with elderly waitresses, saluting parish priests jovially, ordering a revolting plate of cakes for me as if I were a favourite nephew out on a treat, laughing with his teeth at his own jokes.

Suddenly he became serious. 'Ye must objectivise the situation,' he said. 'Ye must learn to see it as part of the historical process. I want to feel the cutting edge of your mind on your problems.'

The cutting edge of my mind had in fact long since given up my problems in despair and nowadays it confined itself to making faint gnashing noises in the middle of the night, but I forebore.

'I want to feel from your writing that you feel you're part of the dialoctic process. I'm going to rescue you. I'm going to rescue you. I'm going to make you a part of the main stream of Irish life, so that your mind will become as infollible a guide to the forward-looking elements in the prosent, historical, dialoctic situation as . . . as MacMurkagaun's,' he concluded, naming a minor peasant novelist of the day. He paused, flung out an arm and seized a passing parish-priest. Was mother Church to be enlisted to aid this project? I wondered, but it was only an exchange of pleasantries of the cloth, lay and clerical, dialoctic and theological, and of tips for the dogs at Harold's Cross. 'Ond we're winning in Korea,' he shouted, pumping the reverend gentleman's hand in farewell, swung back to me and demanded: 'Are ye wulling to consider it if I can arrange it with—?' He named a politico known to have cultural aspirations.

I did not know quite what I was supposed to consider and visions of varying probability came to me. He had, I knew, a lot of friends in high places, old republican comrades through whom he shared in the proceeds of certain of the smaller state monopolies: sweeptickets, clay-pipes, horn rosary-beads, shamrock for Americans. Cousins had given me the general picture. Was I to be made a director of one of these enterprises? Or was I, more likely, to be offered a hazardous and minor post, to be asked for example to smuggle sweep-tickets into England, to spend my life making endless return trips on the Liverpool boat, amid the smell of puke and porter, and the strains of Galway Bay? Surely not, I thought, on reflection; we are, after all, men of letters, and the main stream must be a literary matter. He is going to give me a contract for articles on emigration, inshore fishery, re-afforestation, rural depopulation, housing conditions. I could see my days passing in a miasma of misinformation, a damp fog of inaccurate and out-of-date statistics. But Prunshios banged the table so that the cutlery jumped, the waitresses glared and about forty parish priests turned warning glances in our direction.

'The key to the whole matter,' he shouted, 'is in the rubbish-baskets.'

'The rubbish-baskets?' I queried with that look of intelligent anticipation which is the stock-in-trade of aspiring subordinates. He became confidential.

'Do you realise thot there are twenty thousand rubbish-baskets affixed to lomposts in the coty of Dublin?'

'Twenty thousand!' I breathed in admiration, but still in the dark.

'Twenty thousand,' he repeated emphatically. 'And overy one of them can be a window for the forward-looking mind. Twenty thousand at ten and sixpence is eighteen thousand. . . .' His lips moved in a silent rapture of calculation, while I gazed at him across the cups, his empty for the third or fourth time, mine still full to the brim with the bedraggled remains of a cigarette afloat in the cream.

He outlined his plan. It appeared that there really were twenty thousand rubbish baskets affixed to lampposts in the city of Dublin; that his friend the politico, then serving a routine term of office as Lord Mayor had, as a gesture to Irish literature, offered him an exclusive right to the letting of advertising space on these baskets, the proceeds to be devoted to the expansion and resuscitation of the *Trumpet*; that I was to be the principal agent of this renaissance; that, in short, I was being offered the post of editor.

The fatal step is taken because we are hypnotised and weak; rarely, if ever, because we are really the victims of force or circumstance. Prunshios was waving a roll of tenners the size of a bookmaker's ransom in the air, my eyes, the eyes of the parish-priests and the eyes of the waitresses following every oscillation. He peeled off a tenner. 'Here's a month's salary in advance,' he said. 'Ye'll need to buy a few things and get a room for yourself. Here lassie, give us the bill and congratulate this yong fella on the future.' He hurled back his chair.

'Don't stir, don't stir. Finish yer cakes. Finish yer cakes.'

He advanced towards the cash-desk in a whirl of activity, frieze coat, fistful of tenners, patriotic hat and slaps on the back for chosen parish-priests all flying about.

At the swing-doors he turned. 'Get a room in a slum,' he shouted. 'A real slum. Get wurred in.'

He was gone and I was an editor, a wage-slave once more: the richer by a tenner it was true, but an editor nonetheless. I sat alone among the somnolent clergy, brooding on the awful fact, while the heel of my cigarette luxuriated in the cream.

And being an editor with Prunshios was not, on the whole, pleasant, though it had, I suppose, its consolations. For one thing we rarely saw each other since he spent most of his time in various coffays, all rather similar, always surrounded by droves of parish priests. Sometimes I would be summoned to one of these establishments and would sit there silently while he discussed whether I was more or less wired in than last time. The light of desperation was clearly in his eye, but this seemed to increase his generosity rather than diminish it and though my wage would have put most of the more salubrious slums out of reach, a tenner was the recognised reward for an editorial conference in a coffay.

The *Trumpet* had been a smart literary and sociological magazine during the war, when it had been edited by a peasant historian rather more sophisticated than Prunshios, and when Ireland itself had been the home of flourishing artistic movements. It had carried a deal of documentary reportage and statistics about fishing as well as poems like abbatoirs, full of bones and sinews and thighs and hearts, and jerky short-stories about unevenly articulate peasants whose utterances varied from monosyllabic grunts to phrases like, 'when you shook out the bright scarf of your laughter'.

It had not thrived under Prunshios. For one thing with the end of the war the cattle-boats had been crammed with departing writers, standing knee-deep amid the puke and porter, quietly forgetting about O'Flaherty and O'Faolain and rehearsing their line on Connolly, Kierkegaard, Kafka and Scotty Wilson. For another, he lacked, let's face it, the flair. He had perhaps too many things on his mind, what with the dialoctic, dog-racing on alternate nights at Harold's Cross and Shelborne Park, shadowy creditors preventing his attendance at the office and former republican comrades outstripping him in the minor monopolies racket, while he clung with a strange and chivalrous obstinacy, to his out-moded and ever more confused marxist opinions. Cousins alleged darkly that his only interest in the continued existence of the *Trumpet* was so that hollowed-out bundles of it could be used to smuggle sweep-tickets into England, but even for this some sort of circulation was necessary, and it was when the circulation was falling to practically nothing barring the mythical hundreds for whom the hollow copies were destined that I was called in, having been recommended by Cousins as an up and coming young man. But besides the danger to the smuggling trade Prunshios was quite genuinely, like many who have long since abandoned composition themselves, motivated by a desire for a movement. And also there was the Lord Mayor, a man of similarly confused opinions, presumably expecting great things to come of his rubbish-baskets.

Prunshios would summon me to a coffay and make the most impossible demands about the availability of the so-called young.

'Have ye found the seeds yet?' he would shout, as if I had mislaid them somewhere. Then he would mix the metaphor. 'If you let the fresh wund of your mind blow through the *Trumpet* ye'll find the seeds springing up everywhere.' 'You can bring great things to birth,' he would declare, but his eye had begun to wander uneasily.

The only young writers I knew were Japanese and American rentiers who commuted between Dublin and Paris. Sometimes they abandoned a girl in Dublin, to be devoured by the girl-hungry locals; occasionally they could be touched for small sums; but their knowledge of peasants and fishermen was limited to the Japanese or Californian variety and their writing could scarcely be called constructive, so Prunshios rejected their contributions indignantly.

In quiet desperation I made an inventory of all the native writers remaining in the country. I found that these were almost without exception employed in the radio-station, a large and gloomy building in the principal street, where they occupied positions varying in importance from that of doorkeeper to that of director, depending on the number of novels they had published and the orthodoxy of their religious views. I consulted a friend of mine, an atheist who had once written a short-story and who now had a permanent and pensionable post in the radio-station as a lavatory attendant. After some consideration he arranged a meeting in a pub for me with a dramatist who had once had a one-act play performed in the Abbey but who had signed a letter of protest when a schoolteacher of mildly heretical views had been stoned to death by a mob urged on by the Bishop of Ballyhamnis. This man had some sort of a job on the roof of the radio-station, something to do with the flag poles, I think, or the lightning conductors, in any case he was up there in all weathers and it seemed to drain him of his talents, and though he offered to introduce me to the Protestant essayist who, he said, operated the ventilating system, or was perhaps assistant to the operator of the ventilating system, the whole thing came to nothing. And though in the later, wearier days at least I would gladly have filled the whole magazine with the flag-pole man, the lavatory attendant and the assistant to the ventilating man, they exhibited, in fact, a marked reluctance to write, perhaps fearing promotion, for near the top competition was said to be especially keen, and a man had to attend mass on weekdays and publish at least one peasant novel every four years if he was to keep his job.

They remained, in solitary crane-like eminence among the natives, my friend Mahaffey, a poet and indubitably a genius, a gambler and therefore, perennially short of cash. He expressed himself as willing to turn himself into a movement or anything else if Prunshios would pay him enough; but, willing though he was, his prose, for some strange reason apparently outside his control, always took the form of savage attacks on Prunshios and other peasant novelists. Frequently articles on inshore fishery turned, by some odd process or other, into satirical stories about a character called MacMurkagaun, an all too thinly disguised version of an intimate friend of Prunshios's. If these had simply confined themselves to the so-called MacMurkagaun's sexual proclivities I would have risked it, but since they were concerned to the point of monotony with the fact that the so-called MacMurkagaun had no sexual proclivities at all and was only pretending to have because he considered it essential for a Catholic novelist influenced by Mauriac to wallow in an orgy of sin and remorse, I dared not. One morning, however, when, by a miracle, both Prunshios and I were in the office together, Mahaffey arrived and flinging a gargantuan manuscript on the desk, announced that he had 'done it at last'. A glance at the object showed me that it was a mildly charming pastoral concerning rural life in Cavan about eighty years before, and something in the incredibly aged and tattered appearance of the manuscript also aroused my suspicions; but since McGonaghy was already striding about the office with such words as 'stark', 'forward-looking' and 'dialoctic' on his lips, I held my peace. Later I was to elicit that the novel in question had in fact been written by Mahaffey's maternal uncle, who had been a democratic senator for Wisconsin about fifty years before, and that the manuscript was a sort of family heirloom. By this time however large chunks of it were appearing in the *Trumpet*, giving it, in Prunshios's fevered imagination at least, the proper forward-looking air for several months, the while he informed the reverend gentlemen in the coffays and his friend and patron on the corporation that Mahaffey had 'done it at last'.

Spring became summer. The tulips and the girls flowered in Stephen's Green; the sunlight reached into the furthest corners of the pubs, revealing figures that had slumbered there unnoticed through the long winter. Twilight would come gently to Grafton Street; the summer darkness arrived with closing time and afterwards the bona fides blazed on the mountains; the noise of strong men swearing eternal fealty and eternal enmity being heard in the deserted city like the rumour of a hostile army, the back-slapping like small-arms fire in the larger noise. At ten o'clock the cars swept out along the mountain roads as if all those who could muster transport were fleeing before a plague; at half-past twelve they swept back, awash with song and Guinness, as if the defences of Dublin had suddenly crumbled before a mechanised, drunken horde; and from then till dawn the noise of breaking glass, of splintering wood and cracking skulls would float out over the warm and star-dappled waters of the bay.

But I had no zest for the delights of summer. Though outward bound and inward bound I would cling precariously to fender and running board, or be squashed high near the roof on the outward run and trampled under foot on the return, the responsibilities of editorship were weighing me down. Maddened by the dialoctic, goaded into frenzied action in the coffays by a sudden onset of creditors, a mass seizure of sweep-tickets by the English police or an outburst of hooliganism involving the defacement of large quantities of rubbish baskets, Prunshios raved and gnashed about inshore fishery or the necessity to convert potatoes into electricity. A scheme for paving the streets of Dublin with sods of turf obsessed him and he insisted on writing editorials about it, printing them cheek by jowl with articles on Heidegger by the Japanese and a controversy about Jansenism which his friends from the radio-station, concerned as always with degrees of orthodoxy, were somehow conducting in our columns. The editor of *Furthest Horizons*, the highbrow magazine in whose pages I had formerly appeared, shouted rude jokes about carrigeen moss and dried herrings at me as he drove past with the Japanese and their girls in his large American car; acquaintances who knew me only in my other persona murmured audibly about articles entitled 'Cork Literature: Is It Dead?' or 'The Genius of Sean MacMurkagaun'. I was under pressure from all fronts. I was breaking up and I knew it. I sat so long in the coffays that I had taken to drinking the stuff and was suffering, as I now see, from an advanced form of what the Americans have since diagnosed as coffee-nerves; a little more and I might have become the founder of the hop-head school, seen visions, declared myself if not positively God, at least a minor prophet, but even that was denied me. Prunshios had taken to consorting with a new peasant writer, an enormous oaf with sea-boots, a Kerry accent and a pioneer pin and I was subjected to his diagnoses also in the coffays where we made a curious trio, two all tweed and extroversion, myself giving more and more point to their repeatedly expressed warnings about the dangers of subjectivity. I did not mind printing this sycophant, indeed at that stage I did not mind printing anybody, but I objected to his accent, his conversation and his sneers. At length I ceased to take any part in the discussions, but I had to sit there while they shook their heads over me and mouthed about the dialoctic. I could see this fellow was after my job.

One day at the end of summer, when the leaves had fallen in Baggot Street and the girls had disappeared from Stephen's Green, Prunshios summoned me to the most palatial of his coffays, ordered me a plate of cakes and pronounced my doom.

'A mon of your talents is wasted as an oditor,' he declared with conviction. 'The place for a poet is with the masses. Yer too sheltered. Ye should let the fresh wund of yer mind blow on something else. Immerse yerself in the dialoctic. Take a close look at the life of the people. Do you know what the forward-looking elements are doing at the moment? They're omigrating. It's a necessary part of the historical process. Go to England. Go to England,' he shouted, so loudly that a parish-priest woke up at a neighbouring table and an elderly waitress looked at us with nun-like disapproval.

He pulled out his wad and peeled off four tenners. 'Go to England and live in a doss-house. The prosent dialoctical situation con only be understood in the doss-houses of London.'

He grabbed his hat and his bill. 'Finish yer cakes. Finish yer cakes,' he cried, working his way to the door, slapping elderly clerics absent-mindedly on the shoulders. At the desk he turned.

'Trust yerself to the dialoctic,' he cried, his hat in the air. 'Go to England and live in a doss-house . . .'

Extract from *The Life of Riley*: a Work in Progress.

STEVIE SMITH

Thoughts about the Muse

My Muse sits forlorn
She wishes she had not been born
She sits in the cold
No word she says is ever told.

O Lord incline my worldly ear to hear
The patient mumblings of th' unearthly Muse
For what the trivial gold, the social pause,
These must I also lose if her I lose.
Lord, make me listen, and make her not proud
But speak her thoughts out plain and speak them loud.

Why does my Muse only speak when she is unhappy?
She does not. I only listen when I am unhappy.
When I am happy I live and despise writing
For my Muse this can not but be dispiriting.

VERNON WATKINS

Poem for Conrad

My brothers are just out of eyeshot, conspiring against me.
Let me crawl and surprise them.
What's for me, in this house of their gains?
My sister lies out on the lawn, a pattern of patience.
She lies on a rug, a rug I intend to cross.
But my brothers are plotting, plotting. Their gain is my loss.
They are quick to count chocolate money, and then to eat it,
And they quarrel over their trains.
They are never content to hold nothing, or to divide
Their spoils. They do not lie down; or not for long.
They deal in extreme situations:
The door must be dangerous, bushes are places to hide.
One of them dresses up in feathers
And the other crouches,
Endlessly running wheels over floorboards and carpet
And chanting to make them go.

The third comes in, in his hands a fledgling.
He is gone again, and they are gone after him
To watch it. Now there is nothing
But clumsy furniture.
                Is it enough,
Enough, with extended arms, to master this floor?
I can, and will stand up.
I, too, can walk,
Unsteadily, but in one direction,
Between the wall and the door,
Towards the shouts in the garden.

I saw nothing, but a crane has carried me in.
I am here again, and Dylan is jumping before me.
I laugh, and the louder I laugh, the higher he jumps,
First from the chair, then the table,
His feet crashing, the table's legs giving way.
I bang my cymbals, and one rolls away. He is rushing
At the wall. Chairs are behind him,
And now he is under the chairs, and he throws them up
With balls, dominoes, toys, and the tower of bricks
Falls. The crash and his laughter have made me fall over.

It is wonderful here, but suddenly comes the word *No*,
And it all comes to rest, the see-saw in dancing walls,
And the feathers fallen.

I brush against dark cloth, caught up by a hand.
Snatched up to a shoulder's height,
I am told we are going to the sea.
Now, on the prickly path,
I remember something unpleasant,
The sea interfering with my enjoyment of sand.
They are talking under me, someone banging the gate
Behind us. All is blue in the air I am riding.
There are my brothers, laughing and running ahead,
And a voice behind
Saying: 'Whales have the sea,
And sea-lions, balancing balls, have perfect control;
But that house, those walls were not built to contain the exuberance
Of the performer. Let him loose
And if he continued long enough

His triumph would be complete. This would be said:
"In amusing his brother he destroyed the house." '

On the Margin

An incident last winter which involved a poet published in this magazine and the Poetry Book Society highlighted once again the problem of art patronage through committee. [No need to go back to Ez Pound for a lesson in this dismal business.] In the case we refer to, Brian Higgins forfeited the Poetry Book Society Choice through the fears of the committee that his work might involve the Society in legal action. Significantly enough his publisher was less worried on such grounds. It is a notorious fact that the moment help for artists passes into the hands of bureaucrats the character of the patronage becomes mean and vitiated. In our day when taxation and other difficulties make it hard for individuals to act as once the great patrons of Europe did it is a most unfortunate affair that the efforts of the State to replace such patronage should be so futile. Art patronage IS an essential social factor if there is to be a living continuous tradition of letters, painting, etc. The problem remains how this patronage can be so organised, if organised it must be, in a way that will ensure the best men are not the victims instead of the beneficiaries of the system. It may well be that there is no substitute for enlightened private patronage. From the artist's point of view this is by far the most satisfactory kind. The sort of easy relationship—easy that is when compared with the form filling roundabouts of the committees—that is set up between a man who gives help to an individual because he likes and believes in his work is really a form of friendship which the committee by its nature is incapable of. There is a feeling of profound gloom, not to say indignity, for an artist when he finds himself seated before a table full of rich and cultured do-gooders and is asked or perhaps told how much and whatever he is worth socio-financially speaking. One eminent English painter was actually rebuked for smoking 'Senior Service' by a lady secretary of an institution whose function is to help painters. While abroad, a poet of recognized importance was kept waiting a dreary and unmannerly half hour (under the gaze of his own photograph!) to satisfy some bureaucratic if unwritten law that we all must suffer, when he called at the offices of a government body whose job is to foster British culture in foreign countries. He had come to inquire about a professor who had tried to contact him through this body, and was told it was not an information bureau. A theatre company, however serious or acclaimed, cannot avail itself of the financial support officially held out unless it complies with rules that exclude the activities of those who are prepared to give their time and talent unpaid to experimental work, but are not either 'amateur' nor registered non-profit-making companies. In short the inability of a committee to make an exception, because it must work to rule—no one man being finally responsible—and its incapacity to accommodate the individual dilemma (there being no individual responsibilities) almost totally rules out its usefulness to those who really make art and need help, for these are invariably the exceptional and individual. These cases, mentioned merely in passing and to show how the system even in its details is monstrously unsuited to its function and purpose, do no more than pin-point a difficulty which, so far as we are aware, nothing at all is being done to rectify. Strangely enough the Arts Council's report proves on reading to be a very reasonable document. And in spite of the fact that there is and will be a lot of grumbling about the amount spent we do not think that this is the problem that really needs tackling. It is how this money is used that needs attention—both to whom it goes and the manner of its distribution. It should be possible to devise a means of helping poets and painters so that not only the *acceptable* get some share. This might mean a slight shift in emphasis from the view that holds that audiences should be subsidised to one that says subsidise what brings money to the artist.

Patrick Swift

VI

MALCOLM LOWRY

Be Patient for the Wolf

Be patient for the wolf is always with you.
Listen, little idiot, for the sound of your desire;
Do not be deceived it is not the sea,
The wolf is madness but the moon is light.
God will come out of such ignorance as this,
Not like a jack-in-the-box but like a tree
Turned weeping father in delirium.
The woes of night all have their tragic place,
Half the face of God seeks half its face.
And He will find your genius in the dark
And give it back without a bondsman.

Be patient for the wolf is ever with you,
Ugly and wicked one and yet divine.
Forget the shrieking of the sea
The contemptuous sea curling its lip all day,
Strident as factories of shattering glass.
Pass by the sleek unvintageable sea
For those who drink her deepest are the drowned.
The black snow is piled high under the clock
Where broken tryst meets broken heart in time.
This is a world of worthless mysteries.
Be patient for much much is patient.

Be patient for the wolf is patient,
Whose small shadow has stopped here.
The meadows wait for rainbows to say God,
The shadows wait for you to say the word,
Two pillows look to love to save the world.
The moonlit collier reels at a foul anchor.
The charter waits: the ship freezes in the fjord.
The angel waits: his heart an aching hand
To win you from us to the evening land

Where no one ravens but where things are made,
And where no wolf is nor no thought of flood.

Be patient because the wolf is patient.
The redbreast waits for redress from the dark,
The swallow pines for autumn to say now,
And Echo, for Hero not to reply no.
Only the bell that follows does not wait
Galloping mother-faced across the fields
To abrase you to the bone with a rough chime.
At the beginning of the inferno, in the middle
Of the wood, the image teeters between mother and sea.
Pay no heed to the bell nor to the aged sea
But to the dear kind wolf pay allegiance.

Be patient, because of the wolf, be patient:
The squeaks and woes of night all have their place.
You'll find your blood warm cave and rest at last;
The shadows wait for you to say the word.
Listen now to your own soft cunning step.
Be patient, because of the wolf, be patient—
His step is your own now, you are free, being bereft.

Delirium in Vera Cruz

Where has tenderness gone, he asked the mirror
Of the Biltmore Hotel, cuarto 216. Alas,
Can its reflection lean against the glass
Too, wondering where I have gone, into what horror?
Is that it staring at me now with terror
Behind your frail tilted barrier? Tenderness
Was here, in this very bedroom, in this
Place, its form seen, cries heard, by you. What error
Is here? Am I that rashed image?
Is this the ghost of the love you reflected?
Now with a background of tequila, stubs, dirty collars,
Sodium perborate, and a scrawled page
To the dead, telephone off the hook? In rage
He smashed all the glass in the room. (Bill: $50.)

Reading Don Quixote

A child, I thought summer would solve all things,
But this illusion passed with unseen springs.
The flowers that bloomed at home were dead at school,
And youth was born to die in Liverpool,
Or in Sierra Leone, with the shakes.
The yearning reappeared as spring in books,
The poem read in drugstore magazines,
Half understood—the glass holds what it means—
Then vanished with girls who never turned round,
Fled palette faces sucked into the ground.
The sea came then, cobalt or whisky brown,
The disused longing settled on a town
Always far, and by a different name,
Archangel, Surabaya, or Tlampam . . .
And then I saw that death was all my search,
But reigned up on the threshold of the church,
Angry with hope that one secular dawn
Would bring with it at last enlightened scorn.
Yet for all this I am still at suckle:
The tavern is centre of my circle.

Art and Morality

Prefatory Note

The short answer to the question of the relation of art to morality may strike the speculative mind as being: *none*. Even the most socially responsible of theorisers in this field will admit that making a work of art involves a leap into the unknown which of its nature is incompatible with a systematic morality or a properly observed orthodoxy. Yet any speculation on this subject will have to take account of the curious phenomenon that the poet as often as not turns out on examination to have been ridden by a moral vision, and conversely the great philosopher-ethicist haunted by the Muses. Let us say Dante and Augustine supply two accessible cases. Mr Barker's article remarks on this and among other things strikingly presents the paradoxical apposition of these manifestations of the human mind. It is obvious that the liberal rationalist is going to have a hard time with Dante, who leaves little room for equivocation: 'The purpose of the whole and of this part [i.e., the *Paradiso*] is to remove those who are living in this life from the state of wretchedness, and to lead them to the state of blessedness,' he wrote of the *Divine Comedy*. Mr Cronin in his essay has examined the dilemma which faces the reader of any poetry—how far must he accept the beliefs of the poet? is it necessary to share them to enjoy the work? One might equally ask to what extent the poetic quality of, say, Kierkegaard's prose—i.e. its artistic precision of fact and observation—inclines us to accept his moral imperatives. And it would not be a far leap to question the extent to which our reaction to a work of art is conditioned by the philosophical context, the particular orthodoxy from which we look at it. That is, quite apart from the question of sharing the artist's beliefs, how far are we open to receive the full meaning of the work at all, to what extent are we blinded by the moral prejudices we share (whether liberal-rational or religious and mystical)? Mr Swift takes a fair example of this sort of blindness which expresses itself in fear and results in an attempt to twist the true significance of a work so that it will fit in with the prejudices of the particular orthodoxy involved. For it becomes clear that the whole activity of making art is conditioned, whatever its exact philosophical relationship, by the morality which reigns where it is made. Aquinas is as relevant to Dante as Adams to Pound. And more, the actual social climate created by the dominant moralismus is a factor of real importance: at present, as Mr Sisson concludes from his analysis, we are hag-ridden by the *morality of work*, which is something even worse that the horrible spectre of the consumer-society Miss Hanna Arendt worries about. Endemic realities of the human animal's very nature are involved, and one of these is the innate ambivalence of our attitude to the artistic imagination. What Mr Kavanagh calls the desire to beat the artistic rap. Something which relates closely to Mr Sisson's remark about the social necessity now felt to put poets to work in culture factories.

In the essays which follow the reader need not expect the old ground of social commitment or of existentialist responsibility to be gone over yet again. When Nietzsche saw his devil he found him earnest, thorough, deep and solemn, and the reader should not be surprised or misled by the fact that he will find no ponderable social advice in this anthology of viewpoints. In a way these articles are tangential to the subject but perhaps the better for that. It has been said: 'Decadent art demands salvation, great art expresses gratitude.' The value of systematic speculation applied to art was well demonstrated by Sartre in his book on Baudelaire where he totally failed to comprehend the tragic nature of the poet's fate. Apart from the monstrous proposition that a man is the sum of his actions it is the more serious confusion of art with religion which explains the trouble in this field of thought to-day. In particular the liberal rationalist finds himself tempted to look to art for what he has lost through his rejection of religion, i.e. salvation. What emerges then is a form of moralismus which leaves us worse off than Voltaire found us. And who will deliver us from that sort of pedantic tyranny?

The Hippogryph and the Water-Pistol

The marriage of Art and Morality can only be celebrated in Church.

If there were a sphere exclusive to the operations of the poet a morality could conceivably be constructed upon it. Since, however, everywhere is the sphere proper to these operations, the moral construction is already part and parcel of it. A poem without a bit of morality stuck in its tooth would be a poem without teeth.

The moral conscience of the poet can properly be compared only with the tin can tied to a dog's tail. It warns us that he is around, but it also prevents him from taking us by surprise. Whenever I hear the word Browning I reach for my culture.

An act to which there were no moral consequences is as inconceivable as an act without any consequences at all and this is a contradiction in terms—because an act is a thing that has results. The principal moral consequence of writing a poem is that thenceforth at least one person knows more about himself than he did before, and at most that several people do so.

But the pragmatism of a poem, like the pragmatism of women, works in a very roundabout manner. Thus a poem ostensibly written to show the horrors of war may in truth speak more clearly about the digestive organs of the Upas Tree or about Palladian architecture. Just as a metaphor may become so top heavy as to illustrate not the subject or instance but the analogy or likeness. Poems are extremely disobedient.

When you are dealing with a Hippogryph it is very misguided to use a fishing line and a water pistol. But even these instruments are better than the Decalogue.

Because Society has violated its own conscience so outrageously in the last century or so, it is convinced of the existence of panaceas. But it is precisely those sensibilities which might prove susceptible to such panaceas that society has outraged. At this point one calls in the poet and demands a diagnosis—to call in the priest would be too much like a death bed conversion, or an admission of the Divine Right of Despair.

The diagnosis of the poet in the matter of moral disease would resemble the judgement of a streptococcus upon a spirochaete. The man who has committed suicide is not necessarily the best man to consult about getting rid of graveyards. But if you have a taste for eavesdropping upon the dead then you might learn a little about life from them. It is impossible to know more about life than the dead know, but it is very hard to understand their language.

A poem composed of direct moral judgements would not be a poem because of that but in spite of that. If a Roman Catholic were to read the *Divine Comedy* for its theology he would cease to be a Roman Catholic and become a Quaker listening to another Quaker's speculations upon the Inner Light. Either God speaks or man speaks. It is extremely unlikely that they would both say the same thing.

The only morality that the poet can pursue without expedientality is to speak the truth as he sees it. Here the word truth means whatever he sees, because most of the time most of us are blindfold. But the advocation of a specific or categorical morality operates in direct contradiction to the poetic principle, which is anarchic, neutral and entirely unreliable. Even Wordsworth sometimes changed his singing robes.

For in an act of exploration the navigator does not decline to put in at the wrong islands—he merely calls them by the wrong names. Thus the poet, in the pursuit of a moral paradise, may sometimes come upon such places as the Bay of Noble Conception or the Archipelago of Partial Sanctity, etc. But he does not often discover the Indias of Absolute Revelation he is after.

Perhaps it is even sillier to ask the poet to establish a system of terrestrial morality than to ask the moralist to write poems. But since a morality is a convenience and a poem a luxury, perhaps the best thing of all to do is to stay in bed and repeat quietly to oneself: 'Ama, et fac quod vis.'

The energy of the imagination cannot be anything but hedonistic, consequently any ethic evolved by the imagination will be full of delight, even in its cruellest propositions.

The idea of the imagination in the service of political or even ethical institutions is like harnessing an albatross to a Henderson tractor. It looks nice, it makes everyone think something marvellous has happened, but it is very harmful to the albatross. The albatross is supposed to be shot to death by Coleridges, not shaken to death by conceptual machinery.

Great moralists are among the most poetic of human creatures, just as great poets are among the most moral of them. Rousseau and Alighieri, Penn and Milton, etc. [Think this remark may be true in spite of its demonstrable untruth.]

What is impossible is *not* to get the poet to engage in moral commitments but to get him to disengage himself from them. It would be as easy to forbid him the use of the five vowels as to preclude him from moral speculation. What is wrong is to expect him to believe in the validity of these speculations longer than the duration of poetic composition. All poems are lies, but they are lies native to a country in which the truth does not conclusively exist. *Paradise Lost* is just as morally responsible as *The Waste Land*, but not more so. Because the moral objective of the poem is not the Truth, in its intellectual connotation; it is the valid, in its imaginative connotation. Ripeness is not all. But it was at that moment.

A morality is either a convenient piece of intellectual machinery invented to facilitate our living with or without one another, or it is a necessity arising from the divine dissatisfaction of a creature born without wings. And it can, of course, be both at the same time. But whatever it is, it is cast in the grammar of the imperative, and this is anathema to the imagination just as it is panacea to the intellect. Thus the imagination is permitted to address us in the imperative but we are not permitted so to address it. Moralities simply infuriate the imagination. The imagination simply infuriates us.

Before you decide on a code of behaviour you have to decide why you behave as you do. Or: a morality is evolved because we have an inclination to do certain things and not because it is absolutely authentic. We have certain faculties with which to evolve a morality, or certain faculties with which to apprehend it. In either case we may be misunderstanding the nature of our own faculties, and thus interpreting wrongly what, for us, could never be interpreted rightly. At this juncture only the intervention of the imagination can save us—we have to guess what the god meant when he rendered the vision of a morality even so remotely perceptible. My guess: a crucifixion without a crucifix.

The joy with which an animal that is not naturally masochistic can cast whole cartloads of broken glass ahead of its progress is a joy which arises from its having firstly the cart and secondly the broken bottles. What else is there to do with the spiked railings around the gardens of the ideal save climb them? One can get in. Can one get out?

It seems, sometimes, to certain intrepid minds, that it is better to commit great crimes than to conform to admirable moralities for the reason that the corpses of such minds, hanging from their misdeeds, like magpies from branches, may warn others away from these dangerous places. Is their morality therefore inferior to that of those who do not die? Thus suicides cut their throats in order to prove to themselves that death is in truth total.

DIALOGUE BETWEEN A MORAL PHILOSOPHER AND AN AMORAL POET

M.P. What are you doing out there among so many ferocious temptations?

A.P. Excuse me, out where? This is the human heart I'm in. What are you doing out there among so many ferocious expedients?

M.P. Excuse *me*, this is the human mind I'm in. Come and join me for a moment. The view is remarkable. It's constantly changing. I never know whether I'm looking at the Battle of Brandywine or my brother-in-law making love to my wife. But I'm sure of one thing. If I could just manage to focus my attention correctly, I could see everything clearly for what it is.

A.P. Can you see me quite clearly?

M.P. Well, a moment ago I thought I recognised you. But I'm sure of one thing. You'll get awfully wet if you don't put some clothes on.

A.P. My dear sir, you're mistaken. That isn't rain, it's the Justice of God. And I like it.

M.P. Oh, well, it doesn't matter. It's just that I happen to have an enormous number of umbrellas for sale, and they'll keep anything off you. Not only the Justice of God, but even his Mercy.

'I felt that my slight talents and shallow knowledge were such as could not save the world, and that if Central China was to be overrun, there was nothing I could do to save it.'

It is not so much the moral duty of the poet to seek to influence the behaviour of people as it is his duty to describe what they are being and doing, and what they have been and gone and done: but this far from simple labour, like whistling among glass houses, can produce the most involuntary effects. A parallel could be envisaged between this occupation and the work of the sub-atomic physicist: the moment that molecules and men are subjected to an act of observation their behaviour varies. (Is this why actors seem to be larger than life, because they present a sort of symbolic melodrama of human and even molecular self consciousness?) Since the species is perfectly well aware that a moral judgement is continually directed upon it, how can we know how it would behave if this were not happening? Even the criminal only too often displays his felonies for the purpose of having them admired, no matter how secretly. See Genet.

For the above the title *I Am A Camera* can be criticised for altogether too much audacity or too much abnegation. It is too audacious if it supposes that its 1st Person Singular can be so totally subdued, and if that has in fact been accomplished, then it is too abnegatory. Anyhow, people behave very much worse when cameras stare at them.

If a morality claims no authority other than its expedience, then it seems clear that the anarchist is in for a really high old time. Only the direct word of God out of a cloud could possibly stop most of us from murdering our fathers.

But what, if any, effect upon the poet should—[that paralysing auxiliary]—the prevailing moral code of the social order ideally exercise? Is it the duty of the poet to support the code that prevails simply because it prevails, or is it his duty to subject it to the examination of a presumably superior morality? And if so, where the hell does he get that one from? This is the point of no return where heretical consciences introduce their Aunt Sally: Art as a substitute religion. And once this little Frankenstein has been liberated upon the human scene, it is the very devil to get rid of. For the perfectly simple reason that you then have a so-called religion positively a-dazzle with signs, proofs, omens, and suchlike demonstrations of the direct intervention of the 'divine'.

How could a religion so conclusive to the doubtful mind fail to triumph over: 'To a generation of vipers I will show no sign?' This is the absolute victory of Gresham's Law.

No, for when two men meet in the antarctica of spiritual dereliction, without a compass between them, and with the sun obscured, how do they determine which way to go? The answer is simple, and is another question: what are they looking for?

I have never been able to see clearly why the Marxist wants to incept the mellenium: is it because people ought to be happy, or to celebrate the triumph of Social Justice, or because no one can think of anything else to incept? Is this millenium ipso facto desirable? And if so, how the devil do we know this? No, it is not, of course, a matter of the millenium. But if it is not a matter of the millenium, where is the Marxist idea of salvation located? And without an idea of salvation some where or other, no political philosophy can claim to be realistic: it is simply absurd to go on just for the sake of going on. And this absurdity is full of that moral grandeur—that grandeur of illusion—to which Marxist thinkers are so deeply averse. If salvation does not exist then it is simply up to psychoanalysts to invent it. Poets and priests have invented things almost as difficult. The idea of salvation, for instance. Sometimes the goddess is created in the appalling fires of our necessity. Or our absurdity.

Is a poem that praises well an inferior moral order therefore superior to a poem that praises a superior moral order badly? This is to split the head and the hair as well. Such matters are not the first concern of the poet. For he is not ideally equipped to judge the ascending altitudes of moral orders. I think it is possible only to speak very broadly and to propose that a poet whose poems arise from a seemingly immoral philosophy such as National Socialism in Germany (if such a thing should be possible) could be judged inferior, all else being equal, to a poet whose poems arose from such a philosophy as, say, Platonic democracy. But this is not a proposition I would defend with my life. The Devil would not be dangerous if all his lieutenants were dumb.

I live, let us say, in a little house in a county that I love. I am of the humanitarian persuasion. I like people who like me, and who drink too much. Only a theoretical critic of literature would aspire to instruct such a man as to what kind of poems he should write. The morality of the poem is absolutely pragmatical and unpredictable: what ever such a poet wrote about is what, in truth, he ought to write about. The only interesting point is whether he does it well or badly. When I learn the political convictions of the archangel Gabriel I will do my best to conform to them, but to those of no lesser an evangelist.

For my own part I have not observed that poets in their poems have produced much effect upon the political history of the animal: it is only when they grab a flag and die at the barricades that their poems are sung. This strikes me as quite just: it is harder to die than to rime.

If one celebrates the occasions and ceremonies of the heart, what on earth does it matter which way you vote? For one votes, presumably, with the head; one celebrates, properly, with the heart. The question is one of precedence. The poem begins in the heart, passes, let us hope, through the head, and finishes up on paper. The vote begins in the head, passes, let us hope, through the heart, and finishes up in Parliament. These are two very different itineraries.

It is perfectly possible that the idea of a morality is the instrument with which the gods intend to destroy us. The donkey will follow the carrot over the cliff. For the moral vision, like a ghost, when once seen, can never be forgotten. Why? Because it is the arithmetic upon which the Creator has constructed not, it would seem, Nature, but the lost Paradise.

George Barker

Mob Morals and the Art of Loving Art

We certainly stand just as much in need of a criticism of moral values now as in 1869. But it is unlikely that this proposition which Nietzsche pronounced as an initial philosophical requirement is going to disturb anyone today. Having reached the stage where even morality is left to be decided by majority vote (hereafter to be referred to as the mob) it is doubtful whether the word any longer retains a useful meaning at all.

There are two possible ways in which the term morality has a useful meaning. To begin with there is the meaning granted it religiously and aboriginally: the revealed instructions from the Godhead on how to behave. For someone like myself to whom the God-idea is a logical necessity and an intuitive reality this is understandable. Though I am attracted by the proposition that the God-idea is itself dependent on the human imagination. The second morality-meaning is less interesting but more prevalent; and the mob or majority understands its necessity and will always subscribe to it even though this may lead on occasion to the slave camps of the extreme north or the gas chambers of middle Europe. It is simply the idea of social order; a vague sense of what's proper which nobody can exactly define and which in effect is once more a system of behaviour with a less exalted but practical purpose.

When people speak of morality in the twentieth century, even though they be dressed in black and wear a dog collar, they usually mean the second kind of morality and what they are really saying is that they believe in the police force.

But we should be chary of the accessible pose of belittling orthodoxy. For one thing it is too accessible and too fashionable. And there is something fraudulent about an arrogant speculation which sets out to belittle orthodoxy but which secretly has up its sleeve a perhaps even drearier moral code ready to pop in its place.

The phenomenon can be examined in the pages of any 'liberal' journal these days where, whether the subject be the H-bomb or the female orgasm, the note of moral astringency is very keen.

At this point of history we have enough evidence to show that liberal propositions inevitably cease to be liberal the moment they are allied to power, to make us suspicious of these high-sounding moralisers, however humanistic they may claim to be.

All systematic morality suffers from this categorical distinction that it constricts behaviour and imposes a tyranny of its own. Whether he is crushed in the name of God, the People or the Fuehrer is a matter of merely academic interest as far as the victim is concerned. And as far as these things go there is something, it must be admitted, to be said for the Penny Catechism where at least one can know fairly clearly where one stands.

One thing is discernible and constant whatever the moral code: and that is the violence of the reaction when one of its tenets is flouted or affronted. This is where the liberal and the reactionary meet. And in neither case is there very much clarity as to what exactly they do believe. That mysterious entity the liberal ethic has produced as great bullies and frauds as the Holy Roman and Apostolic has ever done.

And I am not speaking here of great tyrants but of the reactions of the so-called ordinary man who has identified himself with a code of behaviour, with what a majority feel however vaguely to be right: in short with the mob.

Mob reactions can be recognised in that somewhere, if one has an ear for such things, the voice of the preacher of the moral code may be detected adding its dead tone. That note of dead insensibility by which life is reduced to dullness.

Nowhere is this more frequently apparent than in that sort of comment on a work of art which starts out from a position of moral complacency.

For here is a phenomenon one constantly encounters in art discourse: the evident distaste and occasionally the open hatred with which the critic views the personality behind the work he professes to criticise as Art or even to admire.

It is a comic phenomenon and historically is often a pathetic one. When one reads on the faded page Sir Edmund Gosse's comment on James Joyce's prose: 'worthless and impudent, a perfectly cynical appeal to sheer indecency' one recognises the hysteria of the mob reaction; but now it has the pathos of someone making a colossal ass of himself publicly and unconsciously.

But we should resist the temptation merely to laugh: for there is involved in such a case a dilemma in which even a man of sensibility may find himself trapped when he unconsciously slips into the comfortable bog-hole of moral righteousness. Rigorous exercise of the intelligence may save a man. But the human race apart from its exceptions is not really notable for the rigorous exercise of its intelligence.

The dilemma arises from the confrontation of the merely educated mind with an expression of that violent free force which is the human imagination in movement.

It may be said that this is a confrontation of moralities. There is a sense, and a very exciting sense, in which art is moral. When Stendhal says a good picture is nothing but a construction in ethics, one recognises a truth about art which opens up vistas that are at the same time liberating and terrifying. The ethics of art are terrifying because real art by increasing our knowledge of ourselves increases in exactly the same proportion the ethical commitment. This is an indecent thing to do from the point of view of the established moral code. For the moralist like Sir Edmund suspects rightly that the very code itself, like the law of the land which is an extension of it, can be transformed by successful crimes. His alarm is well founded.

There is a rule about this which some good man formulated long ago but which few people perhaps have the intelligence to apply: judge others aesthetically but only yourself morally. The great ethicist put it thus: 'It is intelligent to ask two questions (1) Is it possible? (2) Can I do it? But it is unintelligent to ask these two questions (1) Is it real? (2) Has my neighbour Christopherson done it?'

This is speaking of morality in action, of reality ethically. But it may usefully be thought of in relation to art. Encountering a work of art is in many respects rather like meeting a person. One may not recognise his quality at first, may be put off by a surface aspect and find out later he is quite different etc., but if one's response takes the form of a moral judgement one is unlikely ever to find out anything about him.

It is unrealistic to blame individuals when speaking of widely held moral attitudes. It is more reasonable to speak of the mob as an entity. But I will make use of a fairly typical example of this phenomenon of mob morals in reaction to art—a critique written no doubt by someone no more responsible for his attitudes of mind than the editor of *The Times* newspaper who printed it.

This man is out to praise Toulouse-Lautrec and sets off in the following terms:

There can never have been an artist more difficult to approach dispassionately. His life, his style, his period, his subject-matter all conspire to bring one to his art with a mind heavily encumbered with moral and aesthetic prejudices. His personal legend is a stumbling block from the start. It is of course profoundly relevant to the exact shape the pictures take and to the attitude to life they record that their author was a stunted and physically ridiculous scion of a noble house.

Nobody who is acquainted with the art business will be surprised by the terminology here—an excellent scholarly work on Caravaggio for instance starts off by referring to him as 'an ugly little runt' on the first page—but it seems of some significance that the note of violence breaks out when it becomes necessary to refer to Lautrec personally and that in doing so there is an incidental appeal to the reader that this is normal—the proper attitude. In two unnecessary words the prejudice on which we are to base our point of view is revealed and introduced: 'It is OF COURSE.'

For my part when I read these words my feeling is that it is nothing of the kind. My feeling is that I am in the presence of the unconscious herd instinct of a troubled man who is appealing to me on some presumed common ground. I feel I am in the presence of the *moralismus*.

My man in *The Times* will come around several hundred tortuous words later to the view that Toulouse-Lautrec is OK, but does not feel free to do so without first of all preparing the ground, dissociating himself and getting on proper terms with his readers. For nothing, not even the moralismus, may stand in the way of Art.

What I wish to refer to here however is merely the position, the first position, he takes up when confronted with the spectacle of Lautrec's pictures.

In the first place he professes himself full of doubt. His mind heavily encumbered etc. He is worrying about prostitutes, about licentiousness—if not exactly the female orgasm at least the propriety of the manner of achieving a male one. He is concerned with the way in which Lautrec sees these creatures—for a woman becomes a creature here—'the seamy glamour', 'the rather distasteful hybrid of vulgar decorative taste', 'Lautrec will never allow us to overlook the fact that prostitutes are prostitutes', 'he supplies no other ideal to indicate that he sees other values in the world' etc. Briefly he is full of social concern and the Moral Law.

And then—for we must remember his object is to praise—he reflects that after all since Lautrec was a stunted and ridiculous being it is remarkable that he should have made these pictures at all: 'everything that is clearsighted and compassionate in his art must seem a little nobler in him than it would in the art of normal men' i.e., than if you or I, dear reader, had made the paintings.

All this carries interesting implications. The writer is normal. The reader is asked to recognise that he is NOT like Lautrec who is stunted etc. He appeals without explanation and in a way which to the sceptical mind is quite mysterious, to the laws they both understand. He does not feel that it is necessary to be specific: it is enough to refer to a supposed popularly held view that 'Lautrec recorded a depraved society in a manner that might be likened to a moral squint'. This is not a man speaking for himself for his invocations are far too general and vague, this is the voice of the mob.

The idea of 'normality' is one of the sustaining myths of mob morality. The position therefore may be stated thus. I am normal, you are normal, we are normal. Lautrec by comparison is a stunted ridiculous figure squinting morally at a world of seamy glamour and depravity. And this is profoundly relevant to the exact shape of his pictures. Having got that clear, we are at liberty to enjoy these pictures because they are Art.

Most of the implications of this situation are too trite to bear expansion. What my man in *The Times* does not wish to see is that in the end each man experiences only himself. To refer to your neighbour or twenty million of them for your touchstone of reality is a logical nonsense in the life of the individual person. When one reflects on the personality of Lautrec in these pictures, brave, unconcerned, scornful, and violent, it becomes a monstrosity of sophism to consider his size or shape as relevant factors. The painter celebrates life where he finds it. His morality is the morality of enjoyment, of the continuous development of his own taste without shame or fear. It is a sort of heroism.

The voice of the mob is a worried voice. But one of the most striking characteristics of mob morality is its capacity to assimilate criticism and to transform itself while preserving its fundamental character.

Thus while even in law one can now plead art against morality it is necessary to do so in terms of art being 'wholesome'. An entire school of writers having nothing else in common except an allegiance to a professor of English sprang up in England after the war. Their cry was the *moral basis of literature*. One was allowed to enjoy literature because literature was healthy, rather like taking a brandy for the sake of your stomach instead of to enjoy the taste and the intoxication. This was mob morality at its subtlest and it allowed the normal moral mob member the privilege of reading, without any disturbance of mind or spirit, even contemporary works which if seen clearly as the personal vision of unique minds might certainly upset their peace. The professor invented the method of studying literature without the writer, anonymously and by periods.

The words of the dead are transformed through a monstrous process of analysis into suitable fodder for the living mob.

The techniques for making art thus morally acceptable, of drawing its fangs, are endless; and each generation finds its own. Just now the democratic machinery for rendering art safe is so efficient that it seems that the system can absorb anything. It would be exciting to think that somewhere in Europe there was a man making art which was so violent and true than the system could not take it, someone who had merited complete obscurity and was suffering prophetically the reality of martyrdom on the altar of mob morality. But it would be a very optimistic man who would hold to such a belief—though of course we can always hope since the very condition of his existence demands that we cannot be disappointed in that hope.

Patrick Swift

It Means What It Says

The philosophy expressed by the poems of A. E. Housman is one of pretty thoroughgoing pessimism (I am aware that Housman called himself a pejorist, by analogy with George Eliot's meliorism). That God—a figurative God; Housman also described himself as an atheist—is at worst vindictive and at best remote; that there is no happiness that is not illusion and does not end in pain and remorse; that early death is often a stroke of luck and that suicide is often the best way out: these beliefs fairly obviously underlie much of his verse. Yet Housman is not only a remarkable poet but a remarkably popular poet. It might seem at first as if his readers exercise either some sort of suspension of involvement or suspension of belief in reading him, a suspension of belief that might remind one of Thomas Hardy's remark about the popular outcry that followed the publication of *The Origin of Species:* if he had written it in verse nobody would have given a damn what it implied. Is this a common process: common not only with the popular audience for verse, but among the minority which believes that poetry means something in life?

When we speak of Housman's philosophy we mean, in spite of his declared atheism, something that would be better described as his attitude to life, a pessimism rendered more poignant by a delight in physical beauty. But there are poets who have an actual structure of belief, a formal philosophy or theology on which much of their verse depends. It does seem, at first sight at least, a little odd that so many of Mr Eliot's admirers from *The Waste Land* to the *Four Quartets* should have been the sort of people who are called progressives, who believe in man's perfectibility and the concept of sin as a product solely of the unconscious mind. Conversely, Auden's poem on the death of Sigmund Freud for example would seem to pose a problem for people who do not share the admiration it expresses for Freud's system of psychology, who may regard his basic tenets as not only wrong but pernicious. Yeats' respect for the aristocratic principle would seem to be a stumbling block for egalitarians, even if they care nothing whatever about his astrology and make shift to enjoy the poetry in its despite. And what are most readers to make of Pound's economics, that is if they can make anything of the *Cantos* at all? Whatever else may be said about them they are the product of a mind passionately concerned with a view of history and public affairs which is consistent, urgent and even intolerant; and it is obviously no great compliment to Mr Pound to say, as many critics seem to say, we admire your verse of course but find your views ridiculous.

If what we expect from poetry are satisfactions which can, so to speak, be removed from the poem leaving its content behind as a sort of dress, then no very great difficulty would arise; though on the other hand our satisfactions would seem to be limited. Every reader must decide for himself what he requires from poetry, and every reader would seem to be right; but the reader who to a greater or lesser extent has felt his whole being, moral and intellectual as well as sensual, satisfied in the experiencing of a poem would seem to be the gainer. Unless of course, that is, he is seriously deluded as to the nature of the satisfaction he obtains.

Let us first, to clear some part of the matter up, dispose of the notion of the poet as thinker. When the Victorian partisans of Browning asserted that Browning was a great thinker, whereas Tennyson could not think at all, what they really meant perhaps was that Browning was an acute psychologist with a particular grasp of the process of thought in the human mind; Tennyson had merely a profoundly tragic knowledge of the human mind's capacity to feel emotion. In balance it may even be that Browning's view of life is 'shallower'; but this is to beg the question; what I do wish to suggest is that the idea of 'the thinker' has always bedevilled the questions under discussion; that it is at bottom a nineteenth century notion, associated with the idea of the philosopher as the man who thought things out and the great philosopher as the man who thought things out finally; that it is associated with the idea of progress in the sense that it was believed that final answers were obtainable to certain philosophical questions if we thought long enough and profoundly enough about them and, so to speak, climbed on the backs of previous thinkers; and that such was the prestige of this notion that the prestige of the poet was felt to be threatened; so that from Wordsworth on each great poet was alleged by his admirers to be also a 'great thinker'. Scarcely any eighteenth-century admirer would have denied that Alexander Pope was a man of great intellect; being a 'great thinker' is another matter. Shakespeare has only recently recovered, largely thanks to the efforts of Mr Eliot, from this notion. Wordsworth of course suffered also; but then to some extent Wordsworth may be said to have asked for it.

Let us in this context examine one of Mr Eliot's own first attempts to tackle the problem of poetry and belief. In *Shakespeare and the Stoicism of Seneca* the conclusion appears to be that Mr Eliot is not satisfied that either Shakespeare or Dante did any real thinking at all. They both adopted what was to hand, Dante the Thomist philosophy, Shakespeare 'the mixed and muddled scepticism of the renaissance'; in fact 'the material enforced on each to use as the vehicle of his private feeling'. 'But you can hardly say that Dante believed, or did not believe, the Thomist philosophy; you can hardly say that Shakespeare believed, or did not believe, the mixed and muddled scepticism of the Renaissance'. The relative value of this material 'is of no importance' (we are left to assume that it would serve; as, presumably, Yeats' astrology served); they were both 'occupied with the struggle—which alone constitutes life for the poet—to transmute his personal and private agonies into something rich and strange, something universal and impersonal' (it was the time when Mr Eliot was much occupied with 'impersonality'). 'The rage of Dante against Florence, or Pistoia, or what not, the deep surge of Shakespeare's general cynicism and disillusionment, are merely gigantic attempts to metamorphose private failures and disappointments.'

Two years later, in the preface to Dante, the problem appears to have become a little more complicated. It is asserted 'that we can distinguish between Dante's beliefs as a man and his beliefs as a poet' (I am not quite sure how we are supposed to be able or ought to do this, unless Mr Eliot means that the poet could accept a theology which the man could not, which at first sight would reflect credit on neither of them). However, 'we are forced to believe that there is a particular relation between the two, and that the "poet means what he says". If we learned, for instance, that *De Rerum Natura* was a Latin exercise which Dante had composed for relaxation after completing the *Divine Comedy*, and published under the name Lucretius, I am sure that our capacity for enjoying either poem would be mutilated.'

This seems to raise an unnecessary question which was successfully begged in the earlier essay, a perfect example of the advantages often to be gained from that exercise. Take Dante's sincerity as a man for granted and his sincerity as a poet is surely proved by the fact that he was delighted to use his theology as 'a vehicle for his private feeling'.

However Mr Eliot went on to examine the question of how far the reader need share the poet's beliefs. It is now asserted that 'you cannot afford to ignore Dante's philosophical and theological beliefs. . . . But . . . on the other hand you are not called upon to believe them yourself.' What is needed is assent, 'for there is a difference between philosophical belief and poetic assent.' What is needed apparently is a suspension of belief and disbelief in the interests of understanding. We must distinguish between 'what Dante believed as a poet and what he believed as a man'; though 'practically it is hardly likely that even so great a poet as Dante could have composed the *Comedy* merely with understanding and without belief . . . his private belief becomes a different thing in becoming poetry.' 'What is necessary to appreciate the poetry of the *Purgatorio* is not belief but suspension of belief; a suspension of judgment in the interests of understanding a state of mind in which one sees certain beliefs, as the order of the deadly sins, in which treachery and pride are greater than lust, as possible, so that we suspend our judgment altogether.' Dante's philosophy 'is the philosophy of that world of poetry into which we have entered.'

In an interesting appendix this theory of poetic belief and understanding is said to be similar to that employed by I. A. Richards, and is put forward in the interests of 'the existence of "literature" as well as of "literary criticism".' 'If there is literature, if there is poetry, then it must be possible to have full literary or poetic appreciation without sharing the beliefs of the poet. . . . I deny in short, that the reader must share the beliefs of the poet in order to enjoy the poetry fully.' Nonetheless there are 'difficulties inhering in the theory.' Although if you do not hold it 'you will be forced to admit that there is very little poetry that you can appreciate, and that your appreciation of it will be a function of your philosophy or theology or something else', yet we will have no 'pseudo-statements'. Thus 'Beauty is truth, truth beauty' is meaningless; 'Ripeness is all' has 'a profound emotional meaning, with, at least, no literal fallacy'. And the statement of Dante, 'la sua voluntade e nostra pace' seems to Mr Eliot 'literally true' and he confesses that it has gained in beauty for him since his own experience 'has deepened its meaning'. 'Actually', he winds up, rather suddenly it must be confessed, and in a manner that seems to suggest throwing his hat at it a bit, 'one probably has more pleasure in poetry when one shares the beliefs of the poet', though 'on the other hand there is a distinct pleasure in enjoying poetry as poetry when one does not share the beliefs, analogous to the pleasure of mastering other men's philosophical systems.' It will be seen that there is a good deal of 'if and perhaps and but' about all this, particularly when the ultimate conclusion turns out to be that 'literary appreciation' is an abstraction, and pure poetry a phantom; and that both in creation and enjoyment much always enters in which is from the point of view of 'art' irrelevant.

I intend, after this, to pass over the definite proposition enunciated at the beginning of *Religion and Literature* six years later to the effect that 'literary criticism should be completed from a definite ethical and theological standpoint', not only because it follows logically enough from the above nor even because it was enunciated in the context of a different enquiry; but because it seems to me that Mr Eliot in one of his more recent essays has emerged right out of the sacred wood and, with that startling gift for the profoundly simple statement which he shares with Johnson, has gone a large part of the way towards abolishing the problem altogether.

In *Goethe as Sage* he enters once again upon a prolonged analysis of it, but towards the end he cuts the Gordian knot: 'Whether the "philosophy" or the religious faith of Dante or Shakespeare or Goethe is acceptable to us or not (and indeed, with Shakespeare, the question of what his beliefs were has never been finally settled) there is the Wisdom that we can all accept. . . . For wisdom is communicated on a deeper level than that of logical propositions; all language is inadequate, but probably the language of poetry is the language most capable of communicating wisdom. The wisdom of a great poet is concealed in his work; but in becoming aware of it we become ourselves more wise. That Goethe was one of the wisest men I have long admitted; that he was a great lyric poet I have long since come to recognize; but that the wisdom and the poetry are inseparable, in poets of the highest rank, is something I have only come to perceive in becoming a little wiser myself.'

At this stage of the enquiry then I suggest we are called upon to distinguish between a poet's 'beliefs' (in which word we should include not only his theology, philosophy, astrology or what not, but his attitude to life in so far as it can be formulated in prose, e.g. Housman's 'pessimism') and his 'wisdom'. To go a step further than Mr Eliot—but, let us devoutly hope, in the same direction—we are not concerned with the poet as 'thinker', with the quality of his thought, if he has·any thoughts; but with the quality of his statements, since he makes statements.

Dante's theology, like Wordsworth's ethics, is to many people not only respectable but true. Yeats is perhaps a better, because a more extreme case to take account of. His astrology, his anti-self psychology of the mask and his belief in re-incarnation, his aristocracy, his Parnellism, must when examined purely as beliefs, produce either indifference or antipathy in all but the tiniest minority of his readers. Most people have some idea of the structure he raised upon the spirit messages he began to receive in the early winter of 1917 and made a prose exposition of in the book called *A Vision*. That these ideas played a part in many of the poems he wrote from 1917 onwards is evident; they may serve to illuminate for us the kind of part that belief does play in producing the poem which, so to speak, incorporates the wisdom. According to Yeats' account in *A Vision*, when the spirit messages began, the unknown instructor at first took his theme from a short, just-published book of Yeats' called *Per Amica Silentia Lunae*, in which 'I had made a distinction between the perfection that is from a man's combat with himself and that which is from a combat with circumstance, and upon this simple distinction, he built up an elaborate classification of men according to their more or less complete expression of one type or another. He supported his classification by a series of geometrical symbols and put these symbols in an order that answered the question in my essay as to whether some prophet could not prick upon the calendar the birth of a Napoleon or a Christ.' But *Per Amica Silentia Lunae* is itself a sort of prose exposition of the ideas contained in a poem written two years earlier and called *Ego Dominus Tuus*. It is, I think, a very fine poem; one of the finest Yeats ever wrote, and in fact one of the great poems of our time. But there are two points to be noted. First, the ideas as expounded in the prose essay are—though they contain flashes of illumination—often obscure and occasionally most arguable. Second, though the poem is undoubtedly based on those beliefs the statements it makes are not only more unarguable but more absolute as well:

> HIC Yet surely there are men who have made their art
> Out of no tragic war, lovers of life,
> Impulsive men that look for happiness
> And sing when they have found it.
>
> ILLE   No, not sing
> For those that love the world serve it in action
> Grow rich, popular and full of influence,
> And should they paint or write, still it is action:
> The struggle of the fly in marmalade.
> The rhetorician would deceive his neighbours,
> The sentimentalist himself; while art
> Is but a vision of reality.
> What portion in the world can the artist have
> Who has awakened from the common dream
> But dissipation and despair . . .

Such a statement is acceptable to us or not according to the extent of our own experience. It is not arguable; it is not a mere opinion; it is not a logical deduction from a set of premises that Yeats happened to hold; it is either immediately verifiable by own experience and knowledge of the world or it is not. What part do Yeats' theories about the mask and the anti-self and the phases of the moon then play in the poem? Perhaps the only answer that can be given to that is that the poem depends for its existence on them. It is not an explanation of them; examined inch by inch it can scarcely be said to be about them; but it opens with them and it closes with them; and it could probably not have opened or closed at all without them. It opens with the invocation to the image that will call up the anti-self and it closes on the same note.

Did these beliefs then produce Yeats' statements? Well at least we can say that they in a sense produced the poem. But is the poem about them? The answer to this of course is that nobody can ever really say what a poem is 'about'. A good poem may have as many subjects as it has words. If the poet is properly involved with each image as a living thing or a symbol rather than as an algebraic sign or a dead metaphor, a good poem has certainly as many subjects as it has images. The main theme, if there is a main theme, is a catalyst; and acts of poetic apprehension of the most disparate order are common in the greatest poetry. A love poem can contain, or in fact be, a poem about poverty or cold weather. *A Dialogue of Self and Soul* is one of the finest poems Yeats wrote about the re-incarnation theory, but in the following lines the theme sets off at least six or seven profound statements about human existence whose profundity has nothing at all to do with it.

> A living man is blind and drinks his drop
> What matter if the ditches are impure?
> What matter if I live it all once more?
> Endure that toil of growing up;
> The ignominy of boyhood; the distress
> Of boyhood changing into man;
> The unfinished man and his pain
> Brought face to face with his own clumsiness;
>
> The finished man among his enemies?—
> How in the name of Heaven can he escape
> That defiling and disfigured shape
> The mirror of malicious eyes
> Casts upon his eyes until at last
> He thinks that shape must be his shape?
> And what's the good of an escape
> If honour finds him in the wintry blast?

We may if we like then say that a belief is analogous to a myth, or a plot or a dramatic conflict. It is a causeway for the poem to run on across the morass of personal experience. We may, if we like, regard the poet-as-believer as the persona of a dramatic monologue. The value of the poem for us will depend on the acts of poetic apprehension of the nature of our experience which the poet is capable of; the insights; the shocks of recognition. Auden's Freudianism in the poem mentioned is no more nor less difficult to accept than Yeats' beliefs and the value of such a statement as

> ... the child unhappy in his little State,
> Some hearth where freedom is excluded,
> A hive whose honey is fear and worry,
> Feels calmer now and somehow assured of escape

does not depend on how much Freud really did to rescue him. So *Canto XLV*, which appears to be central to Pound's beliefs, seems to me to be a profound and terrible statement of the effects of the operations of commerce in the contemporary world, and more dependent on the validity of his vision of that world than on the validity of his theories of social credit. Whether that poet be lucky or unlucky who by accident or birth or consanguinity possesses a system of belief is too large a question to enter on here; but there can scarcely ever have been a poet whose mind was not coloured by a habitual and perhaps radical view of human existence; who could not say, as Yeats says in his *Autobiographies*, 'As life goes on we find that certain thoughts sustain us in defeat, or give us victory, whether over ourselves or others, and it is these thoughts, tested by passion, that we call convictions.' Housman's pessimism, with which we began, was an atheology; but it was certainly the agent which, over and over again, produced reactions to the world which are profoundly true and haunting statements of the tragic aspects of human existence; and remain so for us whatever our own ultimate theories about the nature of the cosmos. So too, since we are primarily concerned with the relationship between poet and reader, we may leave the question of the poet as preceptor and missionary with another statement of Yeats's which goes far to sum up the whole matter: 'What came in disjointed sentences, in almost illegible writing, was so exciting, sometimes so profound, that I ... offered to spend the rest of my life explaining and piecing together those scattered sentences. "No" was the answer, "we have come to give you metaphors for poetry." '

Anthony Cronin

Leisure and the Arts

I

Schopenhauer[1] spoke of leisure as an extra need which a few people have in addition to those of hunger and sex which trouble us all. As he saw it, most people are machines that have to be set in motion by some passion; nothing rouses them but some personal interest. When there is nothing to stir them up they have to invent games. This philosopher saw the Europe of his day covered with people playing cards, which gave them little factitious motives when there was no more powerful interest to set their cylinders going. The superior man, on the other hand, took pleasure in knowledge: things interested him as soon as he gave himself up to them. He delighted in natural objects and in the inventions of other superior minds. Those inventions were indeed made for him and existed only for him. For most people works of art and intellect amounted to nothing: they were like whores to an old man, he said brutally. The leisure that most people didn't want was the extra need of the superior people who lived in the intellectual and esthetic world, having escaped from the will.

[1] See *Aphorismen zur Lebensweisheit*, in *Parerga und Paralipomena*.

A German philosopher who was making a system and was resolute enough to illustrate the theories of *Ueber die Weiber* by throwing a woman downstairs could hardly fail to draw the line between men of intellect and the rest somewhat too firmly. But there is an unusual admixture of pure observation in Schopenhauer's theorising. Ordinary people like fusses, squabbles and bothers. If they see trouble coming they rush into it with cries of relief: something is happening at last! It must be admitted that many superior people have the same propensities, not having enough real cares to work off the ordinary human appetite for trouble. But it remains true that a glimmer of intelligence means that there is also, somewhere, a taste for peace. If you really want to read a poem, or look at a picture or even the veins of a leaf you want at some intervals of your life not to be bothering about getting a meal, paying your rates, or exacting deference to your supposed importance. And it is equally true that what is called the leisure time of nearly everybody has to be filled with invented stimuli to the baser or at any rate the more basic passions. There may be an element of contemplation in the activities of the most ferocious weekend gardner; but it is as an ever-renewed threat to an imposed order than the garden is most cherished. And how inadequate the suburban house must have been as a centre of entertainment when the owner could afford to have it painted by tradesmen! Then, the planning and supervision of their labours must have provided his pleasure. Now, he can with good conscience undertake all these labours himself. With wrinkled brow he tells himself (as he bears home his pot of paint and new brushes) that he never has a moment's peace! He need never have: there is always something to do, and when at last he sinks into an arm-chair his residual passions can be kept alive by the sex and violence of the television screen. Should any interval still present itself, he has a car, in which he sits like an electronic device, responding to stimuli, but with the additional advantage that he can rage against the other electronic devices that circulate about him, as if he were in the midst of a battle or of the most exhilarating business deal.

The need for leisure—for those who feel it at all—is a negative matter. It is a demand to be freed from the various impediments to the quiet working of the mind. As such, it is profoundly uninteresting to the social world and it is the last thing that cultural institutions of one sort and another provide for. They, after all, are largely concerned with providing factitious motives for those who like to imagine that they are busy about art. It is unflattering to the great or little public which flood about such institutions, and sit on their committees, to be told, in reply to the question: How can we help the poet or artist? 'You can leave him alone.' And yet that is the most unarguable of the conditions which are requisite for the production of anything worth reading or looking at. The few people who can produce such things have to be given an opportunity to do so. An institution which gave away money for no special reason would be useful. Most cultural institutions entertain the public rather than promote the arts, though one has to admit the possibility that the merchants of culture may occasionally, and as it were by accident, promote an interest which results in the painter selling his picture or the writer his book, so that they might occasionally be the indirect means of giving leisure for meditation to someone who needed it.

II

It would be a mistake to think that a cultural institution, or other self-conscious patron, would be doing what was necessary by giving money to deserving cases. The deserving case, without a doubt, would turn out to be the man who succeeded in producing, at the end of the year or of three years, achievements which could be reported to the committee. 'Twenty-five paintings and three novels have been created under our patronage in the last year', one can imagine the smiling president announcing. One can imagine him also lowering his voice to a confidential tone to add that some of their bets had not turned out so well. A, B and C had proved to be idlers, and there was nothing to show for the grants given to them. To D it had been decided to give one more chance, because he had replied politely to the letter that was sent to him and there was reason to suppose that his book of elegies would be ready in the spring. But money given on conditions—and what public body can give it otherwise?—is a bondage like ordinary wage-earning. Worse, for the man who is patronised for his genius has to justify the faith that is put in him, and which may have been misplaced altogether, or may have been misplaced in time, so that he is exhorted to flower in mid-winter and to ripen his fruits before autumn.

The leisure the poet needs for writing his poems is the least part of the idleness that is necessary to him. If leisure to work were all, few outside the Siberian salt-mines would not have enough for their epics. But the poet no less—how much more!—than the busy social scientist needs time for observation. His observations are not those favoured by the London School of Economics. He does not go round with note-book and pencil counting ages and sexes or asking ten uniform questions of a statistical sample. He is a man who has carefully avoided forming an hypothesis, and he is not interested in finding out matters you can ask questions about before-hand. It is by 'noting things too small for record'—the phrase is Hawthorne's—that he proceeds. How interesting is the conversation of the poet! his admirers may say. But all that is singularly irrelevant. It doesn't matter whether the poet can talk: but he must observe. He will look and listen: it is difficult to believe that there was ever a poet who was not a watchful man. Not a boy scout, who has been taught to count the lamp-posts in the street or to note which houses have empty or full milk bottles exposed before the door. But a man who has in fact walked up the street; or through whose mind the street has made its own itinerary. And to no special purpose. The poet is unlikely ever consciously to use what he has seen. But a few of these perceptions will find their way visibly into his poems. More will lie buried beneath them, hardly a syllable showing. A lot of eating goes to the growing up of a child. It is so with the perceptions and the poem.

Some of these indispensable recordings may well take place in the ordinary fury of practical life. Some cannot take place anywhere else. But it is the nature of practical life to be restrictive of the perceptions. Catching buses or transacting business is done under the guidance of purposes which blind the performer to all but pre-selected stimuli. These are the ones the poet does not want. Reporters and sociologists can observe what happens; the poet is concerned with what was happening while the event is happening.

III

It is not long since there was a considerable class of idle persons in the world.

Great parts of the world are free from the necessities of labour and employments, and have their time and fortunes at their own disposal.

For William Law the distinction between the leisured and the labouring classes was a point to be taken account of at the outset of his *Serious Call*.[1] As to the leisured:

The freedom of their state lays them under a greater necessity of always choosing, and doing, the best things.

But

A slave can only live unto God in one particular way, that is, by religious patience and submission in his state of slavery.

The existence of a leisured class is certainly no guarantee that many will devote themselves to the best things, in any reasonable man's understanding of that term, and no-one has dealt more faithfully than Law with the pitiable follies of nice people. But where there is a leisured class, some

---

[1] *A Serious Call to a Devout and Holy Life* (1728). Law's holiness has so told against him that it is no longer generally known that this book and the *Defence of Church Principles* (his letters to the invisible Bishop of Bangor) contain some of the liveliest prose of the century.

excellencies will be practised by some members of it more completely, and more devotedly, than can ever be possible in a society in which almost everyone is given over to drudgeries. It is not difficult to call to mind what the independence of aristocracy and gentry has contributed directly to letters from Montaigne to Shelley. What it has contributed indirectly is certainly of no less moment. Traherne was the son of a cobbler, but seems to have written his *Centuries of Meditations* as chaplain to a great man, and Jeremy Taylor wrote the *Golden Grove* while employed in a similar capacity. Moreover, the existence of a leisured class gives a respectability to leisure which in our day it has lost. It was long taken for granted that the poor man's son who took to letters would aspire to that condition. Now that the advertised social ideal is the industrious making of money, the ordinary man is bound to ask (and to be unable to answer) why a young man who calls himself a poet should think that other people should work to keep him? The most certain point of morals left is that everybody ought to work.

In a world in which there is so much work to be done—even though not a little of it is in the making of superfluities—this is, naturally, no new idea. There have always been stout protesters. So Thomas Gray:

I am never so angry, as when I hear my acquaintance wishing they had been bred to some poking profession, or employed in some office of drudgery, as if it were pleasanter to be at the command of other people, than at one's own; and as if they could not go, unless they were wound up.

And William Cowper:

But this provokes me, that a covetous dog who will work by candlelight in a morning, to get what he does not want, shall be praised for his thriftiness, while a gentleman shall be abused for submitting to his wants,rather than work like an ass to relieve them.

The social acceptability of such protests has gone with the society that supported them. Instead, it is thought proper that the poet should be put to work in a culture-factory—say the English Department of a university—or at promoting the legitimate diversions of high-brows through the Arts Council. All this is due to a theory of work, not to a theory of art.

C. H. Sisson

On a Liberal Education

A fund is being established to enable young Irish creative artists to further their liberal education.

A liberal education? To enable the net of lies. To arrive at simplicity by the shortest route. To laugh uproariously but with good nature at all propounders of the liberal cliché. To laugh uproariously in the middle of a half-finished poem. To be true to one's own judgement when every journalist says the opposite. Certain kinds of smarmy humanitarians should also be laughed at—the Revd Michael Scott and Albert Schweitzer for example. Yet not to be hard about it, not to make a philosophy out of it. To love all things in literature and life that are gay and happy and to suspect all things that are gloomy and sticky with a purpose and people that are concerned with improving man's lot. I take a moment off here to say that we should also be able at the earliest possible age to see behind the gloomy concern of the various kinds of patriot and worker in good causes to find out if the cause of the gloomy concern is a frustrated peasized ego.

When I was on my way to where I now stand—wherever that may be—I encountered many aspects of The Lie. And no man was ever more wide open to corruption.

I do not feel too bitter over all this; in fact I am always in danger of bursting out laughing. And that's another thing: the majority of people will never forgive you for being comic about the dull little things by which they try to beat the artistic rap.

The Irish Literary Revival as it was called was responsible for many damaging lies. The 'peasant poet'. Having one's roots in the soil. They were all claiming to have their roots in the soil and to be peasants as well—Colum and Corkerry and T. C. Murray, Brinsley McNamara, Frank O'Connor, F. R. Higgins. Yeats was a troubled man because he couldn't achieve peasantry. In his last poems he did manage to move his mount over to the greener going on the stands side if I may use the lingo of the racing game.

It was borne in on me from all sides that I was peasant and a ploughman to boot and that anything outside the peasant in the ploughing field would not carry the authentic Irish note.

So sadly I turned my ploughshare into a pen and in 1936 produced a slim booklet called *Ploughman and Other Poems*. In spite of all the liars around me there are things in that little book which are uncontaminated. However, there must have been enough of the authentic peasant note for I got a front page spread in one of the Dublin newspapers. At the time I couldn't make out why I found that newspaper piece so wounding and offensive. It was an attitude very common in Ireland. I learned in time.

'What do you think of him?' said a man to me in 1957 about a prominent Irish businessman.

'A decent fellow but too fond of poetry' was what I replied. Or so this Boswellian friend told me later. He thought it a witty reply. It is a sharp one with much meaning. Journalists and businessmen and nearly every one in Ireland loves the Muse and won't stop pawing the sweet wee thing.

> I turn the lea green down
> With my plough.

Then there was the all-over lie that was Ireland. Some men of genius have helped to support this lie—Yeats and Joyce in particular.

Because Joyce is passionately obsessed with Dublin many fools imagine that it is Dublin confers the virtuous glory and not the obsession. Yeats too made Ireland his theme. But the work of Yeats which is deliberately Irish in this way sounds awful phoney. Irishness is a form of anti-art. When you meet one of these artists you discover he has no passionate faith in art. The tentacles of allusion which he throws out are aimed at no Promethean theft. A prominent Irish painter recently declared that he and not Jack Yeats was in the apostolic succession of art. If he had said he and not Matisse.

Ireland as a theme like every other formula was something within the reach of the average mediocrity. In spite of what may be said O'Casey is loved in Ireland because however he attacks he always accepts the theme of Ireland. To deny Ireland as a spiritual entity leaves so many people floundering without art.

> My soul was an old horse
> Offered for sale in twenty fairs.

That was more of it. The idea of a poet offering his soul in fairs is quite repugnant to the whole nature of the poet. But the Irish persons love it. Loved they also—

> It would never be summer, always autumn
> After a harvest always lost,
> When Drake was winning seas for England
> We sailed in puddles of the past.

This is painfully Irish but I must confess.

A good critic is one who enthuses over your good points and ignores your bad ones. The Irish critics always enthused over my bad points.

I think too it might have been possible for me to have remained in my native Monaghan and achieved simplicity and the technique which is part of that learning if I had been taught the score. The technique of reserve above all.

I feel that for a moment the mood I have evoked may give the impression that I think what happened to me is very important and that I am important. Nobody is important. Nobody is major. We get to our destiny in the end.

Small as life, not large as life is the proper phrase.

Journalists and university lecturers are another hazard for the liberal education seeker. They do not speak from a raised rostrum but from a hole in the ground. The good liberal education will lift a man up from that hole in the ground.

You will hear them speak of 'the giant figures' of the Literary Revival—Synge, Yeats, O'Casey. And 'major writers' like Frank O'Connor and Paul Vincent Carroll. Remarks of this kind might be likely to frighten the advancing scholar who if he had anything of the poet in him with the poet's arrogance would be just the opposite of the 'hole in the ground' talkers. A certain sort of humility is one form of The Lie.

It is smallness that gives power. Smallness and obscurity and insignificance. I do not however think a man should seek those three cardinal virtues of the poet. If he is one they will be conferred upon him by a grateful press and the other voices of ignorance and The Lie. One big English Sunday paper used to avoid mentioning George Barker's name under the belief that this was bad for him. But of course it is hard to achieve this sort of obscurity. To pursue the matter a little further a man of unique genius in any field will be a man whose name you are tentative and shy about mentioning. Nobody has heard of him. You are speaking in a vacuum. Yet it is good for the soul to practise such courage.

This business of having one's roots in the soil is another thing. Roots in the soil means roots in experience, in love. The roots in the soil that I was told about was knowledge of the accepted formula. The last word in embarrassment in this field that I know of is to be found in Joseph Campbell.

> I have gathered *luss*
> At the wane of the moon
> And supped its sap
> With a yewen spoon.

The principal reason for the existence of powerful bodies of supporters of the off-creative thing is the apparent need for all members of the male (human) sex to project themselves. The search for identity it is called. It is the desire to be somebody. It is awful to be a nobody in a crowd.

This problem was solved in Ireland by diluting the Pierian Spring one part in ten thousand lies. In the past poets proliferated all over the place and even today there are a goodly number.

To satisfy this human need many art movements have been started.

The Irish Literary Revival was essentially one of these. To vary the metaphor a debased coinage to let everybody have plenty of money.

Thirty or so years ago Dr F. R. Leavis of Cambridge aided and abetted by Ezra Pound and T. S. Eliot launched what came to be known as the New or Higher Criticism. More recently the Angry Young Men and more recently still in America there has happened the Beat Generation. People in a more desperate plight in their efforts to beat the artistic rap just go berserk with beards and canvases or go hacking in fury at blocks of wood.

An American, Jackson Pollock, literally threw a pot of paint in the public's face and became a great art name in America. The limit of pathos or bathos was surely reached when an art exhibitor in London poured tar on canvas, set a match to it and there was a work of art.

But to understand all is to love all and the man on the hunt for liberal learning is on the hunt for understanding and the love that goes with it. As I have hinted in the earlier part of this essay this understanding is not going to make a man happy, far from it. Understanding people and feeling for them and laughing naturally and uproariously at their concern with what is not really important is like prying into a mean room. But of course love can go farther and understand understanding. Yes, yes, yes.

On the way towards the final understanding the thing is to know the score as regards the various movements and the different individuals who are not in movements.

Take the New Criticism first.

I know many supposed literary men who are impressed by it and who get bogged down in its intricacies. They haven't the over-all view, they haven't a world in their mind.

The Leavis criticism was criticism as a thing valid in itself and independent or nearly of the original work it purports to deal with. This surely is a form of synthetic insanity. In criticising by the New Critical canon anything goes, anything you say about any work is as good as the next man's opinion. In writing about Hopkin's *Falcon* some speculated that this referred to Christ the King and others that it was the King of England and so on and so on and so on. It was a wonderful idea. I call it artificially induced paranoia. As anybody who has the misfortune to know paranoia or persecution mania produces in the sufferer an inability to stop writing or talking as the case may be. A man once rang me up and asked me to meet him in a Dublin restaurant: he had something he wanted to show me so that I might speak to some editor about it. He warned me, as I entered the cafe and asked him if he was the man, to speak low; he was being watched.

Then he slowly drew out of a large brief case a foolscap MS about three inches thick in single space typing. It was not the whole story of his woes from the time he was sacked as a town clerk of an English town to that present moment . . . it was a précis of the story of his woes.

The New Critics have been able to induce this disease artificially and so you have this fantastic verbal diarrhoea most of which comes from American universities. One of them will turn out a dozen books while you'd be saying F. R. Leavis.

And not only have they induced the verbosity they have also other symptoms: they bring personal relations into the argument. I once knew a well-known N.C. who refused to come to a party because I'd be at it.

The liberal learner should be given a few names to memorise. In America Hugh Kenner, R. P. Blackmur, Lionel Trilling, in England besides the revered founder William Empson, Donald Davie, and in Ireland Denis Donoghue.

It would also be necessary to add that many of these have a lot of real talent, especially an architectural talent, the ability to construct even when the edifice they are constructing may be of little value to mankind.

When one has learned about these prolific critics one can understand what the opposite side is. The side of small output. The side that realises with Rilke that all the best of us has to say is 'after a lifetime's experience a few lines'.

Advising a young creative artist to go to America might appeal to some people. There are many Fellowships which enable a young person to go to America. Yet though America is a most fascinating place socially it is disappointing from the creative view.

With the exception of two little magazines as far as I know—*Poetry Chicago* and a new one, *The Fifties*—there is practically no publication in the United States that will print anything that is not the liberalistic formula or touched with it. This dreary philosophy lies like a dust over the vegetation. *The Commonweal*, edited as a Catholic weekly, leans backward to appear straighter than *Partisan Review*.

The universities and colleges of the United States have all their faculties of creative writing and I cannot imagine a more baneful influence. No standards. No courage to make standards.

In *The Fifties*, the first number brought out in 1958, there is a feature not unlike one I ran in *Kavanagh's Weekly* which I called 'The Old Foolishness', just mere quotation of foolish sayings. Quoted ironically is an extract from an article in another magazine 'The Writer As Teacher'. It is not unfunny and it tells us something about the American cultural scene.

A recent survey showed that nine thousand poems were written in classrooms last year, two thousand of them directly on blackboards. [As compared with only seven thousand written in other places.] The same survey showed that over five hundred poets stopped writing in universities last year as against only two hundred who stopped writing elsewhere; moreover 21 poets committed suicide in the universities last year as against only 2 who committed suicide elsewhere. No one can deny that the writers are in the universities. Now at last poetry has a home; a spiritual home in the spiritual life of the universities. This spiritual life is growing greater ever year; last year for instance our poets spent a total of twenty-eight thousand afternoons listening to their students' problems.

This appears to show an Irish influence. The Assembly at Drumceat had 14,000 poets I think.

The main thing that is wrong with America from the creative point of view is the absence of a humus of repose. In the whole of the United States there are only a few writers of conventionally high talent. John Steinbeck is coarse stuff without that simple rectitude that makes a work of art. Old Robert Frost who was given honours in Oxford and here a couple of years ago writes dull prosy verse. Dead stuff, I would say.

Richard Wilbur constructs artificially like Thomas Kinsella in Ireland. No inspiration. No life. No gaiety. Very popular with the masses of people who worship or pretend to worship what is within the grasp of the mediocrity. From the occasional whiffs of originality and poetic courage that come to me through such little magazines as *The Fifties* and *Poetry* I can see that the dust bowl has not entirely conquered the States.

Some people are of the opinion that going to France or Italy is a cultural education and in so far as the visible is concerned it could be so called. But love is love and love of everything. Standing on the side of a hill in Monaghan, an indifferent landscape of crooked lanes and little humpy hills covered with whins I found love, the kind of love that purifies, a sort of Divine love. Yes—

> The fields that heal the humble.

In more recent years I have begun to love the visible rather than the ideological. I can look for long at a scene. When I was in Rome last I could not do that. I was mentally too strong and arrogant. When one gets physically weaker and so also mentally weaker one enjoys the static pleasures of looking and listening. It was while recovering from a serious illness in the hot summer of nineteen fifty-five as I lay on the bank of the Grand Canal that I learned the pleasures of being passive. The green still water, the light around gables. There are two seats on the canal bank 'Erected to the memory of Mrs Dermot O'Brien'.

> O commemorate me where there is water,
> Canal water preferably, so stilly
> Greeny at the heart of summer. Brother
> Commemorate me thus beautifully.
> Where by a lock niagarously roars

> The falls for those who sit in the tremendous silence
> Of mid-July. No one will speak in prose
> Who finds his way to these Parnassian islands.
> A swan goes by head low with many apologies,
> Fantastic light peeps through the eyes of bridges—
> And look! a barge comes bringing from Athy
> And other far-flung towns mythologies.
> O commemorate me with no hero-courageous
> Tomb—just a canal-bank seat for the passer-by.

It was however a long journey and a dark travail from the little fields of Monaghan that might have saved me had I got the right education and would have accepted it to that July afternoon on the Grand Canal beside Baggot Street Dublin. Surely the purpose of a good education is to prevent one from squandering one's life in useless suffering. Then again is any suffering useless and is there any way home but through it?

I didn't get a liberal education laid on to be absorbed in a couple of years. I got it in the end.

So our seeker after a liberal education is still in Dublin. Certainly he has to get out. I suspect he will be sent to France or Italy because I am sure that the administerers of the fund are convinced that France, Italy or Spain will do the trick. The disreputability of the Continent of Europe is in a way respectable so long as Art is involved. Going to London on the other hand is hardly a thing one of our art patrons would wish to fork out money for. To give a young man a wad of notes with which to stand drinks to poetic loungers in a Soho bar would be even less respectable. And yet I am convinced that the chief place today where the poetic faith is to be found is in some of the bars and clubs and cafes of Soho and also in other spots. You get enthusiastic and sincere people in all sorts of outlying districts. But the main concentration is in the Soho district.

The bar or the club or the cafe with its groups of the poetic faithful is the only place in which a young creative artist can further his liberal education. The only good way to gain admission to such a group is to have talent, to have done something that any one man of the true artistic faith, one of those who will never tell a lie, will like.

The three or four hundred pounds which the fund will provide for our young creative hopefuls will be a useful ice-breaker. Then again the idea of a young man throwing drink into. . . . But one must face the facts. A man from Ireland with a thick roll will be heard coming at London Airport and unless most of the boys are abroad as they often are there will be a fair muster. I would therefore suggest to the Arts Council that someone must be given the job of observer in Soho to report when the fullest muster is likely to be present. This is not meant to be facetious; the best poets and painters today live a great deal of their time in bars and a man with a roll of fivers is a godsend. Whiskey is terribly dear in England and is supplied in what one man has called the 'smallest measure ever moulded for the lips of man'.

Of course there are the groups of industrious mediocrities. . . .

Living and living in pubs at that is part of the poet and painter's work—his experience. The usual mediocrity with his regular output never gestates; he is always dribbling something not life out of him.

We come now to another aspect of the liberal education, another aspect of the corrupting influence that a strong creative character can have on a young man who has not got that diamond hardness that is the poet's. I do not refer to any ordinary corruption. A man's spirit is broken in a different way and he becomes a mere parroter of the master's words and opinions. In many ways there is not much remedy for this and it is possible that a liberal education ultimately consists in copying a selected master. There are only a few originals. This is not a happy condition. I have no answer to it and it may be that there should be no answer to it.

The purpose of a liberal education is to learn to be simple. We begin by being simple and then for years plough through complexities and affectations to come back to where we begin.

All that trouble and here I am again.

Patrick Kavanagh

JOHN HEATH-STUBBS

Use of Personal Pronouns: A Lesson in English Grammar

I

I is at the centre of the lyric poem,
And only there not arrogant.

'You begin every sentence with *I*'—the rebuke was well taken:
But how on earth else am I to begin them?

YOU AND THOU

You are a secret *thou*.
Fumbling amongst the devalued currency
Of 'dear' and 'darling' and 'my love'
I do not dare to employ it—

Not even in a poem, not even
If I were a Quaker, any more.

Beginning as an honorific, the unaffectionate *you*,
For English speakers, has put *thou* out of business.
So, in our intimate moments,
We are dumb, in a castle of reserve.

And He alone
From Whom no secrets are hid, to Whom
All hearts be open,
Can be a public *Thou*.

HE, SHE AND IT

Only in the third person sex raises its
Unattractive—well, 'head' is a fair enough euphemism.
The thought of sex in which you and I
Do not participate is (unless we are *voyeurs*)
Either horrifying or ridiculous. He and she
He it and she it.

But, moving outside the human order,
We observe there is no personality
Apart from gender. Animals are *it*.
But our own cats, horses and dogs are *he* or *she*;
The huntsman's Puss is *she*, Reynard is *he*;
And even ships are beloved as *she*,
Cars and bicycles, even.

For the homosexual queening it in the Gimcrack Bar
His colleagues, objects of his scandal, are *she*,
While the inaccessible youth in the tight jeans,
Three buttons undone in his scarlet shirt,
Is, however, an *it*.

ONE

One thinks of *one* as a pronoun employed principally
At Cambridge, modestly to include oneself
And other people in one's own set,
At Cambridge. One appreciates the French usage
Of *on*; one knows one's Henry James;

One does feel (or, of course, alternatively, one does not)
One must, on the whole, concur with Dr Leavis
(Or, of course, alternatively, with Mr Rylands).
At Oxford, on the other hand,
One tends to become *we*. At Cambridge
One senses a certain arrogance in the Oxford *we*;
A certain exclusiveness in the Cambridge *one*
Is suspected, at Oxford.

WE

'We' said Queen Victoria 'are not amused.'
Subsuming the entire dinner-table into the impersonal
And royal *We*:
No wonder the effect was devastating.

We is also the Editor of *The Times*;
While a Greek chorus is a pattern of dancing *I's*;
The Christian congregation is *I* in the Creed,
Thou in each of the sacraments,
Otherwise solidly *we*. And
'Let Us make man in Our own image.'

We is not amused, nor is it interested
In the possibilities of defeat.

THEY

They is the hellish enemy of paranoiacs
(And even of Auden and Edward Lear);
They is in a conspiracy, is directing hostile thought-waves,
Has got everything fixed *their* way. *They* will not let you.

History a deadly and unending struggle
Of class and national *theys*, except when sometimes
An imperial and oecumenical *We* serenely
Frowns at a barbarian and utter *they*.

But for you and me,
Weeping in our tragic citadel, the horror
Is simply to realise that *they* exist.

BRIAN HIGGINS

On Going into the City

O this sad conurbation which I must visit
Where the lenten murmur is no free moderation
And once I walked, thinking I was honest,
Upon the flags, under the skin of the nation.
And I rose frequently in this assurance
That the pound would not grow greater than my allowance.

Now I am frequently incredulous though I still visit.
Crowds shovelled in teashops have changed,
For under the eye of my intentions their motives are frozen and broken.
When my objections are not heard and silence gathers
I convince strangers that indeed I have been honest
To make fertile the consequential region of my desolation.

And because it is natural to complain and the misunderstanding,
Derives partially from a difference in perspective
I have become polite and beneath other accusations
Accepted my lenten catastrophes as if they were chosen.
Yet, however irrationally, I proclaim it is natural to live.
And is that the only reason I make my visit
To the relatives from whom I long since departed

Having proved a great disappointment to those avuncular spirits
Who thought because I was weak-willed I was feeble-hearted?
O this sad conurbation! Let my journeys be swift and infrequent
I would prefer to conduct my business by letter.

Unfinished

Like Valéry I leave my task unfinished
Perfection has no rival in the real
And yet, I suppose, all things are accurately themselves.
The half-washed teacup growing stains,
The kitchen floor I swept, unworthy of a C.O.'s inspection,
The blankets which obeyed no regulations.

The camp bed, constructed by a distinguished poet,
Tempted the mysterious powers and fell when I reached for his verses.

It had slight rents and a carelessly sewn patch in the centre
(Like Valéry he left his task unfinished).

Autumnal

Better because it has to be
September defines improvement in a golden leaf
Actually brown.
And is not the September sea
Warmer than the sea of May?
O in what sphere of what provincial galaxy
Are we actually thrown?
There is morning, windfall and grief
There is the mistake which tangles the vein,
Irreversible;
And there is silence flooding the talk of the town.

Better still, but only by definition,
Here in the South where there is no room for secrets,
And where it is possible to be jailed for remorse:
No point in curses, justice is not assumed,
Madness jostles success
And work is a frenzy of inanition.
Urbanity cloaks the strategies of force,
Credit blows sky high, founded on good bets.

Climb on the ontology of need
Bleed the gulls (but they will still fly)
The arbitrary has become absolute with a green sign
Autumn burns, and is dryer than we thought.

Elysium crumbles, error has expunged sin;
How long can the gymnast circulate on the ropes
Or the robber escape the collector of taxes
For it is September when the fashion changes
To anger, boredom and the ethics of damnation.

The season is arbitrary, the habit is tangential;
The fixtures are arranged in a commonplace cycle
About which the galactic serpents say nothing.
Will Priapus gain his revenge next time round?
The answer to that will not be found in the constellations of Venus,

Deductions made from the hypothesis of natural selection
Announce only the return of the native.
Friend, Mucker, your guess is as good as my bind.

JAMES LOVELL
Alive, Alive O!

All along we have been talking about the *state* of the theatre, most of this century, and sixty years is a long time to talk. We have reached the conclusion, if it can be called such, that 'the theatre matters', that it is not to be superseded by newer forms of dramatic expression and that it should, failing all else, be supported by public funds or subsidised by corporate patronage.

As far as the public is concerned, the enthusiasm for such a programme resides entirely in the expressions of professional writers on the theatre, in the manifestoes of new theatre companies or in the pages of magazines devoted to the subject, amateur or professional.

The fact remains that only 2% of the population ever go near a theatre, and this figure includes those who exclusively patronize musicals and other forms of light entertainment. It is not surprising that the noise made by those deploring the demolition of a theatre building or clamouring for the establishment of Civic or National theatres should be regarded as being out of all proportion to the importance of the subject by those holding other views, and very often, the purse strings.

As cinema, radio and television flaunt their claims as entertainers of the public this attitude seems rational enough—apart from the persistent nagging doubt that the theatre is not an anachronism and that a place remains for it in the national structure, if only it could be decided what the precise place should be. . . .

From the twenties to the forties we were sustained, those of us who gave a damn one way or the other, by the words and deeds of those who were prominently and energetically active in the cause of the stage immediately prior to August 1914—Craig, Poel, Shaw, Stanislavsky, Granville Barker, Reinhardt, Yeats, Miss Horniman, Barry Jackson and the rest. Such an array of talent and intellectual force rampaging in the twentieth century surely couldn't be misplaced? couldn't be dismissed? If the theatre was, after all, as important as these people clearly believed, then by God, we would dedicate ourselves to its preservation and in the face of advancing materialism we would keep the flame of culture alight, the curtain up, the banner wagging aloft and so forth.

That we misunderstood the nature of these efforts is only recently becoming clear to us. The motivation of this upsurge was not, as we have often supposed, the outward and visible sign of a grand awakening of the theatre after a sleep of three hundred years; such an awakening, we can see now, must have included a sizable section of the people as well as their intellectual leaders which obviously it didn't.

This was not the objective of the Movement, which was, in fact, an effort to raise the devitalized theatre of the time to a place compatable with the prevailing culture. This did not occur either. What actually happened was that a new concept of theatre, completely bourgeois in character and absolutely in tune with the cultural pattern of the time was introduced and imposed on the scene by the energetic efforts of those mentioned above. The irony of this situation might be worth examining at another time; for now, sufficient to say that the existing theatre went sloppily and sentimentally on its way to the tune of The Merry Widow Waltz.

The next generation failed to realise that the voices inspiring their 'very best efforts' were voices that had been raised amongst all the paraphernalia of the socially nondescript, not revolutionary in the least, rather, by declared intent, super conformist. To this day we do not seem to have taken it in that the Edwardian Society, for whom this theatre was being purposefully rigged, passed irrevocably to limbo at the crack of a pistol fired in Sarajevo, and that these same voices to whose reverberating overtones we have been addicted with all the constancy of St Joan at the stake, did not even change their pitch on that occasion, or during the catastrophe that followed, or even three years later, when surely some one might have noticed a red star rising in the east?

The single element that eluded the innovators of 1910 and still tends to bitch the efforts of their successors today, was and is the absence of an acceptable definition of theatre. Just what it is.

The prevalent impression seems to be that there never was one, nor is one possible, that social and historical pressures so condition the context in which actors and dramatists work that what was applicable in 500 B.C., in 1300 or 1600 A.D. differs fundamentally in each instance and will differ again in 1900 and 1960.

Is this true? Or is it only true when, or after, the continuity of a popular concept of theatre is interrupted? A strong Classical tradition may impose restrictions and conventions curbing the adventurous element in a theatrical culture but at the same time will act as guardian of basic principles. In such a context, when the tradition becomes exhausted, a fresh germinal impulse may have to wait longer for recognition but when it appears, it will do so within an organisation ready to receive it. The Oriental Theatre offers examples and the theatre of Molière and Racine, fashioned largely to the requirements of an aristocratic court, does not pass with the aristocracy, because of the persistence of a classical tradition proliferating the national culture as a whole.

The Elizabethan Theatre, supported by Renaissance thought, comes to full flower in a complex pattern the Guildsman of 1300 might have found bewildering but at the same time it remains the logical conclusion to the popular theatre of the Middle Ages. This tradition declines in its own lifetime prior to the closure of the theatres in 1642 and thereafter is lost.

The eighteenth century could not entirely ignore the residue from the previous age, which for practical purposes was the scripts of Shakespeare—the poetry aglow still, but its supporting dramaturgy as obscure to the new critical conception of what a play should be as the hieroglyphics of Egypt before the finding of the key. While the giants of the age of reason squabbled about the uses of the stage the actor moved in and dominated it until the end of the nineteenth century. The popular theatre of the time, for the most part a morass of sentimental rubbish flourished as a vehicle of entertainment, desperately in need of reform, and it was not touched by the Scandinavian concept of theatre brought to combat it; it persisted well into living memory, until the popular cinema took over its function and superseded it.

The theatre that remained, whether the author was Ibsen, Shaw, Barrie, Maugham, Coward or Ben Travers, could only be called 'popular' in the more playful reaches of the Press Representative's verbal abandon. It was, and remains, completely bourgeois without contact of any kind with any popular aspect of life or culture. During the same period some feeble attempts were made to establish a so-called proletarian theatre and failed because by the time it appeared there was no proletariat: but more specifically because any attempt to qualify the constitution of a theatre audience has a debilitating effect on the whole proceedings, rather as if on certain occasions only office workers or debutantes or midwives were permitted to turn out to see the Lord Mayor's Show.

We want to know now if the increased activity in our theatre during the past few years is aimed at refurbishing this middle class toy, long overdue for relegation to the attic, or if some effort is being made, based on valid convictions, to restore the theatre to that place in our national life to which it more properly belongs.

Theatre is an expression of life. It occurs, when it *does* occur, as the result of a collective, compulsive activity in a number of human beings; an activity as curious and mysterious as the behaviour of eels, salmon and birds in their migration. The activating mechanism obviously lies deep in the personality and, like conscience, it has a voice, speaking to two distinct levels of awareness.

To the early children of the earth it seems to say 'You shall sing, dance, inhale, exhale, be aware of, recognise and express the existence of the life within you. Eat, drink and be merry for surely tomorrow you shall die.' Even savages understand as much; they have dug the score and let it rip.

At a higher level of sensibility the voice has a further message; possibly the most important message in the universe as we know it; as persistent as the pulse of the heart, the rhythm of the days and seasons, as compelling as the beat of Rock 'n' Roll, it says:

> This is the way the world starts
> This is the way the world starts
> This is the way the world starts

—the elemental voice of creation, an echo, a statement, a prophecy.

The artist is perhaps the one most keenly conscious of the life-beat within himself, because he is first and foremost a man who has *enjoyed* an object, an atmosphere, a state of mind. Consumed with a great passion to share his experience and as the possessor of a certain talent, equipped to invent a symbol to communicate it, he proceeds to do so. It is important to realise that what the artist *does* is to invent the symbol, not create the elements of the thing symbolised.

If the sign he makes happens to be a Gothic cathedral or a temple on the Acropolis, a poem called perhaps, 'A Midsummer Night's Dream' or 'The Divine Comedy'—if the musician is Bach or Beethoven, the painter Piero della Francesca or the sculptor Rodin, it is likely the sign, the signal he makes, will have been made once, and once and for all. It is likely that such cardinal signs were supremely right for the times in which they were made. It is also likely that they will retain their potency and work their magic and express their truth for ever, that is, as long as the symbols survive and there are men of sensibility aware of their existence.

In the theatre this is not so. There can be no crystalisation of art, no carefully completed object fashioned in the private life of the artist and exhibited to the world when he considers his work finished. Theatre is rather the essence of art itself, on show, demonstrated to the world, made manifest for a short duration of time in the presence of the living. When it is over it is done as surely as Prospero's revels, its components dissipating in vibrations or already on their way to becoming dust and ashes.

The acceptance of this ephemeral nature of theatre and the understanding that it in no way diminishes the importance of the event is a quality required in anyone attempting to define it.

The self-evident constituents of the rest are: an Audience, Actors, a playing space or Theatre and an agreement amongst the actors of what they are going to act—a Play. This last is usually the first in the practical order of things and sets the whole business in motion. Actors may be found, theatres may be had by taking thought or for ready cash and the audience exists all around us.

It is essential to accept this proposition that the audience already exists and accept it without quibble if any progress is to be made in restoring to ourselves a truly popular theatre. A theatre audience should never be regarded as a section of the larger public to whom a particular appeal must be made; it is the whole public to whom a statement is to be made in dramatic terms. Those who pay attention will in the nature of things be a minority of the whole but it is death to condition, or fake the statement on an assumption calculated, for whatever reason, as being acceptable to that minority and it is death and damnation to allow the situation to occur where the minority, or their proxies, are in a position to impose conditions of their own on the organism of the theatre.

Our society is both conglomerate and heterogeneous and the common denominator, as far as the theatre is concerned, lies neither in its social-political nature or the varying degrees of culture governing the use of its leisure, but rather in the biological fact that it is alive today and dead tomorrow and will respond to any heightened demonstration of life primitively, as an affirmation of its identity with the mainspring of its existence. As yet there will not be the numerical response to a play as there would be to a great sporting event but this is only a matter of degree. The element that lies at the heart of the appeal of any public ritual is the element that the theatre possesses *overwhelmingly*, and once acquainted with the fact that it is there, the public response is overwhelming too.

The only move towards the establishment of a public theatre, a theatre for the people, to be made in recent years is that made by Joan Littlewood. Here, to begin with, is an artist, a woman of considerable vision and a master technician. Her first important efforts realised the plays of Ewan MacColl on a basis of theory derived from the innovators of the early century. The ideal of Group Theatre with close analytical study of the psychological motivation of character as expounded by Stanislavsky and the application of physical movement on the stage as taught by Rudolph Laban—one of the really great men of the modern theatre, were primary objectives, and in some measure successfully attained in the early years.

A later phase brought into the repertory a number of English classics; no single Company in modern times has shown consistently the love and consideration for the Elizabethans that Theatre Workshop has; it is only necessary to glance at the titles: 'Edward the Second', 'Volpone', 'Arden of Faversham', 'Richard the Second', 'Eastward Ho!', 'Henry IV', 'The Dutch Courtezan', 'The Alchemist', 'Everyman in his Humour' and read the contemporary notices to realise the truth of this.

Concurrently in these years, there has been much academic work on this subject of the dramaturgy of the Elizabethans. No one will ever understand Shakespeare and his art until he has a wide acquaintance, not only with the works of Shakespeare himself but with the two hundred surviving plays of his contemporaries. This appears to be accepted scholarly practice if the footnotes and bibliographies are to be accepted: but it is far from common practice in the theatre and few theatre people will have had the chance, as Miss Littlewood and her actors had, to come to grips and look in the eye other authors besides Shakespeare belonging to this period.

It is impossible that Miss Littlewood should not have become aware (although she was aware previously of course) of many of the dramatic practices, long fallen into disuse and yet part of our dramatic tradition at the most productive period in its history, embodied in these plays. Nor is it likely she would overlook the many points of similarity in the method of Berthold Brecht as she became acquainted with his plays. It is even less surprising that a woman of her perceptiveness should have hesitated at the attempt to introduce not only these methods but to take what was useful to her purpose from the Commedia, the Music Hall and the comedy of the silent screen and apply them to a contemporary work once the appropriate author appeared.

Dramatists need no longer be deterred by the fear that if their play is not imitation Coward, Shaw or Priestley it has small hope of acceptance for production. No one is as quick to jump on the bandwaggon once it appears safe as the commercial theatre manager, as recent events have shown. Just now these poor men are in something of a fix, they are not at all sure what a play is anymore and a script will no longer be thrown out because the action does not occur in a lounge-hall with french windows to the lawn with characters in evening dress and all the standard lamps on. There is opportunity to treat any theme in any manner but the essential ingredient that must not be missing is the understanding that a play must be something that is proper to the theatre and not something the other mediums can do better. Authors must remember that they are no longer addressing a specific group with specialised knowledge of certain subjects; they are addressing the world against a background of world events of unprecedented significance and the challenge is magnificent.

Theatre when it is great is capable of tremendous things; it is an enriching and energising experience; it comes with quick gladness; it reveals, and not the least of its revelations is the image it restores to man of the innocent heart of his childhood; it excites; it astonishes; it restoreth the soul and it does these things *overwhelmingly.*

ANTHONY CRONIN

'Fairway's' Betting Office, Dublin, 1949

At six to four and five to two
The sun-flecked winners raced
Across the green grass far away
While up and down we paced.

At Kempton Park and Redcar
'Impeccable' and 'Strathspey',
With summer all around them,
Galloped through cheers that day.

Torn tickets, cigarette stubs,
Two up and one to come,
A square of sunlight laid upon
Dirty linoleum.

The third leg third at ten to one.
We blink in the light once more.
Cool consolation waits beyond
MacArdle's open door.

A dray rolls down South King Street,
The seats are warm outside;
A faint sea-breeze in Stephen's Green
Ruffles the typists' pride.

O endless August afternoons,
O grave reality;
Motes in the sun and melancholy
Stretch of eternity.

Responsibilities

My window shook all night in Camden Town
Where through the cutting's murk the sibilant engines
Pounded past slowly gasping in the rain.
Three o'clock was a distant clanking sound.

On Primrose Hill the gasfire in my room
Hissed for more money while the sofa bristled.
The unopened wardrobe stared sepulchrally.
It probably was my predecessor's tomb.

Daily I strolled through leaves to look for letters,
A half of bitter or a chance encounter.
My state was ecstasy, illusion, hunger,
And I was often lectured by my betters.

What wonder that I seldom rose till three
When light was leaking from the grimy primrose
That is the western sky of winter London,
Light in the head, lugubrious, cynical, free.

The past, implausible and profitless,
Is yet a part of us, though I suppose
Gide has the right of it: who have no sense
Of their own history know most happiness.

And yet I set that autumn sunlight down,
That delicate, pale ochre, and that haze;
My eye so idle and the afternoon
So still and timeless with the haze withdrawn.

I could disown them like a thirties poet.
And yet I set inexplicables down;
And scattered images of London when
With a true love I could most truly know it.

The cavernous Rowtons where the footsteps grew
Unsteadily down each corridor and passed,
The stages marked on all my bootless journeys,
A pub, a railing and a short way through.

I groped through bomb-sites on the Finchley Road,
Fog in the stomach, blanketed in cold.
Next morning when the gears began to groan
Whatever else I had I had no load.

No more than when in Hammersmith one morning
The sun lit up the Broadway through the fog.

Incarnadine, transported, I was stalking
Besides the early buses in that dawning.

Nightly the wagons splashed along Watling Street,
Battened down, bound for the pool or for the smoke,
Waiting for lifts I did not know myself,
An avatar, a prehistoric beat.

I saw the landscape of old England like
A man upon the moon, amazing shapes,
Wheels, pulleys, engines, slag-heaps, bricks and dirt,
And furnace sunsets frowning through the smoke.

And heard the poets of old England too
In Watney's pubs repeating cricket scores
And Dylan stories, talk of our medium
And principles and programmes (radio).

The past, predestined, populous and over
Clings in the dampening leaves, the smell of petrol,
On the brown northern heights where I remember
Highgate and Hampstead in a fine October.

CLIFF ASHBY

The Reduced Nanny, Smell of Talcum Powder

The reduced nanny, smell of talcum powder
Still in her nose, opened her napkin-soft heart.
The mistress liked things nice. The breakfast tray
Laid so, her bath, regular as milking time,
The *Telegraph* to graze upon at ten.
Life the same yesterday, today, forever.
The horrors of the war had been most bleak,
Catmeat and cream so difficult to get.
Society evacuating its fecal
Strata into her house, had caused acute
Discomfort to the family doctor.
Life and evening sky seemed set for sunshine,
But came the fat, bullying son-in-law,

Given to public anger, impervious
To the subtle snub and well-bred silences.
Took first the favourite daughter, then the farm,
Crumbled her comfort in his hammer mill,
Offered the solicitor violence.
Now she stumbles in a haze of spirit
With two well-hung dogs, the neutral common.

In the Twilight of her Time

In the twilight of her time,
When every day was dumb
And what was said was not received,
Letters spoke of 'sickness, the crime
Of growing old, head grows numb,
The cold, boredom unrelieved.'

We wrote spasmodically,
Duty bound, 'Children are well,
Don't get round to writing much, we
Apologise.' Did we tell
You of the racked brain and mind
To find words cursory but kind.

No more will rain spoil your day
With spite, nor wind waken you
At night with its malicious play.
The word became flesh and grew,
Assumed a malignant form,
Kept your faded spirits warm.

On the Margin

One would think that only a display of poetic firecrackers unequalled since the early thirties could justify the appearance of yet another Government-subsidized pamphlet on current poetry (*Poetry To-Day, 1957–1960*, by Elizabeth Jennings. Published by The British Council, 3s. 6d.)—especially a survey confined to its achievements in the last three years. Of course the pamphlet claims nothing so exhilarating and indeed hints that another spontaneous combustion of the sort is to be deprecated. But what is of interest is its underlining of the victory of the most depressing phenomenon of the Fifties: the establishment of a standard poetry (here given a semi-official accolade), dedicated to an aesthetic of 'elegance', conformism, and acceptability; confined—to judge from the selection of poets discussed—it would seem almost entirely to graduates of Oxford and Cambridge. Its author observes in tones very near self-congratulation: 'Briefly, there is no one outstanding poet now, I think, who speaks for the age and the spirit of the age . . . There are no prophets now, *nor, perhaps, would we welcome them if they were to appear.*' And in this spirit Miss Jennings, in spite of the awkward necessity of writing about her own merits in the third person, omits mention of some poets whose appearance in the Japanese garden might derange the miniscular perspective.[1] After all the pamphlet was published for a Government body, and Government bodies are notoriously apt to subsidize such exercises in the inflation of minor or inoffensive talent. It would perhaps be invidious to give examples in the case of living poets, but the kind of evaluation that is offered may be judged from this remark on the late Edwin Muir, an excellent but scarcely a major poet. His work, says the pamphlet, 'has an audacity, a power which one can only compare with the later poems of Yeats!' One has to go back to the publicists of the 'New Apocalypse' poets in the forties for a similar specimen of critical rodomontade.

David Wright

[1] While among the elder writers Mr Louis MacNeice, Mr Bernard Spencer, Mr Terence Tiller, Professor C. A. Trypanis, and Miss Anne Ridler are discussed, the existence of Mr George Barker, Mr Vernon Watkins, Miss Stevie Smith, and Mr Patrick Kavanagh is not conceded. Among the younger, that of Mr Christopher Logue is barely registered.

VII

MARTIN SEYMOUR-SMITH

The Administrators

In the administration of culture
Watching our interests, are poetasters
Who wear coloured waistcoats with gold buttons;
Below their suffering countenances,
Like little lights shining upwards,
Sometimes perch bright bow ties.
It is to them we owe those long readings
In public places (we are still allowed to miss them),
Those charming speeches from the stage,
Making us feel at home with the right writers—
A half a glass of *vin ordinaire*,
Rind of high-quality cheese, a stone
(We did not even ask for bread) and a few words with
Themselves: for seven-and-six,
All financed by government grant.

They had their careers planned at sixteen
Down to the finest detail: even to
Those unhappy verses on lust at twenty-two
(We all knew
And their wives too
That they'd done a thing or two
At twenty-two);
To the later more resonant odes,
Suggesting development though no loss of potency,
On the warmth and blessings of married love—
How they brought a hint of romance perhaps,
A sense of Man's High Predicament
To a rare lady's bed;
To the tauter verses of despair:
The agonized song
That the Bomb is wrong;
To the last, maturing, comfortable
Swing to the Right.

By the rays of a setting British sun
They sip their old port at thirty-five,
Headily pretending this is Life . . .
Then, sighing, as though hidden cameras
Were recording their creative privacy—
The unconscious beauty of their bearing
Of life's contrastingly so crude burden—
For eager audiences of student-sensitives
Whose applause rings in their well-trained ears,
They retire to beautifully-appointed studies
('Do not disturb me, Penelope')
To pen longish neat stuff on how they yearn, really,
To give it all up, go back to nature, and so on.
(We should say: 'Dear Aunt: I am looking forward
Very much to my holidays this year';
But we do not know enough about
The transformations and transmutations of Art.)

When in the act of composition,
They forget carefully the furtive adultery
In Hampstead High Street, that awful business
On the Heath itself (this is too personal—
The Muse prefers the more dishonest lads);
Put out of mind the slightly embarrassing
Writings of dead men who led different lives,
Though trapped on their shelves and sealed
With fullest explanatory annotations;
Ignore most studiously of all
The letters of refusal they have to write
To those less fortunate but still living
Whose breathing—is it?—somehow stops their pens.

Request on the Field

When I was broken down and unemployed
You found me bitter, wry and under-joyed.
I would not pay my licenses or dues,
To vote I did improperly refuse.
So captain-like my shoulder-blade you smote
And cried: 'Up lad! Cast off your sullen coat
(And after you have registered your vote)
Get on the pitch among the knaves and fools

And play the game according to their rules—
They're doing, after all, what you won't do.
Respect them then. Later love comes, too.'

I heeded your wise words, and now am on the field
With shirt and socks and red-cross shield.
But before you dribble off, at captain's call,
Could you explain the absence of a ball?

Found on a Building Site

'Dear One:
    I am naked on a building site
In Penge West. It is 1.5 a.m., and cold;
The mist wreathes around me, rising in columns.
I shall have much to think of, but chiefly
What shall I do at dawn?
I am writing this with a piece of coal
On a sheet of a tramp's stained newspaper. . . .
Dum spiro spero: perhaps you will find this
Before the gaunt sirens of daybreak speak.
If not, then think of me, but make no enquiries.'

Thus sometimes the poor spirit.

Living by the River

Nature has left too many relics here.
I lived on what remained of the fresh air;
  Weeds choked development sites
  And not even Human Rights
Could check the river damp. It was unfair.
So my own nature came on, like the rain:
The schoolmaster with his whistle and cane
  Also possessed the Home Life,
  The Garden, the Children, the Wife;
The obstinate and isolated brain.

That day when with bitterness I found
Nothing would grow on my sullen patch of ground
  I felt my life's emptiness,

The morning's lack of progress,
Paper flowers, the open bed like a wound.

I packed and tried to leave, but soon came home.
They said: 'You can't afford to be alone.
  Do what you like in there,
  But remember what is fair:
Property is theft but the dirt's your own.'

I knew what they meant (for cleanliness I sigh),
Did all my washing without asking why;
  But cannot decently depart
  Without mastering the art
Of getting clothes hung out by rivers dry.

The Execution

The big day dawned. They had not told me.
But the warder, cutting the grubby pack
For the last time (I won easily)
Said shyly, 'Me and the boys from the back
Would like to say we'll miss yer. Here mate,
Take what they gave me ter give yer. Yer card.
The public's 'ad theirs. We issued yours late,
Unofficial like, to make it seem less 'ard.'
For weeks now I'd been waiting for sentence,
The first under new laws which couldn't fail:
Condemned for an undisclosed offence,
But pronounced beyond an undefined pale.
And here at last, some clerk's indelible
Filling the blanks, on a yellow hand-out,
It was: 'Beauty is not expendable,
But We cannot preserve Our Parks without
Economies, therefore prisons will end.
Convicted men will now be set the task
Of Nature-Preservation. Duties depend
On men's degrees of guilt, not what men ask.
Case Number One. Name: Seemore. Crime: Extreme.
Task: To the Lions at Regents Park at Noon.
Bus Route 74, St Pancras Steam,
Or tube to Camden Town and walk. Book soon.'

Bracing myself, I shared the warder's joke.
'That Pierpoint's fretting 'isself sick I bet.
It's a noble death, and better than the rope.
Stroll in natural like, with a cigarette.
Give the crowd their sport and keep on smiling
And you'll go down to 'istory ole pal—
Put up a show an' you'll 'ave 'em whistling
Just like at them Roman martyr chaps an' all.'

I do not remember my last steps,
Except weeping women, kids with ices,
The men dressed up, in their best Sunday caps,
And armed with countless applause-devices;
The clang of the gate, and a huge silence.
Recalling the warder's words (what else to do?)
I lit up and strolled to a sleeping-stone
Sat down, and crossed my legs. 'Who in hell are you?
I can see that you're no early Christian,'
Growled the lion, almost inaudibly.
'I suppose you'll have to have some of my meat,'
He added, while sniffing at me rudely.
'It's a circus-trick! What a bloody cheat!'
Someone yelled out. 'We want a refund now!'
And while, though still apprehensive, I began
To talk to the lion, and think out how
I'd refuse its stinking offer—to a man,
The crowd started growling themselves, and went
Slowly home, with the new laws disgusted,
And muttering against the government,
Angry, suspicious and disappointed.

History Lesson

For the master who is limiting freedom
History's not like school any more.
They call out death-dates in the still classroom,
Watch motes in the sun, the afternoon
Wears on; listen contentedly, perhaps,
To the chronicle of justified acts.
For him, though, it's not what went before,
But the shut mind planning to condone
What it now understands, is guilty of.

(All slanderers of freedom or love
Plead 'history, not us!' in self-defence:
'Circumstances, not ourselves, make sense!')

The teacher thinks, 'Should I say more?'
But there's no time: the written lesson
Must begin: 'Write,' he says, 'on the reason
For *Either* this *Or* that necessary war.'

He blinks, remembering the same sun.
His free mind in similar silence
Groping: '*Which war of these, which one, or none?*'
That impulse stifled by a voice like doom:
'Choose now! The time is short. You have the facts.'
And of how he felt so coldly un-alone,
Could write nothing but words never his own.

GEORGE BARKER

On a Distant Prospect of English Poetry & Downing College

The waters we sit by
my dear, and weep
may not be very
wide or deep
but at least we
can see that the harp
is kept well strung
and the pencil sharp
for by this river
many sit
just staring down
into it
sighing because
they see the fish
can't be caught simply
with a wish.
And it's very hard
to land a verse
if your line's baited
with nothing worse

than abstract desire
or megapride
because the poem
like a bride
wants something solid
and upright
to get her teeth in
for a bite.
So fish with the dictionary
and your soul
on the intelligence
like a pole:
for the laws of English
Poetry
reduce themselves
to these three:
(you'll find 'em in
several versions
but all go back
to the Persians)
to speak the truth
and shoot straight
and make the mind
expiscate.

O the cultures are flocking
around the corpse
and *Essays in Cretiny*
gives a few yawps
as Dr Prometheus
in his spectacles
speculates freely on
dialecticals
and the spirits of Downing
street or college
admit they've exhausted
human knowledge
so all that's left
for us to do
(never was so little
done by so few)
is simply to sit
on the ragged rocks

silently sighing
this paradox:
You downy birds,
desist, desist,
or you may find
you really exist.

What can we learn
from a loss so grievous?
Now we shall feel the
rigor leavis.
Abandoned? No,
the homonym
offends the lucid
mind of him
whom even the gods—
reduced to grammar
as inconclusive
as a stammer—
address in an
uncertain manner.
Farewell great doctor
of minor clauses
parentheses and
victorious causes
winged witticisms and
wingless horses.
How can we ever
really thank
a doctor for being
so very frank
that every time
the queen sickens
he simply mutters
What the Dickens
and to our
extreme abhorrence
reveals to us
King Charles' Head
belongs in fact to
D. H. Lawrence.

Now there is nothing
left to do

but sit around
listening to
the memory of
that nurse and doctor
damning us worse
than any proctor,
till, like a toilet,
the vacant silence
(which might be the mind of
Didy Rylands)
fills with a kind of
reptilian hiss and
once again
we know we listen
one and all
to an emission
so full of gall
it sounds like pissing
against a wall.

Farewell master of
Eliot
(I mean the lady
of course, not
that rival critic)
farewell master of
the mephitic,
master of crafty arts
and farewells,
but master of absolutely
nothing else,
we hang on your word.
It never tells.

WILLIAM CLARKE

The Widow

Once he told me, and in secret,
At Casino he had flirted
With a girl and there had happened
What could never be averted.

This by all men is forgotten
But by me, and when the Widow
Takes my hand for consolation
Falls between us like a shadow.

Old People's Home

I asked him could his children not
Provide a home for him instead
Of leaving him up here to rot?
It didn't worry him, he said.

He used to wish them miles away
When they were kids and made a row;
It was to be expected they
Should turn the tables on him now.

Mission Hall

When times were hard and men were out
Of work the Mission Hall was full.
It wasn't we were more devout;
The coffee suppers were the pull.

But since the Welfare State became
Accepted as the people's right
There are no sinners to reclaim,
The place is empty every night.

Military Cemetery

One thing's more than a guess
In a world of changing friends
Jock won't change his address
Here the road always ends

At a bare stone portal
Without bell or letter-box
But there's more than mortal
In this house of Jock's.

MARTIN SEYMOUR-SMITH
C. H. Sisson

I

It is not difficult to see why, when *The London Zoo* came out a few months ago, it was ignored.

> I have no person fit for resurrection
> Destroy then rather my half-eaten frame
>
> But that you will not do, for that were pardon
> The bodies that you pardon you replace
> And that you keep for those whom you will harden
> To suffer in the hard rule of your Grace.

What can the weekend critics make of this? Lacking Sisson to discuss it with over their midweek pale ale, they must realise that its life is located in an area which they long ago abandoned. After all, surely they are not being paid to praise something that makes their bread—butter, jam and all—taste like the self-destroying stuff it is?

Sisson's gloom exists in its own right; it is creative; we cannot disagree with it. To do so would be like saying that Swift had no value because he had perverse feelings as a person. We do not have to agree or disagree, because we are presented with an entity that we have to acknowledge. We can say that there are other aspects of existence; but we do not deny this one, or wish to—not once we have understood it. To most stories and verse we cannot respond at all; but to some novels and poems we do respond; that Sisson's work may rip an unwilling and discomforting response from some literary hack who had almost forgotten he was alive is not a criticism of the writer, but a measure of his importance.

But there is a further reason why Sisson's pessimism is valuable to us, if only we can accept it; it has to do with the truth-possessed nature of all authentic creative writing. Sisson is, in a special and important way, what might be called an anti-preacher. There is a sense in which official love-mongers, and paid optimists, those uneasy lackeys of Public Religion and Culture—from the Archbishop of Canterbury to the Minister of Education—provide an effective insulation for corruption. They jolly humanity along by helping to keep the myth that people are trying; and all the time, of course, they are helping to keep the veil over a reality that is both unpleasant and difficult. Everyone is involved in this—the romantic assertion that 'the poet' is not, represents a serious falsehood, and those who hold this view, and understand it, do not understand the nature of poetry. Thus the unusually carefully written blurb of

Sisson's book of poems, *The London Zoo*, says: 'The title poem is a satire which derives force from the author's involvement in what he denounces.'

Neither Sisson nor anyone else who tries to be a poet wishes to call poetry therapeutic, or to draw that kind of attention to it at all. But people other than poets are so keen on praising the health-giving properties of their own goods that it is fair to point out that Sisson's 'gloom' looks after itself in much the same way as some of us know poetry does.

II

Sisson's pessimism is not absolute. His poems are explorations of reality; and while this activity is involuntary, it could soon be stopped by the exercise of serious ambition.[1]

Sometimes the positive factor is only to be found in the beauty or truth the poems achieve; but there is a kind of positive release in a sadness such as this:

> . . . in this machine world
> No one can die lonely.
> . . .
>
> It is possible that the musk ox
> Descending the glacial valley
> Enters the dying vision
> Of the effete hunter, or the bell
> Of the emerging church-tower marks
> A point in the gathering mists.

The certainty that the truth stumbled upon in a poem will be shared (it does not matter by how few) is in itself a denial of absolute despair; the record, if it is an honest one, is enough.

Good poems speak for themselves; they defy too much analysis. The best we can do is to suggest how they may most fully be read: how all that they have to offer may be extracted from them.

One of Sisson's most memorable poems, *Ellick Farm*, describes a meeting between the small boy and the mature man of affairs he has now become:

> He would have known certainly all that I know
> Seeing it in the muck-strewn cobbles below.
>
> (Under the dark rim of the near wood
> The tears gathered as under an eyelid.)

---

[1] The fact that Sisson has become a very senior Civil Servant demonstrates his lack of ambition.

> It would have surprised him to see a tall man
> Who had travelled far, pretending to be him.
>
> But that he should have been turning verses, half dumb
> After half a lifetime, would least have surprised him.

Sometimes Sisson indicates from where he derives his power as a novelist, as in the weirdly dramatic and alarming *Cranmer*, which ends:

> One evening he came over the hillock
> To the edge of the church-yard already filled with bones
> And saw in the smithy his own fire burning.

With the exception of a long poem in couplets, *The London Zoo*, Sisson does not use verse as a vehicle for satire. In poems the complex suppressive procedures of his prose are suspended:

> This is the pot-bellied bankrupt
> Naked upon the stage
> With a porridge of news-talk
> Obscuring his grimace.

The economic, deceptively simple *The Art of Living*, which I give in full, is a kind of primitive blueprint for his novel, *Christopher Homm*:

> The child can grow
> Only by being blind
> He owes his greatness
> To his fumbling.
>
> The mind askew
> From the appetite that drives him
> The youth gives reasons
> And has destination.
>
> The old man's waltzing nerves
> Misdirect his hand
> Aphasia, medicine, hope
> Obscure his end.

Just as in his critical prose Sisson is scrupulous in his definition of terms, so his poems will be found to be as precise as hard work can make them. Consider the care that has gone into these two stanzas from *In Honour of J. H. Fabre*, without in any way spoiling or altering the original impulse:

> My third trick was to love
> With the pretence of identity
> Accepting without proof
> The objects 'her' and 'me'.

> My last trick was to believe
> When I have the air
> Of praying I at least
> Join the mantis its prayers.

In the short poem, *In Kent* (given in full), by a wholly original use of ellipsis and suggestion, he conveys the mad randomness of history, its moving pointlessness:

> Although there may be treacherous men
> Who in the churchyard swing their mattocks
> Within they sing the *Nunc Dimittis*
>
> And villagers who find that building
> A place to go of a Sunday
> May accidentally be absolved
>
> For on a hill, upon a gibbet
> And this is Saint Augustine's country.

This poem, incidentally, supplies a clue to the already mentioned blandness of much of Sisson's prose. It strongly suggests the kind of violence that may lie beneath—or even prompt—a situation of gentleness.

These poems are difficult, but they will repay the closest attention.

III

Sisson himself is an ironist; but let us not forget the supreme irony, his excellence.

The culture-clerks, professional evaluators and purveyors of reputations are all of them members of what might be described as the Allowed Minority—creatively about as active and useful as the 'opposition' that was once ordered into existence in Turkey by a dictator who, unlike Sisson, suffered from a bit of part-time *Weltschmerz*. No writer could more obviously be outside Establishment Culture than Sisson. Nor does he belong to the anti-Establishment—which is, in itself, a kind of Establishment; just as a censor is, must be, needs to be and wants to be exactly as pornographic as the most pornographic of pornographers—or perhaps a little more, so as to know just that little bit more. Sisson would have succeeded (in the vulgar sense) more had he been angry; the angry ones can usually be absorbed. But if you tell a Civil Servant that a Society supposedly founded for the good of poetry, has not been able to award the prize it felt was deserved because of its fear of being legally proceeded against (this did happen), he is not going to exhibit surprise. Why should he?

> Here lies a civil servant. He was civil
> To everyone, and servant to the devil.

The last thing he would expect of the clerks who serve Culture is that they would ever, under any circumstances, be prepared to stand up for anything—let alone a poet. And Sisson's view is right. What may seem vicious or 'gloomy' to the officers of this or that Society for the Propagation of Culture is really a lesson in self-control and wisdom to those of us who have felt rancour about it. It is unlikely that any committee will give truth a prize.

But the greatest irony of all is that this writer, whose learning, sharpness of mind and awareness of foreign literature (not a set subject these days) makes most of the clerks, columnists (sport, verse or both) and verse-makers look silly, should himself come from Whitehall. While the makers and breakers of reputations are busy making and maintaining a Civil Service of their own, the Ministry of Labour has brought Sisson forth.

IV

In an autobiographical essay called *Natural History* Sisson has summed up another aspect of the same problem in two memorable sentences:

> One should not write more poetry than one must, and some formula has to be found for passing the time between poems. The conduct of affairs is one, though probably not the best.

At first sight this supremely ironic statement may suggest an almost childishly romantic pessimism—but, although we are indeed dealing with a pessimist, we shall find that lucidity rather than romanticism is his chief characteristic. Sisson makes no vulgar or distracting claims, either for himself as poet or for poetry as a whole; instead he says, 'one can only go on living, and be grateful for this by-product when it comes.'

This kind of writing about poetry, with no *Weltschmerz* or sentimentality about it, and quite without philosophical possibilities (I am reminded of Graves's poem saying how he had learned to talk 'less philosophically') is immediately recognisable as the authentic utterance of a creative writer of experience and integrity. It is as unavoidably true, in its limited prose sense, as his superb line of poetry:

> Untie my ligaments, let my bones disperse.

This is the true poetry of a despair personal and unphilosophical enough as to be meaningful to us all.

His novel, *Christopher Homm* (not yet available), is one of the grimmest books of this century; grimmer, in its way, than *The Human Age*. It has seemed to me, and to some others, to be a masterpiece. It resembles no other novel; the influences that have gone to form its style are almost entirely non-literary (in the fashionable sense of this cruelly used word), arising from Sisson's unsanguine temperament and his devotion to accuracy rather than to what he often makes us realise are the silly luxuries of pity. (It should be remembered that new literature is made out of individual experience rather than out of the pronouncements of critics about influences. *Christopher Homm* will reduce the more ordinary type of reviewer to his proper silence.)

Technically a *tour de force*, *Christopher Homm*, on the story level, gives an account of the death, squalid life and birth of a working-class man, brought up in a nonconformist family. Before we had read this, which traces the life of its subject backwards, with the most telling effect, 'ordinary' was a vague and generalizing adjective that we tried to avoid. This novel gives it a new and horrifying meaning: for, in trying to define the type of life that is here described, we are continually driven back to its use. With skill and unobtrusive power Sisson has given us, at once, a panorama of social history, a witty and often very funny account of what can only be described as the normal passions, and a description of the life of a man—the name Homm is not, of course, without significance; but the nature of the resemblance is part of what Sisson would almost certainly call 'the joke'. If *Christopher Homm* puts readers off (and there is some evidence that it does) then this is certainly due to its gloom; for compelling readability is one of its features. It is at least as readable as any novel by Beckett; it is extraordinary, and startling in fact, that Sisson can do the same kind of work as Beckett within such representational, such English, limits. Sisson's lack of pretension, his gift for the bland and unexceptionable statement, with its hidden store of explosive irony, is one of his most formidable weapons; we know, when we have succumbed to the effect of his gloom, that we have not been tricked. We are face to face with an aspect of our condition. This writer has maintained the integrity to tell the truth about himself; now, and because of that integrity, we can see something about ourselves. There is nothing negative about such an achievement.

That is one reason why Sisson's gloom should not put us off. But there are others, equally cogent: as with all good writers, investigation of the nature of his achievement is fruitful; our recognition of this and of his creative power is the kind of magic that it is a waste of time to try to define; but, just as a kind action spreads beneficial ripples throughout its environment, so the positiveness of this achievement enriches the minds of those who pursue the reasons for it.

The productions of a creative mind do not seek to persuade; they merely exist, in a sense in which, for example, a pickthank description of the latest poetry books in a Sunday newspaper, or the most recent actions of the Foreign Secretary, do not. These latter are informed with a kind of emptiness (and a corresponding sense of importance): they were one thing yesterday; now they are something else today; tomorrow they will have changed again. Sisson possesses more than the knowledge, rare enough in itself, that total immersion in affairs (what is sometimes called, if only by the most blatant of self-advertisers, 'commitment') is anti-poetic: his creative achievement shows that he possesses enough self-discipline to avoid the local demands of time. If Sisson's writing is gloomy and pessimistic, we must remember that its concern is with the prospects for the survival of this kind of integrity. 'Nor is it written,' wrote Laura Riding, 'that you may not grieve. There is no rule of joy.' The ironic gloom of the last statement in *Christopher Homm* (Christopher is crouched in the womb) '. . . if he had known how bitter the journey was to be he would not have come,' is justified; it is cruel, but it is inevitable. The fact of the story being told backwards adds to this inevitability—I cannot do more than pay tribute to its technique (if, as Sisson would say, that is what you want to call it), and to hope that the book will very soon be published.

An Asiatic Romance, Sisson's only published work of fiction, is slighter than *Christopher Homm*. The figure of Sir Bertram Sligh, the pompous higher Civil Servant, is light-hearted by comparison with anything to be found in the latter. But it is still a book of great significance.

Briefly, the story concerns Curly, a corporal, Dacres, a subordinate official, and Sir Bertram Sligh, a higher Civil Servant. The two latter are serving on a Commission in some unidentifiable part of Asia when news comes through that Europe has been destroyed. Together with Curly, they flee. Eventually they find themselves in the domains of a Prince; Sligh attempts to ingratiate himself, and in the end is given some work to do. There is some sharp satire on the British administration of Asia: the ridiculous figure of Sligh, who does not care who or where he is so long as he can toady and be toadied to, becomes representative of British administration, with all its lack of imagination, good intentions, failure of understanding and basically dishonest zaniness. To a certain limited extent Sisson identifies his own unease in this specific situation (he was in India during the war) with Dacre's attitude; at one point there is even a hint of the familiar but not invalid philosophical position: 'I am responsible for all these evils around me.'

But at a profounder level *An Asiatic Romance* is a fable about the writer in society: Sligh represents bumbling authority, the psychological censor, the ruler, the administrator, the man-not-man; Curly is the 'ordinary creature' (we see him later much more clearly as Homm) and Dacres represents the real man, who is involved because he does not protest, but is merely bewildered as to how he could protest. Sligh and Curly return, having learnt nothing from their encounter with Asia, or from their adventures (they are shown in league at the end, Sligh smiling down from his Whitehall office at Curly as he passes beneath with a tart, winking and giving the thumbs up sign). Dacres, on the other hand, returns to make further explorations, having resigned from the Civil Service. *The Times* says that 'it is denied that the journey has any political significance.'

The meaning is obvious. Sligh, Curly and Dacres had originally been tricked into thinking that Europe had been destroyed by the significantly named Captain Bridgewater. Bridgewater, a man whose home is in native territory, and who 'has connections', is really giving the three men the chance, by his trick, to experience some reality. The pure, non-Europeanized Asian existence that the three encounter represents the jungle of human existence, raw reality. But when Sligh and Curly return to England they make up the kind of story that will be acceptable only to the ears of the non-realists; they are glad to re-enter the world of unreality, and they take care not even to acknowledge reality. But Dacres returns to explore reality, in the company of Bridgewater, for 'non-political' reasons.

Here *An Asiatic Romance* ends; but two significantly italicized passages have given us the Sissonian view of the reality the two men have gone back to explore.

The Prince rapes his wife's sister by a trick, and then cuts out her tongue. His wife and her sister revenge themselves on him for this by making him a stew of his own son, which he eats before they tell him of its contents.[1]

This is, of course, pessimistic or worse.... But there is nevertheless a hint of hope in the fact that Dacres gives up his comfortable life of unreality in order to try to understand. This is a remarkable book, and it deserves to be read more than most that have been published since the war. It is, for example, at least as good as *Lord of the Flies*, and far superior to *Pincher Martin*.

V

The criticism of Sisson as 'unnecessarily gloomy' (and one can hear this being said) is about as valid as the charge that Erik Satie, in *Socrate*, shows by the austerity of his music that he is indifferent to the murder of Socrates, or that Bosch is merciless because he shows men being merci-

---

[1] The significance of the fact that this story is to be found in Ovid is no more than that it is very old and ought to be familiar.

less. The exact nature of Sisson's unique pessimism and restraint is important and revealing.

That Swift's savagery arose from self-hatred and self-knowledge is not at all concealed in his writings; and it would be surprising if one of the sources of *A Modest Proposal* were not Swift's own sexual predilection for cannibalism.[2] Beyond the satire and the flaying irony there is sheer pleasure in cruelty—a pleasure the reader shares. Again, in the writing of another ironist and satirist, of comparable stature, Wyndham Lewis, there is a joy in hatred—and a sensuously self-indulgent complexity of texture in the writing.

I do not, of course, mention these characteristics as an attempt to subtract from the achievements of either Swift or Lewis, nor do I want to indulge in any fruitless and irrelevant evaluative comparisons; what I wish to bring out is the originality of Sisson's irony. For here we have a writer whose style is deliberately anti-sensuous. When Swift says, 'last week I saw a woman flayed, and you will hardly believe how much it altered her person for the worse', he is playing (magnificently) on all sorts of emotions; basically, he is pointing an accusing finger at those who do not react to its ironic content—he is 'flaying'. He knows, and we know, what the 'mad' Lear knew when he said:

> Thou rascal beadle, hold thy bloody hand!
> Why dost thou lash that whore? Strip thine own back;
> Thou hotly lust'st to use her in that kind
> For which thou whipp'st her. . . .

Sisson's procedure is different: more intellectually controlled, he practises a discipline of acceptance of the human condition. (This is not at all the same as pretending to have reached acceptance, as a person.) This means that all pity, or inversion of pity (as in Swift), is withdrawn. The effect is disturbing and uncanny. He consciously wishes to exclude 'local' feeling—and by local I mean such poetically unmeaningful, 'nonexistent' things or events as the Foreign Secretary's activities or what's on telly—from his writing. This explains some effectively angry adaptations (there are modern references) of Heine's political poems, published in 1955; the genuine indignation here displayed is instructive, because rigid suppression of emotion is a main feature of Sisson's original prose.

---

[2] The bad news, for some, is that such knowledge is only incidental.

C. H. SISSON

The Nature of Man

It is the nature of man that puzzles me
As I walk from Saint James's Square to Charing Cross;
The polite mechanicals are going home,
I understand their condition and their loss.

Ape-like in that their box of wires
Is shut behind a face of human resemblance,
They favour a comic hat between their ears
And their monkey's tube is tucked inside their pants.

Language which is all our lies has us on a skewer,
Inept, weak, the grinning devil of comprehension; but sleep
Knows us for plants or undiscovered worlds;
If we have reasons, they lie deep.

Things Seen

When the bomb has fallen
And the land is scored
With burns over its once delicious green
Time will be erased from these walls
And not even the written word
Call back things seen.

Look your fill while you may
Burying your face in woods as among the dew
And turn home at night-fall
Where the children's voices promise no posterity
Or as much as a cat where they grew
And the only certainty is that night will fall.

Adam and Eve

They must be shown as about to taste of the tree.
If they had already done so they would be like us;
If they were not about to do so they would be
Not our first parents but monsters.

You must show that they were the first who contrived
An act which has since become common,
With head held high when it is conceived
And, when it is repented of, dangling.

There must be not one Adam but two,
The second nailed upon the tree:
He came down in order to go up
Although he hangs so limply.

The first Adam, you will recall, gave birth
To a woman out of his side;
For the second the process was reversed
And that one was without pride.

By the Lift Gate

Well I can understand your contraction
The lines by your eyes and your pointed nose
You pull your coat about you (but I can guess)
Advancing one foot with suspended toes.

The melancholy at the approach of winter
Is not for the season but the summer lost
Your juices retracted, but not yet gone
The moment, you would probably say, passed.

But whether you reached for that moment
And so fell headlong into the abyss
Or waited on the brink, all is one in the end:
You are approaching forty and no peace.

I have hunted your eyes like weasels among the ferns
Who can say when there is an end of hope
Or what peace there would have been in satisfaction?
Close the lift gate and go up on the end of a rope.

Great Down

With the great book of nature open upon your knees
You sit like a comptometer on the hill-side,

Reckoning the church-spires. Is what the machine
Records a proper object of pride?
Is it more than the animal can scent?
Is there also human consent?

The naked Bororo divides his village
And without this geometry loses his faith:
Others have trudged in the course of the sun.
Mechanical compulsions are not of this age.
The best rule is that you should seek to please;
Go down on your back or on your knees.

How were you taught when young to be you?
You had not been invented before, there was no pattern.
Your parents invented you as you grew;
They gave you a name and their love and you learned
That there was no alternative to being a person,
Never suspecting the sense of that tradition.

You will deny that you were born to ask
That your few feet of flesh should have hope.
Proud fool! You think you are degraded by asking
And yet, of all the mind's movements, this is the top:
First, for what I may give you in your womb,
And then, for what you will find for yourself in the tomb.

Grandmother

Grandmother wheeling a perambulator
With outstretched arms and senescent leer,
What reason for hope have you here?
Shame on the body at fourscore!

Only Christ can have mercy on you now;
You can look for none from Venus or Lucina.
The boy's stout finger admonishes you
What a danger to women he intends to be.

Turn up the pram and let him tumble upon
The flat silk front that covers your dugs.
You are glad to feel the strength of his legs;
He is harmless in your lap as others were not.

Once you gave your body to the poor.
That will sustain you now more than any prudence.
Now you may give it to this young impotent
As he laughs and kicks but you know more.

Grandmother you may perambulate
With broken spokes and distorted frame;
You are cheerful and it may be half crazed
Not for what you have but for what you gave.

A Young Woman

You straddle in the street like Atalanta.
You were somebody's daughter not long ago,
Now mother to this brood.
You extend one hand to a straw-haired child;
Another trips over your long back leg
As you run laughing towards a third.

There is a cave in your athletic belly
From which these made their way to the fragrant world.
Now they are like petals but the lines gather
Already about your eyes;
The flesh you took into your bridal bed
Is already such that the boys no longer whistle.

Soon you will understand that hope
Which you at present pursue
Has to be carried like water in a cup.
At last you will hold it so,
The race having turned to mere knowledge
And you by the fire or fingering the turned-down sheet.

The Nature-Lover

Where the hare with her slight thoughts
Passes and the badger leaves his bones
My eyes fill with them and the fields,
But this boy with the gun has the right idea:
It is by killing that we join in their fun.

BRIAN HIGGINS

A Triumvirate

The sea runs on its iron bed
And whispers through the waving springs
Where fishes lie in voiceless calm
And ghosts of ships avoid the storm
The sea runs on where no voice sings
And Davy Jones lies dead.

Above the sky gaunt angels move
In anxious nightgowns floating
They watch the cities and the streams
And try to understand the dreams
Of those who, fired by radiant love,
End up simply voting.

Beneath the earth devils range
Whose limbs are rusty steel
Their eyes, malevolent and fierce,
Stare through the scarlet gloom and pierce
The acrid corridors where strange
Lost bands of sinners kneel.

This is the trinity of doom
Oblivion, Guardian Fate, Damnation.
Between the three of them they set
As many problems as you'll get
By living sadly in one room
And looking at the nation.

The Corrupt Man in the French Pub

'I'm corrupt' he said to me in the French
'I think I live in corruption's stench.'
Did this mean something about pay
Or those he was about to betray?
Was he selling out for a screw with a wrench
Or selling his wife six times a day?

'I'm corrupt' is a big thing to say
Though your chair is not a park bench.
I know that I am called corrupt myself
When seen around in good health
(By journalists usually)
And also because I get away
With 'not working' and such
Soi disant words in inverted commas.
So in the common eye my form is
Perverted. An accusation to be ignored
Only the mind can be corrupt with a word.
So I asked him what he meant by corruption.
He said he was drinking too much.

The Accidental Purity

New days go by but still old times return
Thoughts foregone and equipment dumped
I quiver in the morals or the matter
And dream of peace each time my head is thumped.
I came to the sad city as my brother
Hoping my refusals would be paid.
No argument can prove what is assumed
(Except for this geometry would fade)

Where was my equipment that day
I jettisoned man's best excuse, that he is good?
Hearing arguments of rates of pay,
Hearing of justice, what is understood?
Mutual respect I daresay.
But those voids are too huge for respect
Which are stated to exist, where swing
The monkeys of commerce who are not the elect
But they hold the ropes about which I would like to cling
Just a little when they come my way.

Baedeker for Metaphysicians

Having written several poems which I will not publish
And having on my hands two problems which I do not relish
I find literature is a side issue to survival,
But, having survived, will that obtain my arrival

At the courts of peace? I suspect I travel with broken gears
Over a country which was not made for this journey
For it seems that we drive on sex or money
And unless these are properly articulated together
One does not call a sunny day good weather
And if the parts that relate them are stolen from the store
You might survive alright, but what for?
Though you look on the mountains and rivers and such marvels
And take a child with you on your travels
You might not find this observance or natural creation
Sufficient. And you will not get consolation
Offering lifts to those who have other secrets
And seem to be travelling, you would say, without cheating
You will not obtain the solution by holding a meeting
To swop travelling advantages that cannot be pooled
It is essential to arrive while you travel, then you will
See, when you have stopped, that the journey is completed.

MARTIN GREEN

Coming up for Air

Hope had foundered, time had lost its place
And I could suck in but one breath of air
To keep my lungs and heart in time to face
That I was living only on despair.

I didn't know that I would slowly heal
Alive that I was glad to take a breath
Once more to pleasure in what makes me feel
And glad once more that I could think of death.

For who fears death can only value life
And highest moments of awareness are
When we can comprehend the thrust of knife
That cuts through everything and stops the hour.

CLIFF ASHBY
Please Don't Laugh

I have given up trying to be grown up
I spend my time in adolescent joys:
Finally thrown my 'I am Jesus' face off
And gone out to the boozer with the boys.

One time I took my stand a little distant
Listened to their jokes and felt superior,
Quivered at the mention of a pair of tits;
Coloured from my toe to my posterior.

For many years I looked round for a model
And two or three times thought I had found one,
But when I tried to pin them down to study
A boy remained, I found the man had gone.

The first one had a pride that stank like mine did,
The second had a nibble with a tart,
The third one curried favour with the wealthy,
The fourth, poor sod, became obsessed with art.

One more said that he would pin his faith in love
To rid the world of adolescent strife,
But quickly called me outside for a punch-up
When some kind neighbour said I'd jumped his wife.

My mother thought the world was growing rotten,
That God would take His loved ones for His own
Perhaps that's why I sometimes feel so lonely
Playing blues records on the gramophone.

Last week I went out walking in the country
And heard the turtle dove call from a tree,
I didn't stop to listen to his love-song
I knew he wasn't singing it to me.

As I came home I had to pass a cripple
I thought I ought to smile as I went by,
'Now there's someone that you should try and love son,'
I walked straight past, I couldn't meet her eye.

A candidate for office came to our house
'Just look and see sir what my party's done,'
I pointed to a block of flats like barracks
And trees that stood there weeping for the sun.

Kind Dr Best's the one who'll cure my sickness
In his still waiting-room I sit and pray,
He'll give me Soneryl to help the night on
And heart-shaped Drinamyl to cheer the day.

So farewell to the purple-headed mountain,
The family house, the river running by,
Exotic over-ripe fruits in the winter,
The atom bomb that lightens up the sky.

O Father will you cross my brow with water
And place my tired hands upon my chest,
Remove my testicles and their appendage
And teach me how to love with what is left.

Fountains Abbey

We start as all the popular programmes start
With the commercials at the gate, the picture postcards,
Presents, films, the omnipresent lolly
Clutters up our history with our past.
In natural sequence to the world of commerce,
Authority demands its twentieth of a poem
To let the inheritors view their heritage.
All formal rites performed we now are free—to enter
And wander down to where a restless river
Fails to bear all our sins away.
There in the soft green meadow, mellow in the sun,
Stone upon prayer upon torn finger nail feels for the heavens

And crumbles in its own inadequacy,
My daughter asks how many men have died
Creating this high monument to pride?
God knows! If all the men who died in its defence,
Were laid—with proper reverence—side by side
Within its longest shadow, this shallow valley
Would be levelled to its highest hill.

And still they come the concubines of truth.
The machinist, standing on the Abbot's tomb,
Baring her teeth into the camera's eye,
Has poised stiletto heels above his heart,
And in the infected blood the world may see
The adumbration of its history.

PATRICK KAVANAGH

The Cattle Fair

'I say—give me your hand, give me your hand, give me that hand.'

No response from owner of hand.

I have just been thinking that I have never seen in print a proper description of a traditional deal in cattle in a country fair. To remedy this defect I have gone to the typewriter on more than one occasion, and on each occasion I failed. A deal in cattle or other animals went by a strict formula; the lies the actors said never varied, but the emotions put into them swept all the strings. I must confess that I was never much good at a deal. I used to imagine that I was doing everybody a good turn by cutting out the divides and the hand claps, not realising that I was betraying Shakespeare's instruction to the Players. I was looked upon as an iconoclast, a spoil-sport.

'Here give me that hand?'

The hand of the potential buyer is given reluctantly. The seller stares at the buyer's palm in a meditative way. As he holds the buyer's hand by the tips of the fingers, the other hand goes up and down in a wavy motion. 'Here, I tell you what I will do, I tell you what I will do, I tell you what I will do—twenty-seven all up and you'll have luck in my baste.'

'And you'll have luck in my money.'

The seller reminisces: 'I know your people and I know yous are dacent people and . . . sure I knew your mother and like that I'd like yous to get her.'

'And sure wouldn't I like to buy ot you. Don't I know all ablongin' to you and they were a credit to the country.'

'And they were nothing to the people ablongin' to you.' Traditional courtesy obliges a man to repeat the mispronunciations of his neighbour. 'As dacent a people as stood 'ithin the parish of Donaghmoyne.'

'Twenty-five if you like now, if you like now.'

At this the seller becomes very dramatic. He is no longer holding the other person's hand in a slack casual manner. He is no longer whispering; he is shouting, and we feel that some fantastically generous offer is coming.

'Here, here, I'll be as good a sport as you, I'll be as good a sport as you.' Down comes the palm with a mighty slap. 'I'll be as good a sport as you—twenty-seven with a crown luck.'

The buyer takes his cue: he grabs his opponent's hand and shouts 'And I'll be as good a sport as you.' Voice dies to a whisper. 'Twenty-five all up.'

It might well happen that neither of these was a genuine buyer or seller, that they were merely putting on a show for some slow-witted mother's son: this was quite a common occurrence. At this point a third party turns up. Sometimes he is the actual owner, who is there to carry the play further. The three-card lads are only trotting after these men.

Generally, however, the deal was on the level and the middleman, the 'tangler', was authentic too.

Enter the tangler. 'What's atween yous?'

'There's nothing atween us,' both say.

The tangler delivers his speech:

'I know yous both and yous are both dacent people and yous'll both do as I say—divide what's atween yous.' Both principals remain mute, standing stiffly to attention. 'It's you that has the right pair of good looking daughters that id keep a fella out of the gutter, and begod you might be buying more than a cow.' Sudden excitement again. Tangler grabs both parties' hands, with a great struggle brings them into contact by the skin of the tips of the fingers. The deal is made.

Aye 'deed aye, them was the days. How well I remember the Sparrow Madden. He was a dealer in gorries (local name for bonhams). He was a thin little fellow, couldn't write his name, but is a rich man now, thanks to the Border. In gorry markets, where it was usual to find the husband and wife on opposite sides of their little cart of bonhams, the Sparrow would go up to an old man who had a young wife and in his pretended drunken voice—pretending he didn't know them too—he would say:

'How much for them chaps?'

The man would answer humbly. The Sparrow would replace the sheet on the cart, and then had a short confab with the wife. At that he would turn again to the husband and shout: 'You'll do as your daughter says, you'll not break your daughter's word.'

This would embarrass any normal man, but it was seldom it embarrassed any of the hungry scradins of farmers who were to be found guarding donkey carts full of bonhams in that part of the country. Oh hell to the embarrass or embarrass!

And then there was the horse dealer from Crossmaglen who once paid a tribute to my innocency of expression. This man dealt in crooked horses—and he, too, is in the money today, thanks to the same Border—but as he was so well known, very few people would dream of approaching a horse that had Mr X or one of his well-known friends at its head. So he employed young, innocent looking chaps to stand by his vicious horses and sell them for him. I occupied this post on one occasion and proved that I was never meant to be rich. A poor woman and her gowdy of a son came up to me. Mr X was in the vicinity, but for all that I gave her the wink as secretly as I could.

The son didn't take the wink as quickly as his mother and the result was that I was never asked to sell a horse for this horse dealer again.

Just after the war I happened to be travelling north—travelling first class on that occasion—when I fell into conversation with a very gay fellow on the opposite seat.

It was my old friend the horse dealer, and I had told him all about my experiences with him before I remembered him. He enjoyed the joke immensely. Indeed he was a very cultured fellow in the generous traditional way that is to be found in rural Ireland. He had heard a lot about me; he had read everything I had written. He himself had made a stack since those distant days of the early 'thirties.

'How did *you* do?'

'Aw, sure ther's no money in the job I'm in.'

'Aw, just the same.'

THOMAS BLACKBURN
A Small, Keen Wind

My wife, for six months now in sinister
Tones, has muttered incessantly about divorce,
And, since I'm fond of the woman, this dark chatter
Is painful as well as a bit monotonous.
But marvel one must, when she fishes out of that trunk
Like rags, my shadier deeds for all to see,
With, 'This you did when sober, and that when drunk!'
The remarkable powers of human memory:
For although I wriggle like mad when she whistles up
Some particularly nasty bit of handy work
From my past, the dirty linen I cannot drop
Since 'Thomas Blackburn' is stitched by the laundry mark.
So I gather the things and say,'Yes, these are mine,
Though some cleaner items are not upon your list,'

Then walk with my bundle of rags to another room,
Since I will not play the role of delinquent ghost
And be folded up by guilt in the crook of an arm.
I saw tonight—walking to cool the mind—
A little moonshine on a garden wall,
And as I brooded, felt a small, keen wind
Stroll from the Arctic at its own sweet will.

Teaching Wordsworth

I'm paid to speak, and money glosses
Irrelevance; to keep their places
Students are paid, and so the burden
Is lightened of our mutual boredom
And if the gain's not much, the damage
Is slight within this northern college.

'Since for the most part it's subjective
Verse is not anything you might have
In hand or a bank, although it is
Important to some (it is on *our* syllabus)
Concerned with life's outgoing towards death,
Such as our theme today, the poet Wordsworth;

Who, since not alive, still I disinter
For the sake of a question you will answer,
For the sake also of the vagrant lives
He was involved with, and the wind when it raves
Round such unmarketable places as Scawfell.
An unsociable man and often dull,

He lived for a long time posthumous
To the flashing shield, to the great poet he was,
Busy for the most part with pedestrian exercise,
However you will not be questioned on those days,
Only the time when with stone footfall
Crags followed him, winds blew through his long skull.

That, of course, is known as 'The Great Period'.
Though one hesitates to apply the word 'God'
To a poet's theme—it is so manhandled—
Gentlemen, I can offer you nothing instead;

If he himself never applied it to what occurred
When 'the light of sense went out' this useful word
Though inaccurate will cut my lecture short
Being the full-stop which ends thought,

And consequently for our purposes useful;
For its brevity you should be grateful.
Anyway for those who *know* what the man meant,
My words are (thanks to God) irrelevant.
Take notes is the advice I bequeath the rest,
It is a question of self-interest,

Of being as Shakespeare says 'to oneself true',
For the right marks will certainly benefit you.
After all in the teaching world exam and thesis
For the *right* posts provide a useful basis
And in this sense poems are as good as money.
This man's life was a strange journey.

Early deprived of both father and mother,
To the rocks he turned, to lapping water,
With a sense by deprivation made so acute
That he heard grass speak and the word in a stone's throat;
Many of course to silence address their prayer
But in his case when it spoke he chose to answer.

And he wrote down after a certain time lag
Their conversation. It is a dialogue
Almost unique in any literature
And a positive goldmine to the commentator,
For although his poems mention what silence said,
It can almost any way be interpreted.

Since to find a yardstick by which the occult
Language of stones can be measured is difficult,
Also that 'something far more deeply interfused'
Must be belittled by critiques, if not abused,
There being no instrument with which to measure
This origin of terms and formula,

Which, together with the birth and deathward aim
Of the life in us and things was this man's theme
As he grew and dwindled into a worse

End of life. (As regards verse.)
My conclusion is, most words do violence
To what he said. Listen to silence.'

PATRICK KAVANAGH

Mermaid Tavern

No System, no Plan,
Yeatsian invention
No all-over
Organisational prover.
Let words laugh
And people be stimulated by our stuff.

Michaelangelo's Moses
Is one of the poses
Of Hemingway
Jungle-crashing after prey
Beckett's garbage-can
Contains all our man
Who without fright on his face
Dominates the place
And makes all feel
That all is well.
Yet without smuggery
Of the smirk of buggery

Or any other aid
We have produced our god
And everyone present
Becomes godded and pleasant
Confident, gay—
No remorse that a day
Can show no output
Except from the gut.

In the Name of The Father
The Son and The Mother
We explode
Ridiculously, uncode

A habit and find therein
A successful human being.

HUGH MACDIARMID

From 'In Memoriam James Joyce'

The ancestors of oysters and barnacles had heads
Snakes have lost their limbs
And ostriches and penguins their power of flight
Man may just as easily lose his intelligence.
Most of our people already have.
It is unlikely that man will develop into anything higher
Unless he desires and is prepared to pay the cost.
Otherwise we shall go the way of the dodo and the kiwi.
Already that process seems far advanced.
Genius is becoming rarer,
Our bodies a little weaker in each generation,
Culture is slowly declining,
Mankind is returning to barbarism
And will finally become extinct.

On The Margin

Discussions about Culture, the Arts and Society etc., seem to reveal two diverging points of view. One, the more widely held, being that so far as Art goes everything is O.K.—the problem is to get the stuff correctly diffused, to get more Festivals, Clubs, Culture Circles and so on. In short to bring the benefits of present-day Art to the masses. A certain priggish element involved here, and anyone whose telly tolerance quotient is at all high will have seen and heard a great deal of this along with a lot of discussion of Class. The new Oxbridge Man Of Culture is very keen on this lark.

The other point of view is expressed by Mr Hugh MacDiarmid's verses printed above and is far more pessimistic. For he sees that were

> . . the great masses of mankind given
> Ample incomes and freed for 'higher things'
> They could no more live than fish out of water

They could not sustain life on that level
—Or on any level worthy of Man at all.

As to the masses (not a very useful word any more, and one that is noticeably absent from those culture discussions referred to) we may leave the problem to those educated (and let it be added, paid) for the task. But the more serious part of this pessimism which MacDiarmid voices is the belief that genius (a word we are really not supposed to use any more,—in itself perhaps a symptom?) is becoming rarer, that there is an absolute decline in the quality, the incidence, the influence of real vision, imagination, truth-telling. Those things which raise man above the beasts, on which the survival of the race really depends.

These two points of view are therefore divided by the central thing which concerns them, in the first quantity and diffusion, and the second quality and depth. One sees the deterioration of language and the collapse of human relationships, and this induces a certain pessimism and in fact is so dreadful that the spectacle can only be contemplated through the Comic vision, while the other more or less feels that our culture is 'healthy' and the problems are subsidiary ones as 'worker's theatres' or 'the two cultures' and such.

One cannot blame the purveyors of culture (though one can certainly make fun of them as Mr Seymour-Smith does in his poem *The Administrators*) for feeling that all that's needed is a bit of jollying along, a bit of democratic spreading around of the New Wave etc. After all the popular art of the last ten years or so has been one of protest—and protest is a healthy radical thing. One protest has followed another written by young men and girls who had, it seemed, a lot to complain about. Illegitimate babies, terrible jobs, awful husbands, wives, brothers, sisters, uncles; God knows what. And as the crowds flocked to the local cinema to see the latest version of last year's protest play or novel, it is understandable that many should feel that all that was needed to produce the millennium was a little more strenuous attention to the propaganda aspect of the matter. And since intellectually and electorally the Left is hard up for some workable ideas this tended to become a Leftish agitation. Intrinsically it is doubtful whether these aspirations towards the enlightenment of the working man are any longer peculiar to Socialism. And the working class has not necessarily a monopoly of stupidity so that it is unlikely that the unreal stuff about which these protests are made will ever get further than the make-believe world of the escapist cinema.

And yet the system under which we live has one thing about it which no one will wish to deny, it is arid and barren from any but the most elementary and material point of view. And it is impossible not to believe—so perverse is the human creature—that in this machine which is modern prosperity there are those who will burn even this dross in the imagination, will tell the truth about their situation. Those suffering the *reality* not the *idea*. And the reality is the personal continuing occupation of a situation which denies the truth of a man's mind. The Job which requires that he give up everything but his sleeping hours to triviality or lies, and degrades even the concept of a human relationship.

Let us postulate two kinds of writer: one, a familiar bird of passage, writes a strong attack on the 'corruptions of the age', is put on the stage and before we know where we are we are reading about the sort of sports car she prefers and how many film scripts she will be writing next year. The other merely writes because he feels like it, tries to tell the truth, and since the truth never, or hardly ever, takes the form of a large protest this does not affect his situation: he does not as a result of writing a few verses find himself going up in a lift to a new pent-house flat. He lives to the full the life he is writing about. He does not have to give us dramatic surface detail, he gives us a distillation from his experience. Such a bird is rare. It may be it gets rarer. But it is certainly a different bird from the Oxbridge fowl which arrives from that venerable institution quacking about culture and the analytic mind.

All this boils down to a distinction between writing which is all surface glamour, full of matters of the moment, and writing born out of a slowly developing personal life (as opposed to public life, communal life etc.).

Nowadays the latter kind of writing is mostly characterised by that gloom and pessimism which Seymour-Smith in his essay on C. H. Sisson draws attention to. But this gloom is gloomy merely in the philosophical sense—in the vague and inaccurate way of conceptual thinking—inwardly the poems are laughing. It is interesting that C. H. Sisson who is so 'modern' in this way should have been writing consistently for thirty years and the culture audiences know nothing of him. He is a higher civil servant and the author of *The Spirit of British Administration*, a book which is simultaneously a masterpiece of comic irony and the last word on administration; he has also written perhaps the best novel since Wyndham Lewis's *The Human Age*: no one will publish it.

The point of the above remarks is to give some indication of the sort of thing this journal is interested in. If we are prepared to risk (which of course we are) the charge of being mystical, religious, or too *serious* we might say that the reason that it is worth having a magazine like X is because certain historical laws seem still to operate: the laws which exiled Dante, jailed Villon, put Tasso in the nut-house, hanged de Nerval, and broke Christopher Smart. There are certain kinds of men who do not fit into the 'pattern of the age' and the British Council is not much help to them. In short, in a world where we have to endure the antics of Dons who write verses, on wireless and telly, and ridiculous stage-Irishmen who con the culture-public from top to bottom it seems there are still some things NOT wanted.

Perhaps we have pitched this a bit high. But the other day a famous Man of Culture and editor of a famous magazine, said on the telly (one of the minor rewards of a high t.t.q.) that it is impossible to have a literary periodical to-day without mixing in some sociology and politics—in other words without telling lies. And this leads us to the announcement which we have now to make: that X will cease publication.

Patrick Swift

ACKNOWLEDGEMENTS

Dannie Abse: 'The Magician'. Reprinted by permission of the author.

Craigie Aitchison: *Fragments From A Conversation*. Reprinted by permission of the author.

Michael Andrews: *Notes and Preoccupations*. Reprinted by permission of the author.

Cliff Ashby: 'The Reduced Nanny, Smell of Talcum Powder'; 'In the Twilight of Her Time'; 'Please don't Laugh'; 'Fountains Abbey'; from *Plain Song*. Reprinted by permission of Carcanet Press Limited.

George Barker: 'How to Refuse a Heavenly House'; 'The Hippogryph and the Water-Pistol', reprinted from *Essays* (MacGibbon and Kee, 1970), by permission of Grafton Books Limited, a division of The Collins Publishing Group; 'Circular from America'; 'III Roman Odes'; 'On a Distant Prospect of English Poetry and Downing College' from *Collected Poems*. Reprinted by permission of Faber & Faber Limited.

Samuel Beckett: 'L'Image' first published in *X* volume one, number one, November 1959. Reprinted by permission of Les Editions de Minuit.

Thomas Blackburn: 'A Small, Keen Wind' and 'Teaching Wordsworth' both reprinted from *Selected Poems* (Hutchinson, 1975). By permission of Century Hutchinson Limited.

David Bomberg: from *The Bomberg Papers*. Reprinted by permission of the copyright owners, Dinora Davies-Rees and Juliet Lamont.

William Clarke: 'The Widow'; 'Old People's Home'; 'Mission Hall'; 'Military Cemetery'. Reprinted by permission of Harry Chambers, Peterloo Poets, on behalf of the author.

Anthony Cronin: '"Fairway's" Betting Office, Dublin 1949' and 'Responsibilities' reprinted from *Selected Poems*. By permission of Carcanet Press Limited.

David Gascoyne: 'Remembering The Dead' from *Collected Poems 1988*. Copyright © David Gascoyne 1988. Reprinted by permission of Oxford University Press.

Alberto Giacometti: *The Dream, the Sphinx, and the Death of T*. Text and illustrations copyright © A.D.A.G.P. Used with permission.

Robert Graves: 'November 5th Address'. © Robert Graves 1960. Reprinted by permission of A. P. Watt Limited on behalf of The Executors of the Estate of Robert Graves.

Martin Green: 'Coming Up For Air'. Reprinted by permission of the author.

John Heath-Stubbs: 'Use of Personal Pronouns'. Reprinted by permission of David Higham Associates.

ACKNOWLEDGEMENTS

Geoffrey Hill: 'Annunciations' from *King Log* (1968). Reprinted by permission of André Deutsch Limited.

Patrick Kavanagh: 'Living in the Country'; 'Lecture Hall'; 'Mermaid Tavern' from *Collected Poems 1964*; essay pp. 66ff.; and *The Flying Moment, On a Liberal Education*, and *The Cattle Fair*. All reprinted by permission of Martin Brian & O'Keeffe Limited.

Malcolm Lowry: 'Be Patient for the Wolf', 'Delirium in Vera Cruz', 'Reading Don Quixote', and *Art and Morality*—Prefatory note. Copyright © 1962 by Margerie Lowry. Reprinted by permission of Sterling Lord Literistic Inc. (New York).

Hugh MacDiarmid: essay pp. 63ff. Reprinted by permission of The Literary Executors Valda Grieve and Michael Grieve; 'Reflections in a Slum', 'In Memoriam James Joyce' from 'The Snares of Varuna', both reprinted from *The Complete Poems of Hugh MacDiarmid* by permission of Martin Brian & O'Keeffe Limited.

André Masson: 'Misurina IV', and 'Misurina VI'. © Dacs 1988.**

Ezra Pound: 'Conversations in Courtship' from *Translations*. Reprinted by permission of Faber & Faber Limited.

C. H. Sisson: 'Natural History'; 'The Profession of Letters, or Down With Culture'; 'Leisure and the Arts' all from *The Avoidance of Literature* (1978); 'Money'; 'Moriturus'; 'Sparrow Seen from an Office'; 'Ightham Woods'; 'Family Fortunes'; 'Epictetus'; 'The Nature of Man'; 'Choses Vues'; 'Adam and Eve'; 'By The Lift Gate'; 'Great Down'; 'Grandmother'; 'A Young Woman'; 'The Nature-Lover' from *Collected Poems*. All reprinted by permission of Carcanet Press Limited.

Stevie Smith: 'My Muse' reprinted from *Me Again* by permission of Virago Press Limited; 'The Last Turn of the Screw', 'The Person from Porlock' and 'Thoughts about the Muse'* from *The Collected Poems of Stevie Smith* (Penguin Modern Classics). Reprinted by permission of James MacGibbon, Literary Executor.

Vernon Watkins: Aphorisms on pp. 64ff. and 'Poem for Conrad'. Reprinted by permission of the copyright owner Mrs Gwen Watkins.

*lines 5-10 as printed in *X* were omitted when the poem was reprinted in *Collected Poems*.

Every effort has been made to contact copyright holders before publication. However in some cases (**) this has not been possible. If contacted the publisher will ensure that full credit is given at the earliest opportunity.

INDEX

Abel, Niëls Henrik, 63
Abse, Dannie, *The Magician*, 164–5
Aitchison, Craigie, *Fragments from a Conversation*, 111–14
Alvarez, Alfred, 55
Amis, Kingsley, 55, 57
Andrews, Michael, xvi
  Notes and Preoccupations, 58–63
Aristotle, 80
Arnold, Matthew, 139
Ashby, Cliff, xviii
  Fountains Abbey, 254–5
  In the Twilight of her Time, 225
  Please Don't Laugh, 253–4
  The Reduced Nanny, Smell of Talcum Powder, 224–5
Auden, W. H., 56, 192, 196
Auerbach, Frank, *Fragments from a Conversation*, 22–6

Bacon, Francis, xvi
Barker, George, 206, 226n.
  A Shower in Rome, 140–2
  A Sparrow's Feather, 143–4
  A Visit to Lake Albano, 142–3
  Circular from America, 1–6
  How to Refuse a Heavenly House, 45–51
  On a Distant Prospect of English Poetry & Downing College, 232
  The Hippogryph and the Water-Pistol, 180–7
Baudelaire, Charles, 129, 131, 132
Beckett, Samuel, *L'Image*, 26–8
Bell, William, 51
Berger, John, 126
Berry, Michael, Baron Hartwell, xv, xviii
Betjeman, Sir John, 56
Blackburn, Thomas:
  A Small Keen Wind, 257–8
  Teaching Wordsworth, 258–60
Blackmur, R. P., 208
Blake, William, 100
Bomberg, David, xvi, 25
  The Bomberg Papers, 86–93
Bowness, Allan, 126
Braque, Georges, 20
Bridges, Robert, 78
Browne, Sir Thomas, 138

Browning, Robert, 116, 119, 139, 193
Budgen, Frank, 119–20
Buffet, Bernard, 18
Burne-Jones, Sir Edward, 95–6

Campbell, Joseph, 206
Campbell, Roy, xiii
Carroll, Paul Vincent, 206
Cézanne, Paul:
  disdained, 100
  'La Vieille au Chapelet', 92–3
  moral discipline, 124
  nonconformist, 17
  not fully appreciated, 21
  personality, 91
  shocking individuality, 129
  works in isolation, 19–20
Chesterfield, Philip Stanhope, 4th Earl of, 139
Clarke, William:
  Military Cemetery, 236
  Mission Hall, 236
  Old People's Home, 236
  The Widow, 235–6
Coleridge, Samuel Taylor, 138
Colum, Padraic, 204
Congreve, William, 137
Conquest, Robert, 54
Constable, John, 88
Corkerry, Daniel, 204
Cowper, William, 203
Crabbe, George, 119, 121, 151
Craig, Gordon, 216
Cronin, Anthony, xviii
  A Question of Modernity, 114–23
  'Fairway's' *Betting Office, Dublin, 1949*, 222
  Getting Wurred In, 165–72
  Goodbye to All That, 52–8
  It Means What It Says, 192–9
  Responsibilities, 222–4
  The Notion of Commitment, 6–15

Dante, Alighieri, 193–5, 196, 263
Davie, Donald, 208
De La Mare, Walter, 78
Delacroix, Ferdinand Victor, 17, 100, 124, 129

Denis, Maurice, 95–6
Donoghue, Denis, 208
Donne, John, 119
Dryden, John, 137, 151

Einstein, Albert, 49
Eliot, T. S., 139, 151, 192
  and art of poetry, 48–9
  and Dante, 193–5, 196
  and Goethe, 195–6
  Graves's opinion of, 78
  and literary revolution, 115, 121, 122
  New Criticism, 207
  Prufrock, 119, 121
  quality of his poetry, 11, 14
  and Shakespeare, 193–4, 196
Empson, William, 54, 208

Flaubert, Gustave, 116
Ford, Ford Madox, 151
Fraser, G. S., 52, 53, 57
Freud, Lucian, xvi
Frost, Robert, 209

Gascoyne, David, xiv, 11–14, 56
  Remembering the Dead, 44
Gauguin, Paul, 20
Genet, Jean, 132
Giacometti, Alberto, *The Dream, the Sphinx and the Death of T.*, 34–5
Goethe, Johann Wolfgang von, 195–6
Gosse, Sir Edmund, 188, 189
Graham, W. S., xiii
Granville-Barker, Harley, 216
Graves, Robert, 48, 56, 130
  November 5th Address, 75–81
Gray, Thomas, 203
Green, Martin, *Coming up for Air*, 252

Heath-Stubbs, John, xiii
  Use of Personal Pronouns, 211–13
Herbert of Cherbury, Edward Herbert, 1st Baron, 150–1
Herbert, Sir George, 138
Herbert, Sir Alan, 136
Higgins, Brian, xvii, 175
  A Triumvirate, 250
  Accidental Purity, 251
  Autumnal, 215–16
  Baedeker for Metaphysicians, 251–2
  Cartons, 71–2
  I Have No Comrades, 73

Letter to a Literary Professor, 75
My Mother was a Burler, 72–3
On Going into the City, 214
The Corrupt Man in the French Pub, 250–1
The Only Need, 73–4
The Social Realists, 73
Unfinished, 214–15
Higgins, F. R., 204
Hill, Geoffrey, *Annunciations*, 152–3
Hodgson, Ralph, 78
Horniman, Annie Elizabeth, 216
Housman, A. E., 192, 199
Hull, Tristram, xiii
Hutchinson, Mary, xiv, xix
Huxley, Thomas, 192

Ingres, Jean Auguste Dominique, 129

Jackson, Barry, 216
Jennings, Elizabeth, 225–6
Johnson, Samuel, 139
Jonson, Ben, 117
Joyce, James, 97
  early attitude to poetry, 116, 117–18
  and literary revolution, 114, 115, 119–23 passim
  obsession with Dublin, 205

Kandinsky, Vasily, 21
Kavanagh, Patrick, xiii, xvi, 66–7, 226n.
  Come Dance with Kitty Stobling, xiv
  Lecture Hall, 30–1
  Living in the Country, 28–30
  Mermaid Tavern, 260–1
  On a Liberal Education, 204–11
  The Cattle Fair, 255–7
  The Flying Moment, 81–6
Keats, John, 118
Kenner, Hugh, 208
Kinsella, Thomas, 209

Laban, Rudolph, 220
Larkin, Philip, 57, 123
Law, William, 202 and n.
Leavis, F. R., 207
Lewis, Wyndham, 241, 263
Littlewood, Joan, 220, 221
Logue, Christopher, xiv, 11–14, 226n.
Lovell, James, *Alive, Alive O!*, 216–21
Lowry, Malcolm:
  Be Patient for the Wolf, 177–8

Delirium in Vera Cruz, 178
Reading Don Quixote, 179

MacColl, Edward, 220
McCooey, Art, 67
MacDiarmid, Hugh, xii, xvi, 63-4, 261-2
   In Memoriam James Joyce, 261
   Reflections in a Slum, 15-16
McGahern, John:
   The End or the Beginning of Love, 153-63
   X discovers, xviii
McNamara, Brinsley, 204
MacNeice, Louis, 226n.
Mangan, James Clarence, 121
Marvell, Andrew, 138
Masefield, John, 78
Masson, André, *Dissonances*, 94-100
Mauve, Anton, 129
Meissonier, Jean Louis, 17
Michelangelo, 93
Milton, John, 138
Mondrian, Piet, 21
Monet, Claude, 92
Montaigne, Michel Eyquem de, 203
Muir, Edwin, 226
Munch, Edvard, 100
Murray, T. C., 204

Nerval, Gérard de, 263
Newton, Eric, 126

O'Casey, Sean, 205-6
O'Connor, Frank, 204, 206

Perugino, 100
Picasso, Pablo, 18
Pissarro, Camille, 91
Pollock, Jackson, 97, 207
Pope, Alexander, 137, 151, 193
Pound, Ezra:
   Cantos, 192-3, 198
   Conversations in Courtship, 103-7
   Graves's opinion of, 78
   and literary revolution, 114-19 *passim*
   metric verse, 151
   New Criticism, 207
   and profession of letters, 139
   quality of his poetry, 11, 14
Proust, Marcel, 132

Rachewiltz, Boris de, 103
Raleigh, Sir Walter, 151
Raphael, 100

Read, Sir Herbert, 78, 129
Redon, Odilon, 97, 100
Reid, Phillipa, xiv
Reinhardt, Max, 216
Rembrandt, 17, 20, 92, 124
Renoir, Auguste, 91, 124
Richardson, Samuel, 139
Riding, Laura, 78
Ridler, Anne, 226 n.
Rimbaud, Arthur, 46, 94
Rousseau, Jean-Jacques, 139

Schopenhauer, Arthur, 199, 200
Seymour-Smith, Martin, 262, 263
   C. H. Sisson, 237-45
   Found on a Building Site, 229
   History Lesson, 231-2
   Living by the River, 229-30
   Request on the Field, 228-9
   The Administrators, 227-8
   The Execution, 230-1
Shakespeare, William, 119, 121, 151, 193-4, 196
Shaw, George Bernard, 216
Shelley, Percy Bysshe, 119, 203
Shirley, Evelyn, 67
Sisson, C. H., xvii-xviii, 263
   A Young Woman, 249
   Adam and Eve, 246-7
   article by Seymour-Smith on, 237-45
   By the Lift Gate, 247
   Epictetus, 110
   Family Fortunes, 109-10
   Grandmother, 248-9
   Great Down, 247-8
   Ightham Woods, 108
   Leisure and the Arts, 199-203
   Money, 107
   Moriturus, 107-8
   Natural History, 144-52
   Sparrows Seen from an Office, 108
   The Nature Lover, 249
   The Nature of Man, 246
   The Profession of Letters, 135-40
   Things Seen, 246
Smart, Christopher, 263
Smith, Stevie, xiii, xvi, 68-9, 226n.
   Not Waving But Drowning, xiv
   The Last Turn of the Screw, 31-3
   Thoughts about the Muse, 173
   Thoughts about the Person from Porlock, 33-5
Soutine, Chaim, 131

Spencer, Bernard, 226n.
Spenser, Edmund, 138–9
Stanislavsky, Konstantin, 216, 220
Steinbeck, John, 209
Stendahl, *Peinture en Italie*, 124
Stevens, Alfred, 88
Swift, Patrick:
  Mob Morals and the Art of Loving Art, 187–92
  Official Art and the Modern Painter, 16–22
  The Painter in the Press, 124–33
Swift, Patrick, xvii–xix *passim*
Swinburne, Algernon Charles, 119
Synge, John Millington, 206

Tasso, Torquato, 263
Tate, Allen, 135–6
Taylor, Jeremy, 203
Tennyson, Alfred, Lord, 119, 139, 193
Thomas, Dylan, 56
Tiller, Terence, 226n.
Toulouse-Lautrec, Henri de, 189–91
Traherne, Thomas, 203
Trilling, Lionel, 208
Turner, J. M. W., 100

Van Gogh, Vincent, 20, 91, 92, 100, 129
Vaughan, Henry, 138
Vermeer, Jan the younger, 17
Villon, François, 263
Voltaire, François Marie Arouet de, 137

Wain, John, 54, 55, 57, 58
Watkins, Vernon, *Poem for Conrad*, 173–5
Watkins, Vernon, xvi, 64–6, 226n.
Wilbur, Richard, 209
Wolfe, Humbert, 78
Wordsworth, William, 119, 193, 196
Wright, David,
  Adam at Evening, 100–2
Wyatt, Sir Thomas, 139

Yeats, W. B.:
  effect of his beliefs on his poetry, 196–8
  Graves's opinion of, 78
  lacks 'peasantry', 204
  and Literary Revival, 206
  and literary revolution, 114, 115, 121
  and poet's quandary, 45
  quality of his poetry, 11, 14
  quoted, 199 *bis*
  theatre, 216
  theme of Ireland, 205